THE UN'S ROLE IN NATION-BUILDING

FROM THE CONGO TO IRAQ

James Dobbins, Seth G. Jones, Keith Crane, Andrew Rathmell,
Brett Steele, Richard Teltschik, Anga Timilsina

RAND
CORPORATION

This research in the public interest was supported by the RAND Corporation, using discretionary funds made possible by the generosity of RAND's donors and the fees earned on client-funded research.

Library of Congress Cataloging-in-Publication Data

The UN's role in nation-building : from the Congo to Iraq / James Dobbins ... [et al.].
    p. cm.
    "MG-304."
    Includes bibliographical references and index.
    ISBN 0-8330-3589-4 (pbk. : alk. paper)
    1. Democratization—Case studies. 2. United Nations—Peacekeeping forces—Case studies. 3. United Nations—Military policy—Case studies. 4. United Nations—Economic assistance—Case studies. 5. United Nations—Technical assistance—Case studies. 6. Peace-building—Case studies. I. Dobbins, James, 1942–

JZ4984.5.U534 2005
341.5'84—dc22

2004027669

The RAND Corporation is a nonprofit research organization providing objective analysis and effective solutions that address the challenges facing the public and private sectors around the world. RAND's publications do not necessarily reflect the opinions of its research clients and sponsors.

RAND® is a registered trademark.

Cover design by Stephen Bloodsworth

Published 2005 by the RAND Corporation
1776 Main Street, P.O. Box 2138, Santa Monica, CA 90407-2138
1200 South Hayes Street, Arlington, VA 22202-5050
201 North Craig Street, Suite 202, Pittsburgh, PA 15213-1516
RAND URL: http://www.rand.org/
To order RAND documents or to obtain additional information, contact
Distribution Services: Telephone: (310) 451-7002;
Fax: (310) 451-6915; Email: order@rand.org

The cover photographs are of UN Secretary-General Dag Hammarskjöld in the Congo (left) and UN Special Envoy Sergio Vieira de Mello in Iraq (right). They are the two most senior representatives to have given their lives in the course of UN nation-building operations over the last 60 years. This work is dedicated to them and their many colleagues who have made that ultimate sacrifice.

PREFACE

This study contains the results of research on best practices in nation-building. It is intended to complement a companion volume, *America's Role in Nation-Building: From Germany to Iraq,* which focuses on U.S.-led nation-building efforts. Its purpose is to analyze United Nations military, political, humanitarian, and economic activities in post-conflict situations since World War II, determine key principles for success, and draw implications for future nation-building missions. The study contains the lessons learned from eight UN cases: Belgian Congo, Namibia, El Salvador, Cambodia, Mozambique, Eastern Slavonia, Sierra Leone, and East Timor. It also examines the nation-building effort in Iraq.

This study was sponsored by the RAND Corporation as part of its mission to conduct research in the public interest. The effort was made possible by the generosity of RAND's donors and the fees earned on client-funded research. RAND is a nonprofit institution that helps improve policy and decisionmaking through research and analysis. The research was conducted within the RAND National Security Research Division (NSRD). NSRD conducts research and analysis for the Office of the Secretary of Defense, the Joint Staff, the Unified Commands, the defense agencies, the Department of the Navy, the U.S. intelligence community, allied foreign governments, and foundations. For more information on the National Security Research Division, contact the Director of Operations, Nurith Berstein. She can be reached by e-mail at Nurith_Berstein@rand.org; by phone at 703-413-1100, extension 5469; or by mail at the RAND Corporation, 1200 South Hayes Street, Arlington, Virginia 22202-5050. More information about RAND is available at www.rand.org.

CONTENTS

FIGURES

TABLES

The first volume of this series dealt with the American experience with nation-building, defined therein as the use of armed force in the aftermath of a crisis to promote a transition to democracy. It examined eight instances in which the United States took the lead in such endeavors. This volume deals with the United Nations' experience with comparable operations, examining eight instances in which the United Nations led multinational forces toward generally similar ends.

For the United States, post–Cold War nation-building had distant precursors in the American occupations of Germany and Japan in the aftermath of World War II and its role in fostering the emergence of democratic regimes there. For the United Nations, the comparable precursor was in the early 1960s in the newly independent Belgian Congo.

The Republic of the Congo failed almost from the moment of its birth. Within days of the Congo's independence its army mutinied, the remaining white administrators fled, the administration and the economy collapsed, Belgian paratroops invaded, and the mineral-rich province of Katanga seceded. These developments cast a serious shadow over the prospects for the successful and peaceful completion of Africa's decolonization, at that point just gathering momentum. On July 14, 1960, acting with unusual speed, the Security Council passed the first of a series of resolutions authorizing the deployment of UN-led military forces to assist the Republic of the Congo in restoring order and, eventually, in suppressing the rebellion in Katanga.

Given the unprecedented nature of its mission and the consequent lack of prior experience, existing doctrine, designated staff, or administrative structure to underpin the operation, the United Nations performed remarkably well in the Congo. Significant forces began to arrive within days of the Security Council's authorization—performance matched in few subsequent UN peacekeeping missions. The United Nations was quickly able to secure the removal of Belgian forces. Over the next three years, UN troops forced the removal of foreign mercenaries and suppressed the Katangan secession while civil elements of the mission provided a wide range of humanitarian, economic, and civil assistance to the new Congolese regime. Measured against the bottom-line requirements of the international community—that decolonization proceed, colonial and mercenary troops depart, and the Congo remain intact—the United Nations was largely successful. Democracy did not figure heavily in the various Congo resolutions passed by the UN Security Council; there was, in any case, no agreement during the Cold War on the definition of that term. The Congo never became a functioning democracy, but large-scale civil conflict was averted for more than a decade following the United Nations' departure, and the country more or less held together for two more decades, albeit under a corrupt and incompetent dictatorship.

UN achievements in the Congo came at considerable cost in men lost, money spent, and controversy raised. For many people, the United Nations' apparent complicity in the apprehension and later execution of Prime Minister Patrice Lumumba overshadowed its considerable accomplishments. As a result of these costs and controversies, neither the United Nations' leadership nor its member nations were eager to repeat the experience. For the next 25 years the United Nations restricted its military interventions to interpositional peacekeeping, policing ceasefires, and patrolling disengagement zones in circumstances where all parties invited its presence and armed force was to be used by UN troops only in self-defense.

HEALING COLD WAR WOUNDS

The conclusion of the Cold War ended this hiatus in nation-building and presented the United Nations with new opportunities and new challenges. By the end of the 1980s, the United States and the Soviet Union had begun to disengage from proxy wars in Latin America, Africa, and Asia and were finally prepared to work together in pressing former clients to resolve their outstanding differences.

The early post–Cold War UN-led operations in Namibia, Cambodia, El Salvador, and Mozambique followed a similar pattern. The international community, with U.S. and Soviet backing, first brokered a peace accord. The Security Council then dispatched a UN peacekeeping force to oversee its implementation. In each case, the UN mission's responsibilities included initiating an expeditious process of disarmament, demobilization, and reintegration; encouraging political reconciliation; holding democratic elections; and overseeing the inauguration of a new national government. Operations in each of these countries were greatly facilitated by war-weary populations, great-power support, and the cooperation of neighboring countries. The United Nations became adept at overseeing the disarmament and demobilization of willing parties. The reintegration of former combatants was everywhere more problematic, for nowhere did the international community provide the necessary resources. Economic growth accelerated in most cases, largely as a result of the cessation of fighting. Peace, growth, and democracy were often accompanied by an increase in common crime, as old repressive security services were dismantled and demobilized former combatants were left without a livelihood.

All four of these operations culminated in reasonably free and fair elections. All four resulted in sustained periods of civil peace that endured after the United Nations withdrawal. Cambodia enjoyed the least successful democratic transformation and experienced the greatest renewal of civil strife, although at nothing like the level that preceded the UN intervention. Cambodia was also the first instance in which the United Nations became responsible for helping govern a state in transition from conflict to peace and democracy. The United Nations was ill prepared to assume such a role. For its part, the government of Cambodia, although it had agreed to UN administrative oversight as part of the peace accord, was unwilling to cede effective authority. As a result, UN control over Cambodia's civil administration was largely nominal.

Despite the successes of these early post–Cold War operations, a number of weaknesses in the United Nations' performance emerged that would cripple later missions launched in more difficult circumstances. Deficiencies included

- the slow arrival of military units

- the even slower deployment of police and civil administrators

- the uneven quality of military components

- the even greater unevenness of police and civil administrators

- the United Nations' dependence on voluntary funding to pay for such mission-essential functions as reintegration of combatants and capacity building in local administrations

- the frequent mismatches between ambitious mandates and modest means

- the premature withdrawal of missions, often following immediately after the successful conclusion of a first democratic election.

COPING WITH FAILED STATES

During the early 1990s, the United Nations enjoyed a series of successes. This winning streak and a consequent optimism about the task of nation-building came to an abrupt end in Somalia and were further diminished by events in the former Yugoslavia. In both instances, UN-led peacekeeping forces were inserted into societies where there was no peace to keep. In both cases, UN forces eventually had to be replaced by larger, more robust American-led peace enforcement missions.

Although the Cold War divided some societies, it provided the glue that held others together. Even as former East-West battlegrounds, such as Namibia, Cambodia, El Salvador, and Mozambique, were able to emerge as viable nation states with UN assistance, other divided societies, such as Somalia, Yugoslavia, and Afghanistan—which had been held together by one superpower or the other, and sometimes by both—began to disintegrate as external supports and pressures were removed. Not surprisingly, the United Nations had a harder time holding together collapsing states than brokering reconciliation in coalescing ones.

The original UN mission in Somalia was undermanned and overmatched by warring Somali clan militias. The U.S.-led multinational force that replaced it was built on a core of 20,000 American soldiers and marines. This force was quickly able to overawe local resistance and secure the delivery of famine relief supplies, its principal mission. Washington then chose to withdraw all but 2,000 troops. The United States passed overall responsibility back to the United Nations and supported a radical expansion of the UN's mandate. The previous UN and U.S. forces had confined their mission to securing humanitarian relief activities. Even as the United States withdrew 90 percent of its combat forces and saw them replaced by a smaller number of less well equipped UN troops, it joined in extending the mission of those remaining forces to the introduction of grass-roots democracy, a process which would put the United Nations at cross purposes with every warlord in the country. The result was a resurgence of violence to levels that residual U.S. and UN troops proved unable to handle.

Insuperable difficulties also arose in the former Yugoslavia, where UN peacekeepers were again deployed to an ongoing civil war without the mandate, influence, or firepower needed to end the fighting. UN deficiencies contributed to the failure of its efforts in Bosnia, as they had in Somalia, but at least equal responsibility lies with its principal member governments: with Russia, for its stubborn partisanship on behalf of Serbia; with the United States, for its refusal to commit American forces or to support the peacemaking initiatives of those governments that had; and with Britain and France, the principal troop contributors, for failing to enforce the mandate they had accepted to protect the innocent civilians entrusted to their care.

The failure of UN missions in both Somalia and Bosnia, when contrasted with the more robust American-led multinational efforts that succeeded them, led to a general conclusion that, although the United Nations might be up to peacekeeping, peace enforcement was beyond its capacity. This conclusion, not uncongenial to the United Nations' own leadership, is belied by that organization's performance 30 years earlier in the former Belgian Congo. Its subsequent conduct of small, but highly successful peace enforcement missions in Eastern Slavonia from 1996 to 1998 and in East Timor beginning in 1999, suggested that the United Nations was capable of executing a robust peace enforcement mandate in circumstances where the scale was modest, the force included a core of capable First World troops, and the venture had strong international backing.

Eastern Slavonia was the last Serb-held area of Croatia at the end of the conflict between these two former Yugoslav republics. The United Nations once again became responsible for governing a territory in transition, in this case from Serb to Croat control. The UN operation in Eastern Slavonia was generously manned, well led, abundantly resourced, and strongly supported by the major powers, whose influence ensured the cooperation of neighboring states. Not surprisingly, given these advantages, the UN peace enforcement mission in Eastern Slavonia was highly successful.

American-led multinational missions in Somalia and Bosnia contrasted positively with the UN missions that had preceded them, primarily because they were better resourced and more determined in the employment of those larger capabilities. Had the United States been willing to provide a military commander and 20,000 American troops to the UN-led operations in Somalia or Bosnia, those earlier efforts would likely have fared better, perhaps obviating the need for the subsequent multinational interventions.

NATION-BUILDING IN THE NEW DECADE

In the closing months of 1999, the United Nations found itself charged with governing both Kosovo and East Timor. The latter operation proved an ideal showcase for UN capabilities. Like Eastern Slavonia, East Timor was small in both territory and population. International resources, in terms of military manpower and economic assistance, were unusually abundant. Major-power influence secured the cooperation of neighboring states. A multinational coalition, in this case led by Australia, secured initial control of the territory and then quickly turned the operation over to UN management. Remaining combatants were disarmed, new security forces established, a local administration created, elections held, and a democratically elected government inaugurated in less than three years.

Even this showcase operation exhibited certain chronic UN deficiencies. International police and civil administrators were slow to arrive and of variable quality. Once ensconced, UN administrators were a trifle slow to turn power back to local authorities. These were minor blemishes, however, on a generally successful operation.

In less benign circumstances, such weaknesses continued to threaten the success of UN operations. In Sierra Leone, inadequate UN forces were inserted in 1999 as part of the United Nations Mission in Sierra Leone (UN-AMSIL) under unduly optimistic assumptions. They encountered early reverses and eventually suffered the ultimate humiliation of being captured and held hostage in large numbers. Poised on the verge of collapse, the Sierra Leone operation was rescued by the United Kingdom and turned around thanks in large measure to extraordinary personal efforts by the UN Secretary-General. British forces arrived, extricated UN hostages, intimidated insurgent forces, and began to train a more competent local military. The United States threw its logistic and diplomatic weight behind the operation. The regime in neighboring Liberia, highly complicit in Sierra Leone's civil war, was displaced. Additional manpower and economic resources were secured. Thus bolstered, the United Nations was able to oversee a process of disarmament and demobilization and hold reasonably free elections.

QUANTITATIVE AND QUALITATIVE COMPARISONS

Nation-building can be viewed in terms of its inputs—which, broadly speaking, are manpower, money, and time, and its desired outputs—which are peace, economic growth and democratization. Needless to say, outputs depend on much more than the inputs. Success in nation-building depends on the wisdom with which such resources are employed and on the susceptibility of the society in question to the changes being fostered. Nevertheless, success is also in some measure dependent on the quantity of international military and police manpower and external economic assistance, and of the time over which these are applied.

The first volume of this study compared inputs and outputs for seven U.S.-led nation-building missions: Germany, Japan, Somalia, Haiti, Bosnia, Kosovo, and Afghanistan. Drawing on that earlier work, this volume compares data from the eight UN missions described herein, the eight U.S. missions from the previous volume, and data from the current operation in Iraq.

Military Presence

Military force levels for UN missions ranged from nearly 20,000 UN troops deployed in the Congo and 16,000 in Cambodia to 5,000 in Namibia and El Salvador. UN missions have normally fielded much smaller contingents than American-led operations, both in absolute numbers and in relation to the local population. The largest UN mission we studied is smaller than the smallest U.S. mission studied.

Duration

UN forces have tended to remain in post-conflict countries for shorter periods of time than have U.S. forces. In the early 1990s, both U.S. and UN-led operations tended to be terminated rather quickly, often immediately following the completion of an initial democratic election and the inauguration of a new government. In this period, the United States and the United Nations tended to define their objectives rather narrowly, focusing on exit strategies and departure deadlines. As experience with nation-building grew, however, both the United Nations and the United States came to recognize that reconciliation and democratization could require more than a single election. By the end of the decade, both UN- and U.S.-led operations became more extended and peacekeeping forces were drawn down more slowly, rather than exiting en masse following the first national election.

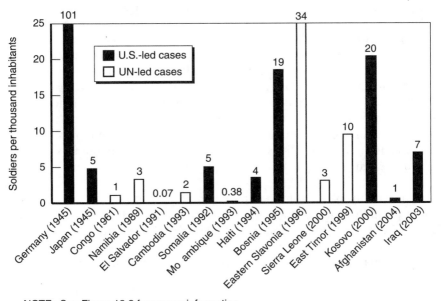

NOTE: See Figure 12.2 for source information.

RAND *MG304-S.1*

Figure S.1—Peak Military Presence Per Capita

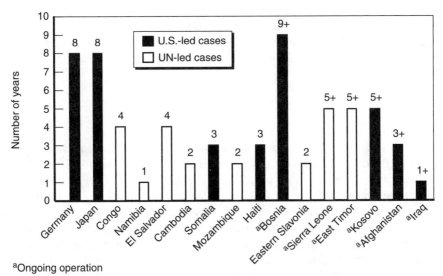

[a]Ongoing operation

NOTE: See Figure 12.3 for source information.

RAND *MG304-S.2*

Figure S.2—Duration of Operations

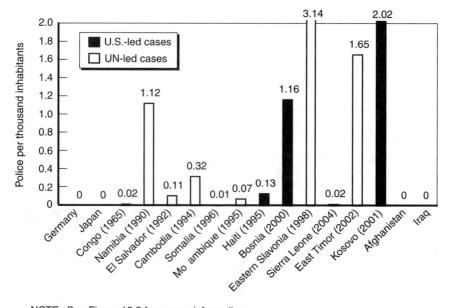

NOTE: See Figure 12.5 for source information.

RAND MG304-S.3

Figure S.3—Peak Civilian Police Presence Per Capita

Civilian Police

International civilian police are an increasingly important component of most UN nation-building operations, in some cases representing 10 percent or more of the overall force. UN civilian police forces usually left with the troops. However, in El Salvador, Haiti, and Eastern Slavonia they stayed a year or more after the military component withdrew. The United States pioneered the use of armed international police in Haiti but looked to the United Nations to supply police for the NATO-led operations in Bosnia and Kosovo. The United States did not include civilian police in its last two nation-building operations, Afghanistan and Iraq.

Combat-Related Deaths

Casualties suffered are a good measure of the difficulties encountered in an operation. Missions with high casualty levels have been among the least successful. Among UN cases, the Congo had the highest number of casualties, reflecting the peace enforcement nature of the operation. After the Congo, the Cambodian operation, lightly manned as a proportion of the population, had the highest casualty level, followed by Sierra Leone.

Following the loss of 18 U.S. soldiers in Somalia in 1993, the United States took great precautions through the rest of the decade to avoid casualties. The United Nations was slightly less risk averse. Through the end of the 1990s, casualty rates in UN-led operations were consequently a little higher than American. In the aftermath of the September 11, 2001, terrorist attacks, American sensitivity to casualties diminished. At the same time, the United States abandoned its strategy of deploying overwhelming force at the outset of nation-building operations. Significantly lower force-to-population ratios in Afghanistan and Iraq than in Bosnia or Kosovo have been accompanied by much higher casualty levels.

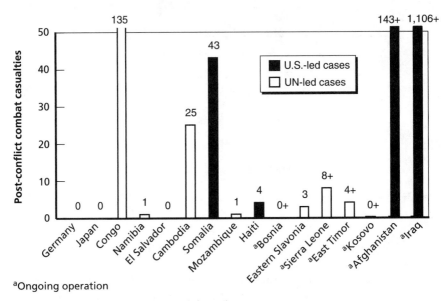

aOngoing operation

NOTE: See Figure 12.7 for source information.

RAND MG304-S.4

Figure S.4—Post-Conflict Combat Deaths

Sustained Peace

Peace is the most essential product of nation-building. Without peace, neither economic growth nor democratization are possible. With peace, some level of economic growth becomes almost inevitable and democratization at least possible. As Table S.1 illustrates, among the 16 countries studied in this and the preceding volume, eleven remain at peace today, five do not. Of the eight UN-led cases, seven are at peace. Of the eight U.S.-led cases, four are at peace; four are not—or not yet—at peace. These categorizations are necessarily provisional, particularly for the ongoing operations in Afghanistan and Iraq. Peace in Bosnia, Kosovo, East Timor, and Sierra Leone has been sustained but so far only with the ongoing presence of international peacekeepers.

Table S.1
Sustained Peace

Country	At Peace in 2004
Germany	Yes
Japan	Yes
Congo	No
Namibia	Yes
El Salvador	Yes
Cambodia	Yes
Somalia	No
Mozambique	Yes
Haiti	No
Bosnia	Yes
Eastern Slavonia	Yes
Sierra Leone	Yes
East Timor	Yes
Kosovo	Yes
Afghanistan	No
Iraq	No

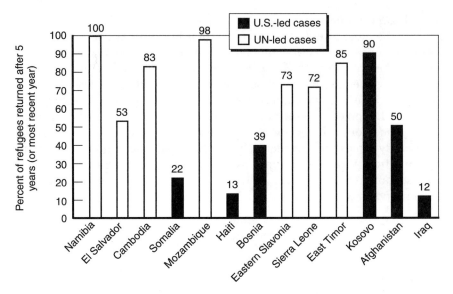

NOTE: See Figure 12.8 for source information.

RAND *MG304-S.5*

Figure S.5—Refugee Returns After Five Years

Refugee Return

Success in stemming the flow and facilitating the return of unwanted refugees is one of the chief benefits provided to the international community by nation-building and often a major incentive to launch such operations. Most nation-building missions have been highly successful in this regard. Low rates of refugee return are often a sign of continued conflict in the society in question (e.g., Somalia, Iraq, and Afghanistan) but are sometimes indicative of the significantly better living conditions in the places of refuge (e.g., the United States for Salvadoran and Haitian refugees).

Democratization

Below, we characterize each of the sixteen societies studied as democratic or not based on codings from Freedom House and the Polity IV Project at the University of Maryland. Among the U.S.-led cases, Germany and Japan are clearly democratic; Bosnia and Kosovo are democratic but still under varying degrees of international administration; Somalia and Haiti are not democratic; and Afghanistan and Iraq are seeking to build democratic structures in exceptionally difficult circumstances. Among the UN-led cases all but the Congo and Cambodia remain democratic, some of course more than others.

Table S.2
Democractic Development

Country	Democracy in 2004	Polity IV (0 low, 10 high)	Freedom House (0 low, 10 high)
Germany	Yes	10.0	10.0
Japan	Yes	10.0	10.0
Congo	No	0.0	2.9
Namibia	Yes	6.0	8.6
El Salvador	Yes	7.0	8.6
Cambodia	No	3.0	2.9
Somalia	No	–	2.9
Mozambique	Yes	6.0	7.1
Haiti	No	1.0	2.9
Bosnia	Yes	–	5.7
Eastern Slavonia[a]	Yes	7.0	8.6
Sierra Leone	Yes	5.0	5.7
East Timor	Yes	6.0	7.1
Kosovo	Yes	–	–
Afghanistan	No	–	2.9
Iraq	No	0.0	1.4

[a] Since neither Polity IV nor Freedom House had data for Eastern Slavonia, we used Croatia as a proxy.

External Assistance

UN-led operations have tended to be less well supported with international economic assistance than U.S. operations, in both absolute and proportional terms. This reflects the greater access of the United States to donor assistance funds, including its own, and those of the international financial institutions to which it belongs. In effect, the United States can always ensure the level of funding it deems necessary. The United Nations seldom can. Many UN operations are consequently poorly supported with economic assistance.

Economic Growth

The presence of international peacekeepers and their success in suppressing renewed conflict, rather than the level of economic assistance, seem to be the key determinants of economic growth. As the present situation of Iraq illustrates, security is a prerequisite for growth, and money is no sub-

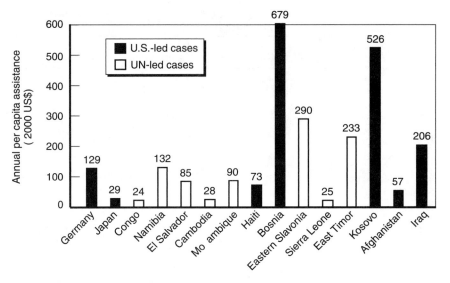

NOTE: See Figure 12.10 for source information.

RAND *MG304-S.6*

Figure S.6—Annual Per-Capita Assistance After First Two Years

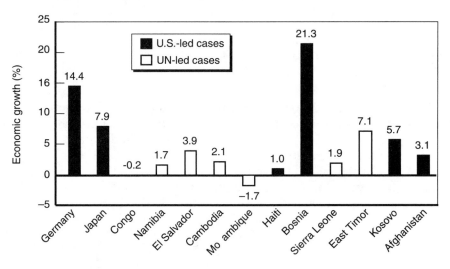

NOTE: See Figure 12.11 for source information.

RAND *MG304-S.7*

Figure S.7—Average Annual Growth in Per Capita GDP During First Five Years After Conflict

stitute for adequate manpower in providing it. Indeed, security without economic assistance is much more likely to spur economic growth than is economic assistance without security.

THE U.S. AND UN WAYS OF NATION-BUILDING

Over the years, the United States and the United Nations have developed distinctive styles of nation-building derived from their very different natures and capabilities. The United Nations is an international organization entirely dependent on its members for the wherewithal to conduct nation-building. The United States is the world's only superpower, commanding abundant resources of its own and having access to those of many other nations and institutions.

UN operations have almost always been undermanned and under-resourced. This is not because UN managers believe smaller is better, although some do. It is because member states are rarely willing to commit the manpower or the money any prudent military commander would desire. As a result, small and weak UN forces are routinely deployed into what they hope, on the basis of best-case assumptions, will prove to be post-conflict situations. Where such assumptions prove ill founded, UN forces have had to be reinforced, withdrawn, or, in extreme cases, rescued.

Throughout the 1990s, the United States adopted the opposite approach to sizing its nation-building deployments, basing its plans on worst-case assumptions and relying on overwhelming force to quickly establish a stable environment and deter resistance from forming. In Somalia, Haiti, Bosnia, and Kosovo, U.S.-led coalitions intervened in numbers and with capabilities that discouraged significant resistance. In Somalia, this American force was drawn down too quickly. The resultant casualties reinforced the American determination to establish and retain a substantial overmatch in any future nation-building operation. In the aftermath of the September 2001 terrorist attacks, American tolerance of military casualties significantly increased. In sizing its stabilization operations in Afghanistan and Iraq, the new American leadership abandoned the strategy of overwhelming preponderance (sometimes labeled the Powell doctrine after former Chairman of the Joint Chiefs of Staff General Colin Powell) in favor of the "small footprint" or "low profile" force posture that had previously characterized UN operations.

In both cases, these smaller American-led forces proved unable to establish a secure environment. In both cases, the original U.S. force levels have had to be significantly increased, but in neither instance has this sufficed to establish adequate levels of public security.

It would appear that the low-profile, small-footprint approach to nation-building is much better suited to UN-style peacekeeping than to U.S.-style peace enforcement. The United Nations has an ability to compensate, to some degree at least, for its "hard" power deficit with "soft" power attributes of international legitimacy and local impartiality. The United States does not have such advantages in situations where America itself is a party to the conflict being terminated, or where the United States has acted without an international mandate. Military reversals also have greater consequences for the United States than for the United Nations. To the extent that the United Nations' influence depends more on moral than physical power, more on its legitimacy than its combat prowess, military rebuffs do not fatally undermine its credibility. To the extent that America leans more on "hard" than on "soft" power to achieve its objectives, military reverses strike at the very heart of its potential influence. These considerations, along with recent experience, suggest that the United States would be well advised to resume supersizing its nation-building missions and to leave the small-footprint approach to the United Nations.

The United Nations and the United States tend to enunciate their nation-building objectives very differently. UN mandates are highly negotiated, densely bureaucratic documents. UN spokespersons tend toward understatement in expressing their goals. Restraint of this sort is more difficult for U.S. officials, who must build congressional and public support for costly and sometimes dangerous missions in distant and unfamiliar places. As a result, American nation-building rhetoric tends toward the grandiloquent. The United States often becomes the victim of its own rhetoric when its higher standards are not met.

UN-led nation-building missions tend to be smaller than American operations, to take place in less demanding circumstances, to be more frequent and therefore more numerous, to have more circumspectly defined objectives, and—at least among the missions studied—to enjoy a higher success rate than U.S.-led efforts. By contrast, U.S.-led nation-building has taken place in more demanding circumstances, has required larger forces and more robust mandates, has received more economic support, has espoused more ambitious objectives, and—at least among the missions studied—has fallen short of those objectives more often than has the United Nations. Table S.3 summarizes nation-building operations since 1945.

Table S.3
Major Nation-Building Operations: 1945 – Present

Country	Years	Peak Troops	Lead Actors	Assessment	Lessons Learned
West Germany	1945–1952	1.6 million	Led by U.S, British, and French	Very successful. Within 10 years an economically stable democratic and NATO member state.	Democracy can be transferred. Military forces can underpin democratic transformation.
Japan	1945–1952	350,000	U.S.-led	Very successful. Economically stable democratic and regional security anchor within a decade.	Democracy can be exported to non-Western societies. Unilateral nation-building can be simpler than multilateral.
Congo	1960–1964	19,828	UN-led	Partially successful, costly and controversial. UN ensured decolonization and territorial integrity, but not democracy.	Money and manpower demands almost always exceed supply. Controversial missions leave legacies of "risk aversion."
Namibia	1989–1990	4,493	UN-led	Successful. UN helped ensure peace, democratic development, and economic growth.	Compliant neighbors, a competent government, and a clear end state can contribute to successful outcome.
El Salvador	1991–1996	4,948	UN-led	Successful. UN negotiated lasting peace settlement and transition to democracy after 12-year civil war.	UN participation in settlement negotiations can facilitate smooth transition.
Cambodia	1991–1993	15,991	UN-led	Partially successful. UN organized elections, verified withdrawal of foreign troops and ended large-scale civil war. But democracy did not take hold.	Democratization requires long-term engagement.

Table S.3—Continued

Country	Years	Peak Troops	Lead Actors	Assessment	Lessons Learned
Somalia	1992–1994	28,000	UN-led peacekeeping mission, followed by US-led coalition, followed by UN led peacekeeping mission	Not successful. Little accomplished other than some humanitarian aid delivered to Mogadishu and other cities.	Unity of command can be important in peace as in combat operations. Nation-building objectives must be scaled to available resources.
Mozambique	1992–1994	6,576	UN-led	Mostly successful. Transition to independence was peaceful and democratic. But negative economic growth.	Cooperation of neighboring states is critical to success. Incorporation of insurgent groups into political process is key to democratic transition.
Haiti	1994–1996	21,000	U.S.-led entry, followed by UN-led peacekeeping mission with large U.S. component	Initially successful but ultimately not. U.S. forces restored democratically elected president but U.S. and UN left before democratic institutions took hold.	Exit deadlines can be counterproductive. Need time to build competent administrations and democratic institutions.
Bosnia	1995– present	20,000	U.S./NATO-led military component, ad hoc coalition civil component, largely U.S. and EU	Mixed success. Democratic elections within two years, but government is constitutionally weak.	Nexus between organized crime and political extremism can be serious challenge to enduring democratic reforms.

Table S.3—Continued

Country	Years	Peak Troops	Lead Actors	Assessment	Lessons Learned
Eastern Slavonia	1995–1998	8,248	UN-led	Successful. Well-resourced operation and clear end state contributed to peaceful and democratic transition.	UN can successfully conduct small peace enforcement missions with support from major powers.
Sierra Leone	1998–present	15,255	UN-led, parallel UK force in support	Initially unsuccessful, then much improved. Parallel British engagement helped stabilize mission.	Lack of support from major powers can undermine UN operations. But even a badly compromised mission can be turned around.
East Timor	1999–present	8,084	Australian-led entry followed by UN-led peacekeeping mission	Successful. UN oversaw transition to democracy, peace, and economic growth.	Support of neighboring states is important for security. Local actors should be involved as early as possible in governance.
Kosovo	1999–present	15,000	U.S./NATO-led entry, followed by NATO-led peacekeeping, UN-led civil governance, OSCE-led democratization, and EU-led reconstruction	Mostly successful. Elections within 3 years and strong economic growth. But no final resolution of Kosovo's status.	Broad participation, and extensive burden sharing can be compatible with unity of command and American leadership.

Table S.3—Continued

Country	Years	Peak Troops	Lead Actors	Assessment	Lessons Learned
Afghanistan	2001–present	20,000	U.S.-led entry and counterinsurgency, UN-led democratization, and NATO-led peacekeeping	Too soon to tell. Democratic elections and decline as a base for terrorism. But little government control beyond Kabul, and rising drug and insurgency challenges.	Low initial input of money and troops yields a low output of security, democratization, and economic growth.
Iraq	2003–present	175,000	U.S.-led entry, occupation, and counterinsurgency	Too soon to tell. Overthrow of Saddam Hussein's brutal regime. But insurgency has slowed reconstruction efforts.	Postwar planning is as important as planning for the conflict.

There are three explanations for the better UN success rate. The first is that a different selection of cases would produce a different result. The second is that the U.S. cases are intrinsically more difficult. The third is that the United Nations has done a better job of learning from its mistakes than has the United States. Throughout the 1990s, the United States became steadily better at nation-building. The Haitian operation was better managed than Somalia, Bosnia better than Haiti, and Kosovo better than Bosnia. The U.S. learning curve was not sustained into the current decade. The administration that took office in 2001 initially disdained nation-building as an unsuitable activity for U.S. forces. When compelled to engage in such missions, first in Afghanistan and then in Iraq, the administration sought to break with the strategies and institutional responses that had been honed throughout the 1990s to deal with these challenges.

The United Nations has largely avoided the institutional discontinuities that have marred U.S. performance. The current UN Secretary-General, Kofi Annan, was Undersecretary-General for Peacekeeping and head of the UN peacekeeping operation in Bosnia throughout the first half of the 1990s, when UN nation-building began to burgeon. He was chosen for his current post by the United States and other member governments largely on the basis of his demonstrated skills in managing the United Nations' peacekeeping portfolio. Some of his closest associates from that period moved up with him to the UN front office while others remain in the Department of Peacekeeping Operations. As a result, UN nation-building missions have been run over the past 15 years by an increasingly experienced cadre of international civil servants. Similarly in the field, many UN peacekeeping operations are headed and staffed by veterans of earlier operations.

The United States, in contrast, tends to staff each new operation as if it were its first and destined to be its last. Service in such missions has never been regarded as career enhancing for American military or Foreign Service officers. Recruitment is often a problem, terms tend to be short, and few individuals volunteer for more than one mission.

IS NATION-BUILDING COST-EFFECTIVE?

In addition to the horrendous human costs, war inflicts extraordinary economic costs on societies. On average, one study suggests, civil wars reduce prospective economic output by 2.2 percent per year for the duration of the conflict. However, once peace is restored, economic activity resumes and, in a number of cases, the economy grows. A study by Paul Collier and Anke Hoeffler looked at the cost and effectiveness of various policy options to reduce the incidence and duration of civil wars. It found that post-conflict military intervention is highly cost-effective—in fact, the most cost-effective policy examined.[1]

Our study supports that conclusion. The UN success rate among missions studied—seven out of eight societies left peaceful, six out of eight left democratic—substantiates the view that nation-building can be an effective means of terminating conflicts, insuring against their reoccurrence, and promoting democracy. The sharp overall decline in deaths from armed conflict around the world over the past decade also points to the efficacy of nation-building. During the 1990s, deaths from armed conflict were averaging over 200,000 per year. Most were in Africa. In 2003, the last year for which figures exist, that number had come down to 27,000, a fivefold decrease in deaths from civil and international conflict. In fact, despite the daily dosage of horrific violence displayed in Iraq and Afghanistan, the world has not become a more violent place within the past decade. Rather, the reverse is true. International peacekeeping and nation-building have contributed to this reduced death rate.

The cost of UN nation-building tends to look quite modest compared to the cost of larger and more demanding U.S.-led operations. At present the United States is spending some $4.5 billion per month to support its military operations in Iraq. This is more than the United Nations spends to run all 17 of its current peacekeeping missions for a year. This is not to suggest that the United Nations could perform the U.S. mission in Iraq more cheaply, or perform it at all. It is to underline that there are 17 other places where the United States will probably not have to intervene because UN troops are doing so at a tiny fraction of the cost of U.S.-led operations.

CONTINUING DEFICIENCIES

Even when successful, UN nation building only goes so far to fix the underlying problems of the societies it is seeking to rebuild. Francis Fukuyama has suggested that such missions can be divided into three distinct phases: (1) the initial stabilization of a war-torn society; (2) the creation of local institutions for governance; and (3) the strengthening of those institutions to the point where rapid economic growth and sustained social develop-

---

[1] Paul Collier and Anke Hoeffler, "The Challenge of Reducing the Global Incidence of Civil War," Centre for the Study of African Economies, Department of Economics, Oxford University, Copenhagen Challenge Paper, April 23, 2004, p. 22.

ment can take place.[2] Experience over the past 15 years suggests that the United Nations has achieved a fair mastery of the techniques needed to successfully complete the first two of those tasks. Success with the third has largely eluded the United Nations, as it has the international development community as whole.

Despite the United Nations' significant achievements in the field of nation-building, the organization continues to exhibit weaknesses that decades of experience have yet to overcome. Most UN missions are undermanned and underfunded. UN-led military forces are often sized and deployed on the basis of unrealistic best-case assumptions. Troop quality is uneven and has even gotten worse as many rich Western nations have followed U.S. practice and become less willing to commit their armed forces to UN operations. Police and civil personnel are always of mixed competence. All components of the mission arrive late; police and civil administrators arrive even more slowly than soldiers.

These same weaknesses have been exhibited most recently in the U.S.-led operation in Iraq. There, it was an American-led stabilization force that was deployed on the basis of unrealistic, best-case assumptions and American troops that arrived in inadequate numbers and had to be progressively reinforced as new, unanticipated challenges emerged. There, it was the quality of the U.S.-led coalition's military contingents that proved distinctly variable, as has been their willingness to take orders, risks, and casualties. There, it was American civil administrators who were late to arrive, of mixed competence, and not available in adequate numbers. These weaknesses thus appear to be endemic to nation-building rather than unique to the United Nations.

CONCLUSIONS

Assuming adequate consensus among Security Council members on the purpose for any intervention, the United Nations provides the most suitable institutional framework for most nation-building missions, one with a comparatively low cost structure, a comparatively high success rate, and the greatest degree of international legitimacy. Other possible options are likely to be either more expensive (e.g., coalitions led by the United States, the European Union, NATO) or less capable organizations (e.g., the African Union, the Organization of American States, or ASEAN). The more expen-

---

[2] Francis Fukuyama, State-Building: Governance and World Order in the 21st Century (Ithaca, NY: Cornell University Press, 2004), pp. 99–104..

sive options are best suited to missions that require forced entry or employ more than 20,000 men, which so far has been the effective upper limit for UN operations. The less capable options are suited to missions where there is a regional but not a global consensus for action or where the United States simply does not care enough to foot 25 percent of the bill.

Although the U.S. and UN styles of nation-building are distinguishable, they are also highly interdependent. It is a rare operation in which both are not involved. Both UN and U.S. nation-building efforts presently stand at near historic highs. The United Nations currently has approximately 60,000 troops deployed in 17 countries. This is a modest expeditionary commitment in comparison with that of the United States, but it exceeds that of any other nation or combination of nations. Demand for UN-led peacekeeping operations nevertheless far exceeds the available supply, particularly in sub-Saharan African. American armed forces, the world's most powerful, also find themselves badly overstretched by the demands of such missions. A decade ago, in the wake of UN and U.S. setbacks in Somalia and Bosnia, nation-building became a term of opprobrium leading a significant segment of American opinion to reject the whole concept. Ten years later, nation-building appears ever more clearly as a responsibility that neither the United Nations nor the United States can escape. The United States and the United Nations bring different capabilities to the process. Neither is likely to succeed without the other. Both have much to learn not just from their own experience but also from that of each other. It is our hope that this study and its predecessor will help both to do so.

ACKNOWLEDGMENTS

Several people made important contributions during the course of the project. David Harland and Paula Souverijn-Eisenberg at the United Nations Best Practices Unit, Department of Peacekeeping Operations, organized a series of fruitful discussions on the case study chapters at the UN Headquarters in New York City. They invited prominent UN officials from missions covered in this study, who read drafts of the chapters and offered frank and insightful comments. Special thanks to all those at the UN who participated in the discussions. We also thank Simon Chesterman, Sarah Cliffe, and Ambassador Peter Galbraith for their valuable comments and Francis Fukuyama and Bruce Pirnie for their thoughtful reviews. Two of the authors taught a class at Georgetown University's Edmund A. Walsh School of Foreign Service on nation-building, and they are indebted to the students for their insights. A number of RAND colleagues offered useful insights: James Thomson, Michael Rich, Nora Bensahel, and Olga Oliker. Anga Timilsina provided key research support and collected data for the charts and graphs. Jennie Breon helped put together the final report, and Karen Stewart provided valuable research and administrative support.

AFRC	Armed Forces Revolutionary Council
ANC	Armée Nationale Congolaise
ASDT	Timorese Social Democratic Association
CDF	Civil Defense Force
CIVPOL	unarmed international civilian police
CJSF-7	Combined Joint Strike Force 7
COPAZ	National Commission for the Consolidation of Peace
CPA	Coalition Provisional Authority
CPP	Cambodian People's Party
DFI	Development Fund for Iraq
DoD	U.S. Department of Defense
ECOMOG	Economic Community of West African States Military Observer Group
ECOWAS	Economic Community of West African States
EU	European Union
FMLN	Farabundo Martí National Liberation Front
FRELIMO	Mozambique Liberation Front
FUNCINPEC	United National Front for an Independent, Neutral, Peaceful, and Cooperative Cambodia
GDP	gross domestic product
HDZ	Croatian Democratic Union
IAF	Iraqi Armed Forces
ICDC	Iraqi Civil Defense Corps
ICRC	International Committee of the Red Cross
IDAS	International Danger Disaster Assistance
IGC	Iraqi Governing Council
IIG	Interim Iraqi Government
IMF	International Monetary Fund
INC	Iraqi National Congress
INTERFET	International Force in East Timor
IOM	International Organization of Migration
ITU	International Telecommunications Union

JIC	Joint Implementation Committee
KDP	Kurdistan Democratic Party
mbd	million barrels per day
MINURCA	United Nations Mission in the Central African Republic
MINURSO	United Nations Mission for the Referendum in Western Sahara
MINUSAL	United Nations Mission in El Salvador
MoD	Ministry of Defense
NGO	nongovernmental organization
OFF	Oil for Food
ONUC	United Nations Operation in the Congo
ONUMOZ	United Nations Operation in Mozambique
ONUSAL	United Nations Observer Mission in El Salvador
ORHA	Office for Reconstruction and Humanitarian Assistance
OSCE	Organization for Security and Cooperation in Europe
PUK	Patriotic Union of Kurdistan
RENAMO	Resistencia Nacional Mozambicana
RUF	Revolutionary United Front of Sierra Leone
SCIRI	Supreme Council for the Islamic Revolution in Iraq
SLA	Sierra Leone Army
SWAPO	South West African People's Organization
TAL	Transitional Administrative Law
TPF	Transitional Police Force
UDT	Timorese Democratic Union
UNAMET	United Nations Mission in East Timor
UNAMI	United Nations Assistance Mission for Iraq
UNAMIC	United Nations Advance Mission in Cambodia
UNAMSIL	United Nations Mission in Sierra Leone
UNCRO	United Nations Confidence Restoration Operation for Croatia
UNESCO	United Nations Educational, Scientific, and Cultural Organization
UNHCR	United Nations High Commissioner for Refugees
UNICEF	United Nations Children's Fund
UNIDR	United Nations Institute for Disarmament Research
UNMIL	UN Mission in Liberia
UNMISET	United Nations Mission of Support in East Timor
UNOHAC	United Nations Office for Humanitarian Assistance Coordination
UNOMSIL	United Nations Observer Mission in Sierra Leone
UNPROFOR	United Nations Protection Force
UNSCR	United Nations Security Council Resolution

UNTAC	United Nations Transitional Authority in Cambodia
UNTAES	United Nations Transitional Authority in Eastern Slavonia, Baranja, and Western Sirmium
UNTAET	United Nations Transitional Administration in East Timor
UNTAG	United Nations Transition Assistance Group
WFP	World Food Program
WHO	World Health Organization

Chapter One

INTRODUCTION

Since the end of the Cold War, the United Nations has invested significant military, political, humanitarian, and economic resources into operations conducted in the aftermath of interstate wars and civil unrest. Numerous studies have been published on various aspects of these operations. But this is the first comprehensive effort of which we are aware to review the major UN experiences in nation-building, compare and contrast the quantitative and qualitative results of these operations, and outline best practices and lessons learned.[1]

This is the second volume in RAND's nation-building series. The first volume, *America's Role in Nation-Building: From Germany to Iraq,* looked at eight U.S.-led experiences in nation-building, therein described as the use of armed force in the aftermath of a conflict to promote a transformation to democracy. It began with the post–World War II occupations of Germany and Japan; continued through Somalia, Haiti, Bosnia, Kosovo, and Afghanistan; and ended with a chapter on the Iraqi operation, just beginning at the time of publication. This volume builds on the earlier effort, adding 8 UN cases and again including a chapter updating the U.S. and UN experiences in Iraq. It then uses data from all 16 cases to draw general conclusions about the efficacy of U.S. and UN efforts in this field. The distinction made herein between U.S. and UN-led nation-building operations is not meant to obscure the fact that the United States has supported, often in important ways, all the UN-led operations studied herein and that the UN has participated importantly in all but the two immediate post–World War II U.S.-led

---

[1] Several studies have examined UN peacekeeping operations in detail, including William J. Durch, ed., *UN Peacekeeping, American Politics, and the Uncivil Wars of the 1990s,* New York: St. Martin's Press, 1996; William J. Durch, ed., *The Evolution of UN Peacekeeping: Case Studies and Comparative Analysis,* New York: St. Martin's Press, 1993; and United Nations Department of Public Information, *The Blue Helmets: A Review of United Nations Peace-Keeping,* New York: United Nations, 1996.

operations. Nevertheless, UN "blue helmet" peacekeeping missions, acting under the operational control of the UN Secretary-General and his local representative, are in many ways qualitatively different from multinational operations under American or NATO command. This volume explores those differences while making clear that UN and U.S. efforts in the field of nation-building have been and will remain highly interdependent.

METHODOLOGY

This study focuses on eight UN cases: the Congo, Namibia, El Salvador, Cambodia, Mozambique, Eastern Slavonia, Sierra Leone, and East Timor. It also examines reconstruction efforts in Iraq. Excluding Iraq, these are the most important instances in which UN forces have been used to pursue nation-building objectives. We have chosen the term *nation-building* because it best captures the elements of the phenomenon we want to study: the use of armed force in the aftermath of a conflict to promote a transition to democracy. Other terms, such as *peace-building* or *peacekeeping,* capture only elements of this paradigm: The former often occurs without the use of armed force; the latter is often employed for less far-reaching objectives.

Some have objected that nation-building implies the construction of a common nationality, defined as a group of people who share the same culture, language, and history. *Nation-building* is the most common American term for the phenomenon we wish to study. Most Americans tend to use the terms *state* and *nation* more or less interchangeably, regarding the United States as both, despite its multicultural and increasingly multi-linguistic nature. As used herein, the term *nation-building* is not intended to suggest the suppression or homogenization of distinct cultures within a given society. *State-building,* the reform and strengthening of institutions for governance, is a central component of nation-building but does not normally or necessarily require the application of military force. Nation-building, by contrast, has become almost universally identified with state-building missions that require the use of such force.

Based on this definition, we did not include the UN missions in Western Sahara, Liberia, Angola, the Central African Republic, or a number of other cases. In those cases, either the UN did not deploy armed military forces or UN forces were used for more limited purposes. The United Nations Mission for the Referendum in Western Sahara (MINURSO) focused on monitoring the cease-fire and helping organize a referendum so that the population could choose between independence and integration with Morocco. The

UN Mission in Liberia (UNMIL) concentrated on observing implementation of the cease-fire agreement and providing humanitarian assistance. The UN verification missions to Angola monitored ceasefires and observed elections. The UN Mission in the Central African Republic (MINURCA) supervised the disposition of weapons retrieved in the disarmament process and provided advice and technical support for elections. Some of these are admittedly borderline cases, and others may well develop into full-scale nation-building efforts.

OUTLINE OF THE STUDY

Chapters Two through Nine are case studies of the eight UN-led operations. Chapter Ten is an update of the U.S.-led operation in Iraq. They are designed to draw out "best practice" policies for democratizing states. To achieve this goal, we adopted a common approach.

In each case study, we first provide some historical context and briefly describe the nature of the settlement that ended the conflict. Second, we describe the major challenges facing the United Nations at the beginning of each operation. In particular, we examine the security, humanitarian, administrative, democratization, and economic reconstruction challenges facing the United Nations at the end of the conflict. Third, we describe the roles of the United Nations, relevant countries, the World Bank, International Monetary Fund, and other nongovernmental organizations during each nation-building operation. What were their objectives? What military, financial, and other resources did they provide? Fourth, we examine how each operation developed over time. Did the security environment stabilize or deteriorate? Were humanitarian needs met? How was a civil administration constructed? How did the process of democratization develop? Did economic conditions improve or decline? Finally, we compile the most important lessons learned from each case study that are useful for current and future nation-building operations.

Chapter Eleven weaves the experiences of the eight UN-led cases in this volume and eight U.S.-led cases studied in the first volume into an integrated narrative. Chapter Twelve examines and compares the inputs and the outputs of all these missions. Five input measures are compared across cases: military presence, police presence, duration of presence, timing of elections, and economic assistance. Five outcome measures are also compared across cases: military casualties; refugee returns; a qualitative measure of sustained peace; a qualitative assessment of whether or not a country's government became and has remained democratic; and growth in per capita GDP. Chapter Thirteen concludes with an examination of the differing ways in which the United Nations and the United States have gone about nation-building.

Chapter Two

CONGO

Belgium granted independence to the Republic of the Congo in June 1960. The Belgian Congo, comprising an area already devastated by the Atlantic slave trade, was officially organized in 1885 as the Congo Free State under the absolute rule of King Leopold II of Belgium. Leopold II forged the Congo into a financially lucrative but politically underdeveloped colony that would come to epitomize the "heart of darkness" of European colonialism, characterized by the brutality of the *Force Publique,* the Belgian-led, Congolese-manned local constabulary.[1] In response to an international outcry over the brutality with which the Congolese were treated, the Belgian Parliament annexed the colony in 1908, removing it from the control of the Belgian crown. Belgian colonial administration henceforth actively promoted the material well-being of the Congolese. Belgian officials continued to monopolize political power above the tribal level until the onset of independence. Church-run primary schools provided a substantial number of children with a basic education, but very few Congolese received secondary schooling—let alone a university education. After strongly opposing independence, the Belgians abruptly acceded to Congolese demands, hoping to avoid an Algerian-style insurrection. Belgian administrators and military officers were authorized to serve the new state as advisors until their new Congolese counterparts learned the government operations necessary to function independently. Within days of acquiring independence on June 30, 1960, however, enlisted Congolese members of the *Force Publique* mutinied. Soldiers attacked local white civilians, looting, raping, and inciting a mass exodus of Belgian officers, administrators, and settlers during the summer of 1960.[2] The troops mutinied on the grounds that newly elected Congolese officials were making themselves rich from government coffers, in contrast to the low wages

---

[1] Adam Hochschild, *King Leopold's Ghost: A Story of Greed, Terror, and Heroism in Colonial Africa,* Boston: Houghton Mifflin, 1998.

[2] Susan Brownmiller, *Against Our Will: Men, Women, and Rape,* New York: Simon and Schuster, 1975, pp. 132–139.

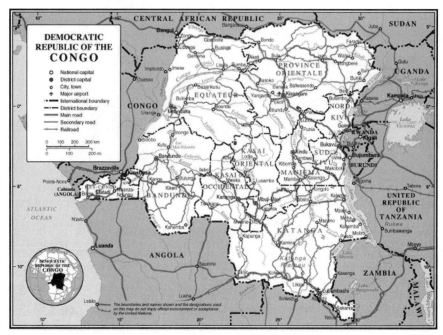

SOURCE: United Nations Cartographic Section, Democratic Republic of the Congo, no. 4007 Rev. 8, January 2004. Available online at http://www.un.org/Depts/ Cartographic/english/htmain.htm.

RAND MG304-2.1

Figure 2.1—Map of the Congo

and poor working conditions provided to soldiers in the *Force Publique*.[3] The newly independent state plunged into chaos. As former UN Undersecretary-General Brian Urquhart aptly described it: "Events in the first days of independence went at a dizzying pace. The army mutinied and threw out its Belgian officers, Europeans were roughed up, and there were reports of white women being raped. The Belgian population panicked and left.... Public administration, law, and order evaporated and were replaced by chaos and anarchy."[4]

The mutiny challenged the democratically elected Congolese government under the leadership of Prime Minister Patrice Lumumba and President Joseph Kasavubu, By August 1960, the Congo's nascent political, social, and

---

[3] M. Crawford Young, "Post-Independence Politics in the Congo," *Transition*, Vol. 26, 1966, pp. 34–35.

[4] Brian Urquhart, "The Tragedy of Lumumba," *The New York Review of Books*, Vol. XLVIII, Number 15, October 4, 2001, p. 4.

economic institutions had collapsed. Katanga, under the leadership of its elected provincial president, Moise Tshombe, declared independence on July 11, 1960, thereby depriving the central government in Léopoldville of export revenue from copper extracted from this rich mining area. The Brussels government, in violation of the Treaty of Friendship between Belgium and the Congo, sent Belgian paratroopers to protect its nationals against mutinous troops from the *Armée Nationale Congolaise* (ANC), as the *Force Publique* was now called.

In response, Prime Minister Lumumba requested that the United Nations dispatch troops to restore order and oust the Belgian "aggressors." Secretary-General Dag Hammarskjöld supported the request and secured a UN Security Council resolution authorizing the dispatch of a UN force, the United Nations Operation in the Congo (ONUC), to restore law and order and promote economic and political stability. Belgium agreed to withdraw its troops but only if they could be replaced by UN troops.

CHALLENGES

The United Nations was called upon to restore order, secure the removal of Belgian forces, and help establish an indigenous government in a nascent country with a mutinous army, a breakaway province, and little experience in self-government.

Security

Despite efforts by newly appointed Congolese officers, the Leopoldville regime could not contain the ANC mutiny. Nevertheless, both Lumumba and the international community regarded Belgium's intervention as the greater threat because it represented a challenge to the whole process of decolonization.

The Katangan secession further deepened the security crisis. Citing the "chaos" in the country, Tshombe declared Katanga independent from the Congo on July 11, 1960, the same day that Belgium intervened militarily. Tshombe hired Belgian military officers and Western mercenaries to prevent government troops from retaking Katanga. Lumumba responded by declaring Tshombe an agent of neocolonial Belgian interests collaborating with the powerful mining company, *Union Minière du Haut Katanga,* and vowed to suppress the rebellion. Katanga's secession was followed by that of Kasai province under the leadership of Albert Kolonji.

Humanitarian

Health services collapsed with the Belgian exodus, leaving only Congolese *assistants médicaux* and Catholic nuns to care for the sick and injured.[5] Public health services to inoculate against and suppress epidemic diseases broke down. Sleeping sickness, tuberculosis, leprosy, malaria, typhus, typhoid, and even bubonic plague all emerged during the summer of 1960.

Prime Minister Lumumba launched an invasion of Kasai province to suppress the newly declared "Mining State" under the tribal leadership of Albert Kalonji. Kalonji, like Tshombe, sought a federal constitutional framework for the Congo that guaranteed provincial autonomy. The ANC invasion resulted in the slaughter of members of the Baluba tribe, who were also attacked by their traditional enemies, the Lulua tribe. More than 350,000 starving Balubas fled the province. Famine throughout South Kasai added to the humanitarian problems. With the intensification of conflict in Katanga, a second wave of refugees fled to Elizabethville, that province's capital.

Even the normal commercial distribution of food was disrupted by the Belgian exodus. After the Belgians, who ran the seaport of Matadi, fled, the port closed and the channel quickly silted up. The blockage of the channel and closure of the port prevented imported food from reaching the Congo, soon leading to serious shortages.

Civil Administration

The Lumumba government had originally authorized the former colonial administrators to remain in the Congo to assist the newly elected politicians and appointed civil servants. Because very few Congolese had sufficient qualifications to assume senior administrative responsibilities, the Belgian expatriates' experience and expertise were crucial. Tshombe kept up such an arrangement in Katanga through 1963 and succeeded in maintaining security and administrative efficiency. With the onset of the ANC mutiny, the Belgian administrative and technical advisers in Léopoldville

---

[5] Gordon King, *The United Nations in the Congo; a Quest for Peace* Washington, D.C.: Carnegie Endowment for International Peace, 1962, p. 67.

quickly deserted their posts, leaving most new Congolese officials unable to cope.

The fiscal challenges facing the new nation would have challenged experienced Belgian officials; they rapidly overwhelmed the new Congolese bureaucrats, who had expected to dispose of the vast sums of money they assumed had previously been controlled by the Belgians. Many of these officials focused on political maneuvers to maximize their personal power and wealth, contributing to the collapse of basic services, including sanitation, the post office, the railroad, air-traffic control, radio communications, and education during the summer of 1960.

Democratization

Democracy in the newly independent Congo meant different things to different people. To the Belgian colonial regime, it had meant organizing parliamentary elections, which resulted in Lumumba's selection as prime minister. To the Afro-Asian and Soviet-bloc states, it meant liberating the Congo from Belgian colonial control. To the United States, it meant ensuring that the country not "fall" to a communist dictatorship. Western, communist, and nonaligned powers all agreed that democracy in the Congo meant a powerful centralized government in Léopoldville that could resist external colonial designs and internal insurgents. Such a consensus, however, did not exist within the Congo. For the rich mining provinces of Kasai and Katanga, democracy meant maintaining strong local autonomy to protect their valuable economic assets from depredation by the military or the central government in Léopoldville. To the central authorities in Léopoldville , especially the supporters of Lumumba, democracy meant maintaining a strong centralized regime to counter the tribal pressures that could fracture the complex array of cultures within the Congo into a number of small, weak nations as subsequently occurred in French Equatorial Africa and French West Africa.

Economic Reconstruction

During the insurrection, the Congo suffered significant losses in human, though not physical, capital. The damage ANC mutineers inflicted on the Congo's physical infrastructure was minimal. During the colonial regime, Belgium had invested substantial sums in transportation infrastructure, agriculture, mining, education, and health. Although the ANC engaged in some looting, this infrastructure remained largely undamaged. Any material losses came from a lack of maintenance of modern machinery during the summer of 1960. Neglected machinery ranged from agricultural machinery, steamboats, and railroad locomotives to communications equipment and harbor-dredging equipment.

Congolese officials had to arrange for the transfer of assets from Belgium to the new Congolese government, a very complicated financial transaction at the time of a looming fiscal crisis. Capital flight in 1959 and early 1960, which occurred because of the initial independence negotiations, had already reduced the Congo's foreign exchange reserves to dangerously low levels. The economic downturn in commodity prices in the late 1950s also fueled high budget deficits. The Belgian Congo's budget deficit reached approximately $40 million by the time independence was declared, roughly 25 percent of the Congo's estimated GDP in 1960. The financial problems grew much worse after the secession of Katanga, the primary source of government revenues.

UN AND OTHER INTERNATIONAL ROLES

On July 12, 1960, the Congolese government asked for military assistance from the United Nations. Two days later, the Security Council asked Belgium to withdraw its troops from the Congo and authorized military assistance. In less than 48 hours, contingents of a UN force began to arrive in the country. The United Nations also rushed civilian experts to the Congo to help ensure the continued provision of public services.

Foreign powers profoundly shaped the Congo crisis. The Soviet Union and a number of Third World countries had encouraged the Congolese to demand immediate independence even though their capacity to administer the country and run large local businesses was inadequate. Belgium sought to protect its economic and political interests in the Congo, especially Katanga, even after independence. Cold War rivalries also fueled the crisis. The Soviet Union under Nikita Khrushchev viewed the Congo as an opportunity to expand communist influence in Central Africa. The People's Republic of China was initially indifferent to the Congo but eventually seized on the crisis to promote Maoist-style wars of national liberation in Africa. This led to China's support of the "Simba Rebellion" in eastern Congo that commenced in 1963. The United States engaged in the new Republic of Congo primarily to resist communist expansion and secondarily to support Western economic interests. Great Britain, Portugal, and France reacted strongly to the Congo crisis, perceiving that unrest there could threaten their control of neighboring colonial territories. Finally, other ex-colonial nations, especially Algeria, Egypt, Ghana, Nigeria, and India, viewed the Congo as a means to promote their international influence as champions of anticolonialism. ONUC was especially dependent on financial and logistical support from the United States and on political and military support from India.

Military and Police
In response to the ANC mutiny, Belgian intervention, and the general breakdown of law and order, the UN Security Council authorized the Secretary-General on July 14, 1960, to

> [T]ake the necessary steps, in consultation with the Government of the Republic of the Congo, to provide the Government with such military assistance as may be necessary, until, through the efforts of the Congolese Government with the technical assistance of the United Nations, the national security forces may be able, in the opinion of the government, to meet fully their tasks.[6]

The resolution also called on Belgium to "withdraw their troops from the territory of the Republic of the Congo." Eight days later, on July 22, 1960, the Security Council passed a second resolution (UNSCR 4405), directing ONUC to ensure the withdrawal of Belgian troops, and calling "upon the government of Belgium to implement speedily the Security Council resolution of 14 July 1960, on the withdrawal of their troops and authorized the Secretary-General to take all necessary action to this effect."[7]

ONUC included a peacekeeping force that reached a peak of nearly 20,000 officers and soldiers. Approximately 30 countries contributed forces and military personnel, including Argentina, Canada, India, Ireland, Pakistan, Sierra Leone, and the United Arab Emirates. In February 1963, a battalion of the Congolese National Army was incorporated into ONUC. The force also included a military police company, which was composed of military

[6] Ernest W. Lefever, *Crisis in the Congo: A United Nations Force in Action*, Washington, D.C.: Brookings Institution, 1965, p. 190.

[7] Lefever (1965), p. 191.

police from Canada, Denmark, India, Indonesia, Ireland, and Norway. The company headquarters was located in Léopoldville, and detachments were located at Kamina Base, Elizabethville, and Léopoldville.

In addition, the United Nations deployed a civilian police unit to assist what was left of the Congolese police in maintaining civil order. A small police unit from Ghana was attached to the force in 1960. It operated in the capital, Léopoldville, but was withdrawn after a few months because of the deteriorating security environment. Eventually, Nigeria sent a 400-member police contingent to the Congo under a tripartite agreement between the United Nations, the Congo, and Nigeria. Most of the Nigerian police contingent were stationed in the capital, Léopoldville, with small units in several of the provincial capitals.

Civil and Economic
The United Nations also assumed responsibility for assisting the Congolese government in providing the essential services of an independent state. It helped with administration and with establishing order. The UN decision to intervene in the Congo was in part a response to Belgian rhetoric that Western colonialism was justified on the grounds that black Africans were incapable of governing themselves. On September 20, 1960, the Security Council determined "that, with a view to preserving the unity, territorial integrity and political independence of the Congo, to protecting and advancing the welfare of its people, and to safeguarding international peace, it is essential for the United Nations to continue to assist the Central government of the Congo."[8] This authorization endorsed the initial agreement that Hammarskjöld had reached with Lumumba on July 29, 1960, whereby the UN operation would involve both military and civil support functions.[9]

WHAT HAPPENED

Fielding forces of up to 20,000 combat troops and spending close to half a billion dollars, the United Nations achieved its principal goals: the departure of Belgian military forces, the preservation of the Congo's territorial integrity, and the avoidance of an East-West confrontation. However, the process proved messy, costly, and controversial. ONUC failed to eliminate,

---

[8] Lefever (1965), p. 193.

[9] Lefever (1965), p. 198

and in some respects contributed to, the constitutional weaknesses of the Congolese government, which succumbed to the highly corrupt dictatorship of General Sese Seko Mobutu in 1965. ONUC did not halt civil war or stop foreign interference after it departed in 1964. This included communist Chinese and Cuban involvement in the Simba Rebellion of the eastern provinces, the use of Western mercenaries to defeat them, and American involvement in Mobutu's final coup d'état. Despite the United Nations' success in achieving its principal objectives, the experience of the Congo generated an enduring resistance within the Secretariat and among member states to peace enforcement and nation-building missions.

Security

When Hammarskjöld organized and deployed ONUC forces to the Congo in July 1960, the primary objective was to end the ANC mutiny and restore basic law and order. These were the conditions Belgium had set for the withdrawal of its forces. ONUC was successful in disarming some ANC units and replacing Belgian troops, even though UN troops were, at this stage, under strict orders to use force only in self-defense and when all other options were exhausted. Suspicions within the Lumumba government and its difficulties in controlling the ANC made it impossible to systematically disarm and retrain the ANC. After secession crises in Kasai and Katanga provinces emerged as serious threats, support for this option further receded. Colonel Mobutu, the newly appointed chief of staff, reinforced the government's unwillingness to trust ONUC with disarming the ANC. He viewed giving ONUC the job of disarmament as a personal loss of face, especially if it involved conceding that the entire ANC was dysfunctional. Both he and President Kasavubu agreed that, in spite of the mutiny, an intact ANC ensured that the United Nations would never attempt to impose a trusteeship on the Congo. Despite these obstacles, ONUC generally succeeded in establishing security in those areas where its forces were deployed in strength, especially in key strategic sites, such as Léopoldville, the airports, and most refugee camps. Such stability dissipated, however, when ONUC withdrew from a particular location or was not aggressive enough in deterring ANC violence, as in northern Katanga.

Difficult as it was to secure Lumumba's cooperation in establishing civilian control over the ANC, a far more contentious problem existed in Katanga. President Tshombe initially refused to let ONUC operate there. Although he eventually allowed Belgian troops to be replaced by ONUC forces, he hired Belgian officers to command the Katanga gendarmerie. This gave him a force that was better disciplined and more combat capable than the ANC. It also fueled Lumumba's charges that Tshombe was a "Belgian stooge." Lumumba charged that Tshombe's criticism of the political centralization embodied in the *loi fundamentale* (the provisional constitutional arrangement) was only a cover for Belgian neocolonialism. So intense were Lumumba's demands for ONUC to remove Tshombe and the secessionist leadership that they provoked an ugly break with Hammarskjöld in August 1960. The Secretary-General resisted having ONUC coerce Katanga militarily on behalf of Lumumba's regime. He felt such a role would destroy any sense of the United Nations' political neutrality—Hammarskjöld's central diplomatic ideal.

President Kasavubu dismissed Lumumba in September 1960, following the Prime Minister's "genocidal" campaign against the independence movement in Kasai and the ANC's poor performance in its initial offensive against the Katanga gendarmerie. Lumumba refused to cede his post, however, provoking a constitutional crisis. The central government was dealt a further blow when Mobutu launched the first of his coups d'état. His declared objective was to neutralize the power struggle between Kasavubu and Lumumba and compel them to cooperate.[10] His action instigated a further breakdown of central political authority. Hammarskjöld responded by authorizing ONUC to close all airports to prevent Lumumba from using loyal ANC units from his political base in Stanleyville to seize control of other sections of the country. In so doing, ONUC effectively supported Kasavubu. Although ONUC maintained a heavy guard to protect the ousted Lumumba from his political enemies, especially those in the ANC, they made no attempt to rescue him from Colonel Mobutu's forces when he was seized attempting to flee to his power base in Stanleyville in December 1961. The same apparent indifference on the part of the United Nations applied when Mobutu and Kasavubu sent the captured Lumumba to his Katangan enemies in Elizabethville, where he was executed by Belgian mercenaries under Tshombe's command.[11]

Lumumba's execution provoked an anticolonialist outcry around the world and provoked the Security Council to order the suppression of the Katangan secession. This determination was expressed in Resolution 4741 of February 21, 1961, directing ONUC to "take immediately all appropriate measures to prevent the occurrence of civil war in the Congo, including arrangements for cease-fires, the halting of all military operations, the prevention

---

[10] Rajeshwar Dayal, *Mission for Hammarskjold: The Congo Crisis*, Delhi: Oxford University Press, 1976, p. 63.

[11] Ludo de Witte, *The Assassination of Lumumba*, London: Verso, 2001.

of clashes, and the use of force, if necessary, in the last resort." This broad mandate provided for the possibility that ONUC might engage in coercive military action. The resolution also called for an international investigation of Lumumba's death and a trial for his murderers, something Kasavubu and Mobuto took as a personal threat. Lumumba's execution also caused Soviet leader Nikita Khrushchev to demand Hammarskjöld's resignation and to provide formal support to the Lumumbist rebellion in Stanleyville under the leadership of Antoine Gizenga. Lumumba's demise was not, however, entirely unwelcome in New York or Washington. Both Hammarskjöld and the Kennedy administration had turned sharply against Lumumba by September 1960, following the his success in securing Soviet logistical support to reconquer Katanga. Both believed that preventing Soviet involvement in Congolese affairs was a primary, albeit unacknowledged, goal of the UN operation.[12] Lumumba's death went far to secure that objective.

It took the United Nations almost two years and three separate offensives to end the Katangan secession and Lumumbist rebellion. In the process of completing this mission, ONUC abandoned all pretense of political neutrality. The first UN military move, in summer 1961, was in support of the newly formed government of Prime Minister Cyrille Adoula against the Lumumbist rebellion in Stanleyville. ONUC played a key role in defusing that conflict by creating a neutral zone between the ANC forces loyal to Léopoldville and those fighting under Gizenga. Nevertheless, the ultimate survival of the politically moderate Adoula depended on his receiving credit for ending the Katangan succession. Frustrations with Tshombe's intransigence and military buildup finally convinced Hammarskjöld, despite pressure from U.S. President John F. Kennedy to avoid coercive force, to move against Katanga in an offensive operation labeled *Rumpunch*. Having steadily built up UN forces within Katanga, the UN Secretary-General's representative, Conor Cruise O'Brien from Ireland, launched a surprise operation on August 27, 1961. It succeeded in arresting and expelling some of the unauthorized Belgian officers and mercenaries from Katanga. Of the 506 known mercenaries, ONUC arrested 300 and repatriated 185 without bloodshed.[13] ONUC justified its offensive action by arguing that it lessened the political pressure on Adoula to launch an ANC offensive against Katanga. Far more controversial was a second UN offensive, Operation Mortar, which O'Brien launched on September 13, 1961. Convinced that prior arrests had sufficiently weakened the Katangan

---

[12] Lise A. Namikas, "Battleground Africa: The Cold War and the Congo Crisis, 1960–1965," Dissertation, University of Southern California, 2002.

[13] Namikas (2002), p. 319.

Gendarmerie, ONUC forces sought to capture the Katangan leadership but encountered unexpectedly heavy resistance. A company of Irish soldiers was forced to surrender at Jadotville, and the Katanga Gendarmerie managed to fight the other, predominantly Indian, units in ONUC to a standstill. Even more humiliating was the United Nations' inability to counter a Katangan Fouga fighter plane that attacked the ONUC forces with impunity. By the third day of the offensive, the United Nations had suffered 7 dead and 26 wounded, compared with 200 dead and 500 wounded on the Katangan side. These latter figures included substantial numbers of civilians caught in the crossfire.[14] To make matters worse, Hammarskjöld was killed on September 17, 1961, when his plane crashed in Northern Rhodesia. He was on his way to meet with Tshombe to negotiate a cease-fire. U Thant of Burma became the new UN Secretary-General. Thant proved far less restrained than his predecessor in the employment of UN military forces to end the Katangan secession.

In the cease-fire that followed Operation Mortar, ONUC rebuilt its forces, acquired fighter aircraft, and permitted ANC forces to invade Katanga. The repulse of the ANC by the Katangan gendarmerie led the ANC to sack the European quarter in Luluabourg, the capital of Kasai province, where all whites were arrested and many women raped. ONUC was powerless to stop these ANC depredations. Matters became even worse in Albertville, where the local ONUC commander persuaded the Katangan commander to withdraw in the face of 1,500 ANC troops, resulting in a devastating sack of that city.[15] ONUC's inability to restrain the anarchy that accompanied ANC offensives culminated with the massacre of 13 of the United Nations' own Italian airmen by ANC elements.

The brutal violence associated with the Katangan secession led the Security Council to direct ONUC, on November 24, 1961, to remove all foreign military personnel from Katanga, by force if necessary. On December 14, 1961, ONUC launched Operation Unokat in response to the establishment of roadblocks by Katangan forces. The ensuing battle between 6,000 ONUC and 3,000 Katangan troops in Elizabethville was intense. ONUC accidentally hit numerous civilian targets with its new air power, including hospitals and mining facilities, as well as the offices of the *L'Union Miniére*, whose tax payments were bankrolling the Katangan secession. The flexible defensive tactics of the Katangan forces succeeded in frustrating ONUC, al-

---

[14] George Martelli, *Experiment in World Government: An Account of the United Nations Operation in the Congo, 1960–1964*, London: Johnson Publications, 1966, p. 147.

[15] Martelli (1966), p. 147·

though ONUC forces slowly gained ground. After a week of combat, ONUC had suffered 10 dead and 34 wounded; the Katangans endured 141 dead and 401 wounded.[16] Operation Unokat left ONUC in control of the Katangan capital of Elizabethville, but the rest of southern Katanga remained loyal to Tshombe. The ANC continued to commit atrocities throughout northern Katanga, including the massacre of 19 Belgian priests in Kongolo, which ONUC again proved powerless to prevent.

The final ONUC offensive against Katanga was Operation Grandslam. This operation followed more than a year of uneasy truce, during which the United Nations, Tshombe, Adoula, and the United States negotiated a new constitution. Tshombe ultimately rejected the "Thant Plan" for national reconciliation, which many considered to be unworkable. Tshombe insisted that only a loose confederation of Congolese states would allow Katanga province to maintain the stability that its mining operations demanded. U Thant grew increasingly impatient with ONUC involvement in the Congo. Unlike Hammarskjöld, who appreciated ONUC's role in developing political and economic institutions in the country, U Thant viewed ending the Katanga secession as the only justification for the ONUC operation. Fighting between Katangan and ONUC troops eventually broke out on Christmas Eve 1962 in Elizabethville. UN forces advanced throughout southern Katanga, including the mining centers of Jadotville and Kolwezi. Tshombe's surrender of Elizabethville in January 1963 signaled the end of the Katangan secession.

The conquest of Katanga by ONUC was not followed by effective steps to discipline the ANC. Both the United States and the Soviet Union offered training programs, but U Thant rejected them to preserve political neutrality. Mobutu successfully lobbied the Kennedy administration to supply arms to loyal ANC units, but he rejected efforts to reform the ANC in order to protect his power base in the ranks.[17] Although ONUC remained in the Congo until June 1964, funded by the United States, the country was still volatile when the United Nations departed. The ANC continued to prey on civilians. It was incapable of mounting disciplined operations in the face of the growing threat to national unity from the Chinese communist–sponsored revolt that commenced in Kwilu Province.

---

[16] Martelli (1966), p. 160.

[17] Sean Kelly, *America's Tyrant: The CIA and Mobutu of Zaire*, Washington, D.C.: American University Press, 1993, pp. 89–90.

Throughout their years in the Congo, UN troops monitored numerous cease-fires and occupied buffer zones between rival Congolese forces. Although the quality of their service differed dramatically, some units, such as the Nigerians in Kasai and the Moroccans in the port city of Matadi, were quite effective in restoring order and maintaining calm.[18] On the other hand, the inability of UN troops to restrain the ANC in Northern Katanga was inexcusable. ONUC also provided essential protection for refugee camps, airports, political centers (especially the Parliament building in Léopoldville), and individual political figures. UN troops served as escorts for UN civilian administrators and provided protection service for ONUC civilian workers. In spite of such service, ONUC was never able to secure the trust of the Congolese military and political establishment. The Congolese never discarded their suspicion that ONUC was guided by foreign designs, rather than operated in the best internal interests of the Congolese.

Humanitarian

In summer 1960, Hammarskjöld made an urgent appeal to the International Red Cross to send teams of physicians and nurses to the Congo. The health crisis there was beyond the limited resources of the United Nations' World Health Organization (WHO). More than 20 nations responded. These medical teams initially served as replacements for the Belgian physicians who had fled, much to the relief of the beleaguered nuns and Congolese *assistants médicaux*. They also instituted a series of training programs to make the Congolese self-sufficient.[19] In addition to on-the-job training, ONUC recruited six medical professors to augment the medical education program at Lovanium University, which the Belgians had established shortly before independence. ONUC also helped establish a Swiss and French program to educate Congolese *assistants médicaux* as full-fledged physicians. Sixty-one students started this three-year accelerated program in 1960, followed by another group of 51 in 1961.[20]

In light of the breakdown of preventive health care services, which had been overseen by Belgian expatriates, ONUC faced the daunting prospect of outbreaks of disease. Intensive vaccination campaigns were conducted to control outbreaks of smallpox in South Kasai during the summer of 1961. ONUC made significant efforts to provide health care to the numerous refu-

---

[18] Arthur M. Bullock, *An Assessment of Peace Operations in the Congo*, Santa Monica, Calif.: RAND Corporation, 1994, p. 45.

[19] King (1962), p. 67.

[20] King (1962), p. 68.

gee camps, especially those of the Baluba. As UN Representative Rajashwar Dayal described it:

> The site that met our unbelieving eyes was one of utter desolation. Thousands upon thousands of refugees, sick and emaciated, their children with bloated stomachs caused by hunger, were crouching under trees or cowering from the rain in the most elementary shelter. The small hospital barracks, which had beds for two-dozen, were crowded with hundreds of seriously ill and dying. The stench was indescribable. Our United Nations doctors were doing a magnificent job and the Indian nursing sisters, the first to volunteer, were like ministering angels to the suffering. Till the arrival of U.N. medical assistance, a couple of Congolese medical assistants had been bravely labouring to give what help they could. But by now international aid was beginning to come in as a result of the worldwide appeal which I had inaugurated.[21]

ONUC, in short, was relatively successful from a medical and public health perspective. This success was matched by the UN effort to provide food relief. The United Nations delivered emergency shipments of food to Léopoldville, in response to the breakdown of internal transportation during summer 1960 and the resulting skyrocketing food prices. Later, ONUC provided sizable quantities of food to refugees in both Kasai and Kivu provinces. Substantial loss of life from starvation and disease was therefore one curse that the Congo was spared.

Civil Administration

ONUC coordinated its efforts to support the civil administration of the Léopoldville regime through the Consultative Group, a civil "general staff" of senior advisors selected from various UN agencies. The Consultative Group was made up of experts in agriculture, communications, education, finance, foreign trade, health, instruction (national security forces), labor markets, law, natural resources and industry, and public administration.[22] Operating within broad UN authorization to offer "technical assistance," they

---

[21] Dayal (1976), p. 166.

[22] Harold Karan Jacobson, "ONUC's Civil Operations: State-Preserving and State-Building," *World Politics*, Vol. 17, No. 1, October 1964, p. 84.

embarked on an ambitious program to train Congolese administrators to manage government functions. They also assisted in long-term planning of central economic, educational, and social services. They attempted to build the bureaucratic institutions that the Belgian colonial regime had neglected to create. The challenges were overwhelming. Not only were the newly appointed Congolese administrators poorly educated, they were constantly distracted by internal power struggles and corrupt political maneuverings in the capital and throughout the provinces.[23] The Consultative Group never received the international political and financial support that the military branch of ONUC enjoyed. Many African and Asian states resented the international subsidization of Congolese institution-building when their own nations suffered from comparable problems. The Consultative Group itself proved to be an awkward experiment in coordination: Most of the members retained their primary affiliation with their specialized UN agencies.[24]

Among the more successful institution-building achievements of the Consultative Group was the establishment of basic training courses at the National School of Law and Administration. The Consultative Group began offering an intensive course in public administration for 300 civil servants during the fall of 1960. The Ford Foundation gave a grant to the National School of Law and Administration in February 1961 to establish a four-year educational program, which ONUC augmented with scholarships to 300 students.[25] ONUC also helped expand and improve secondary education. In October 1961, the Consultative Group organized the Pedagogical Institute in Léopoldville. With a teaching staff furnished by the United Nations Educational, Scientific, and Cultural Organization (UNESCO), they enrolled 76 students to address the urgent shortage of qualified secondary school teachers.[26] ONUC administrators also strove to redirect the religious orientation of the Congolese educational curriculum by recruiting more than 554 new secondary school teachers. An emphasis on vocational training replaced the traditional European focus on the classics.

---

[23] As one ONUC member reported in February 1961, "Preoccupied with political issues, neither the Central nor the Provincial Authorities have seemed to pay sufficient attention to the economic situation under their respective control. In spite of repeated warnings and recommendations by ONUC's advisers, no practical measures have been taken so far to check or alleviate the danger of further disintegration." See UN Secretariat, "Progress report No. 9 on United Nations Civilian Operations in the Congo during February 1961," pp. 1–2.

[24] Robert L. West, "The United Nations and the Congo Financial Crisis," *International Organization*, Vol. 15, No. 4, Autumn 1961, p. 616.

[25] King (1962), p. 71.

[26] King (1962), p. 70.

By the end of 1962, 332 Congolese students had studied abroad with UN support, and over 9,464 Congolese had attended various ONUC training courses.[27] The supply of textbooks and the construction of new schools were severely hampered by the Congo's fiscal problems, although the government did receive financial support for education from UNESCO, the Ford Foundation, and the U.S. Agency for International Development. Between 1962 and 1963, more than 20,000 primary school teachers were simply not paid; the provincial authorities diverted the funds received from the central government to other uses.[28] In light of these problems, it is all the more remarkable that between the Congolese government and ONUC, almost three times as many children were enrolled in secondary schools in 1963 than before independence.

Under the leadership of Paul Gardiner, a prominent Ghanaian economist, the Consultative Group helped design a formal organizational structure for the different ministries. Implementing the plans proved difficult. The national administrators and politicians remained suspicious about accepting ONUC's advice on government administration. Although the Congolese were frustrated by their inability to handle their new responsibilities, they did not hesitate to assert their authority. The corrupt tendencies already in place under the Lumumba regime continued to grow under Adoula. Yet ONUC's institution-building efforts to strengthen the bureaucratic power of the central government relative to the provincial governments were significant. The relative ease with which Mobutu was able to concentrate power appears to have been due in part to the mechanisms of administrative power that ONUC worked so hard to construct.[29]

Democratization
Democratization was never the principal goal of ONUC. Promoting decolonization, avoiding a direct or proxy East-West conflict in the Congo, and preserving the territorial integrity of this newly independent nation were the priorities of Hammarskjöld and U Thant. If the international community were to tolerate the Congo's fragmentation along tribal, ethnic, or other lines, what other newly independent state could stand secure within its equally arbitrary colonial frontiers? As soon as Tshombe surrendered control of Katanga in January 1963, most newly independent states lost interest

---

[27] Jacobson (1964), p. 92.

[28] Basile Mabusa, "The Crisis in Education: A Congolese View," in Kitchen (1967), p. 94.

[29] Jacobson (1964), p. 102

in the Congo operation, preferring to focus their energies on further decolonization campaigns involving the colonies of Great Britain, Portugal, and South Africa.[30]

ONUC did pursue the creation of a democratic government in the Congo. It also insisted on territorial integrity. However, the Congolese government focused on liberating the country from foreign, especially Belgian, interference. ONUC's commitment to maintain the territorial integrity of a former colonial state, which comprised hundreds of ethnic groups scattered over an area approximating the eastern half of the United States, placed the United Nations in direct confrontation with local political aspirations to resist the chaotic rule of the central government. Both Hammarskjöld and U Thant were prepared to intervene in the democratic process to ensure a political outcome that fulfilled their geopolitical goals, including a determination not to let the Congo fall into the Soviet camp. The Secretary General's reaction to the removal of Lumumba as Prime Minister in September 1960 was subtle, but decisive. Lumumba's dictatorial political tendencies, as shown by the massacre of civilians in Kasai province, were augmented by his success in obtaining sizeable quantities of Soviet aid. When President Kasavubu announced Lumumba's removal as prime minister, a constitutionally dubious maneuver, Hammarskjöld directed his temporary representative, Andrew Cordier, to take steps to ensure that Lumumba would be unable to launch either a political or military counterattack.[31] ONUC troops shut down the Léopoldville airport to prevent Lumumba from receiving support from loyal ANC troops in Stanleyville. They also blocked him from using the radio station to broadcast his counterdemands for Kasavubu's ouster.[32] Cordier would later argue that his actions were intended to prevent Lumumba from turning the Congo into a communist state.

Tshombe, in contrast, was viewed as a bastion of anticommunism in Africa. Yet his campaign for a federal Congo made up of a loose confederation of autonomous states earned him much opprobrium from both ONUC and the United States. Tshombe initially convinced Kasavubu to agree to a new federal constitution at the Tananarive Conference in March 1961. This was the first time a basic constitutional agreement had been reached in the Congo without foreign interference. Yet the UN community, includ-

[30] Martelli (1966), p. 216.

[31] Namikas (2002), p. 184.

[32] For a description of Lumumba's anger over this interference in Congolese politics in the name of preventing violence, see Dayal (1976), pp. 53–54. For a discussion of both Kennedy's and Hammarsjköld's determination to have Lumumba removed from power, see Namikas (2002), pp. 168–171.

ing Hammarskjöld, immediately dismissed the accord and helped stoke internal Congolese opposition to it.[33] Hammarskjöld particularly resented the opposition to ONUC expressed in the agreement. Further UN interference in the democratic political process of the Congo occurred during the Lovanium Conference, which sought to reopen the parliament and to elect a new prime minister with the full participation of the rebellious Gizenga. Hammarskjöld was eager to see the conflict between Stanleyville and Léopoldville settled through political reconciliation. Yet he did little to inhibit American manipulation of the conference to ensure the election of Adoula as prime minister and the relegation of Gizenga to the relatively powerless position of vice prime minister.[34] Kennedy was determined not to let the pro-Soviet Gizenga become prime minister.

Economic Reconstruction

Budgetary shortfalls strangled the new republic. Balancing the budget was among the most pressing tasks facing ONUC. During the summer of 1960, ONUC suspended foreign exchange transactions to prevent hard currency reserves from being drained by fleeing refugees. In response to the severe drop in revenue resulting from the secession of Katanga and Kasai provinces, the United Nations gave the Lumumba regime a grant of $5 million to keep his government solvent.[35] This was followed by a grant of $10 million.[36] These emergency stopgap measures were insufficient, however. ONUC helped establish the Monetary Council to monitor central banking operations and to finance public debt. The Consultant in Finance, within the Consultative Group, served as its president. UN financial experts advised the Congolese authorities on the complexities of securing Congolese financial assets from Belgium and played a key role in helping Prime Minister Adoula negotiate with Belgium over the colonial debt and Belgian ownership of private companies operating in the Congo.[37] The Consultative Group also provided intensive financial training to Congolese civil servants and made substantial progress toward developing coherent fiscal policies. Unfortunately, external events derailed their implementation.

---

[33] Martelli (1966), p. 89.

[34] Namikas (2002), pp. 307–308.

[35] West (1961), p. 608.

[36] Jacobson (1964), p. 86.

[37] Jacobson (1964), p. 93.

The secession of Katanga and Kasai, followed by the Lumumbist rebellion in Stanleyville, made it impossible for the central government to meet its budget obligations. Because of the collapse in revenues, the government stopped servicing its debts. Rebellious provincial authorities often illegally transferred funds, and the ANC routinely refused to operate within its assigned budget.[38] Corruption made the fiscal management of the "parastatal" companies, including the public utilities, difficult to control.[39] ONUC found it difficult to recruit qualified financial experts to work in the Congo, especially because the government discouraged the employment of experienced expatriate Belgian managers for political reasons. The unsettled, often dangerous security environment and the exclusion of Belgian expatriate staff left the central government with only a small fraction of the financial experts who had been available to the Belgian colonial regime. Revenue shortfalls, the lack of expenditure controls, and a shortage of trained civil servants led to an inflationary monetary policy.[40] Both ONUC and the new Congolese political leadership proved to be woefully unprepared to fiscally manage the first Republic of Congo.

The physical reconstruction of infrastructure in the Congo was not a major objective for ONUC. Although the ANC had killed, maimed, and looted during the mutinous summer of 1960, it had destroyed relatively few buildings or machinery. Some of the most substantial infrastructure destruction in Katanga was actually the fault of the ONUC. ONUC's primary task in terms of reconstruction lay in putting plants and services into operation again. This included bringing in experienced dredging-machine operators to clear the Matadi channels. Hammarskjöld also convinced the International Civil Aviation Organization to send maintenance workers and air traffic controllers to get the major Congolese airports functioning again. The World Meteorological Organization responded by sending in meteorologists to work as advisors to the Directorate of Civil Aviation in Léopoldville and to train the Congolese assistants of their Belgian counterparts.[41] Functioning airports were a logistical requirement for the ONUC force, in light of the vast territorial domains it sought to control.

---

[38] West (1961), p. 610.

[39] According to Martelli, "Corruption was so common, both among the politicians and officials, as to be regarded as the norm rather than the exception. There was, in fact, almost a moral obligation on anybody in power to make as much out of it as he could, if only so as to enable him to do his duty by his dependents. The attitude was that if you did not take the money yourself, somebody else would, and the general public would be no better off." (p. 213).

[40] West (1961).

[41] King (1962), p. 66.

The International Telecommunications Union (ITU) cooperated with ONUC to restore telecommunications in the Congo. ITU sent engineers to restart telephone, radio, and international telecommunication services, which had all collapsed with the Belgian exodus in summer 1960. Because of the severe shortage of technically qualified Congolese, the ITU engineers started basic training programs.

The collapse in agricultural production was even more serious. The Belgians left the Congolese with large numbers of plantations but with little knowledge of how to operate the modern agricultural machinery. Engineers and agricultural experts assigned to ONUC helped put this equipment into operating condition. Their efforts contributed to a rebound in agricultural output as the chaotic conditions so pervasive in 1960 subsided during the latter half of 1961.[42] ONUC agricultural personnel served in an advisory capacity to the central government's agricultural bureau. They also set up numerous training programs in both horticulture and veterinary medicine, including a new veterinary medicine program at Lovanium University.

LESSONS LEARNED

The Republic of the Congo was a failed state from its inception. Its army was mutinous and the rest of its institutions had largely collapsed. The United Nations, called upon to reestablish security, complete decolonization, and preserve the country's territorial integrity, responded with remarkable speed, force, and decisiveness. In the process of completing these tasks, the United Nations found itself conducting a full-scale peace-enforcement operation and its first, but by no means its last, nation-building mission. The United Nations was successful in meeting its highest-priority objectives. But the costs and controversies associated with accomplishing these goals proved so high that they discouraged future operations on this scale for several decades.

On the positive side, the UN experience in the Congo demonstrated the following:

- Nation-building requires a mix of civil and military capabilities.

---

[42] King (1962), p. 69.

- Unity of command within a nation-building operation is important to knit these various capabilities together.

- Success in UN operations depends heavily upon strong leadership and broad international backing.

On the negative side, however, the United Nations also learned several lessons:

- The money and manpower demands of nation-building almost always exceed the supply.

- Peace enforcement is costly and controversial, even when done well.

- Democratic development can conflict with other priority objectives.

The Congo operation set important precedents. It consolidated the authority of the Secretary-General for the conduct of UN military operations and established the principles of unity of command and the maintenance of civilian control over such missions.

In recent decades, the United Nations has acquired a reputation for being slow, cautious, and bureaucratic. New peacekeeping operations are typically debated at length, budgeted sparingly, manned inadequately, and deployed incrementally. It is worth recalling, therefore, that there was a time when the United Nations could field a substantial and capable force within days of receiving Security Council authorization, conduct an extended military campaign, mount a succession of offensive operations (employing, among other assets, artillery and fixed-wing fighter-bombers), and decisively defeat military opponents. The Congo operation profited from an international consensus on the objectives of the intervention that was unusual, and perhaps unique, for the Cold War era. The mission also received strong, hands-on leadership from two Secretaries-General. The United Nations was able to generate substantial civil and military capacity, drawing successfully upon its family of specialized agencies to field a broad-based interdisciplinary team of experts in all the arts of governance.

As noted, there were considerable costs associated with such robust action. The United Nations was unable to deliver in a few years what Belgium had failed to achieve in as many generations—a viable Congolese state with a functional administration and a growing economy. One Secretary-General lost his life in the attempt. Democratic objectives were subordinated to those of decolonization and territorial integrity. The United Nations was at least passively complicit in the downfall and death of Prime Minister Lumumba. Both the Soviet Union and much of the Third World looked more skeptically upon the use of the United Nations in similar circumstances in the future.

Ultimately, several events cast a pall over the United Nations' achievements in the Congo: the enduring controversy surrounding the death of Lumumba; the costs associated with UN operations to end the Katangan secession, including the loss of Secretary-General Hammarskjöld; and the corrupt and bloody nature of the Mobutu dictatorship. Partially because of its experience in the Congo, the United Nations for the next 25 years limited its military engagement to the rare instances where all the parties to a conflict invited its intervention and where the use of armed force by UN troops could be limited to self-defense.

Table 2.1
UN Operation in the Congo—Key Facts

Population (1960): 16,462,477; Area: 905,365 Square Miles; Capital: Léopoldville (Kinshasa)

Operation	Mandate	Special Representative	Peak Military Size	Peak Police Size	Civilian Components
ONUC (1960–1964)	Resolution 161: Ensure the withdrawal of Belgian forces from the Republic of the Congo	Ralph J. Bunche (United States)	19,828 in all ranks	400 civilian police	Ensure continued operation of public services
	Assist the government in maintaining law and order	Andrew W. Cordier (United States)	Major contributors: Algeria, Egypt, Ghana, Nigeria, India, United States, France, Great Britain, Portugal		
	Provide technical assistance	Rajeshwar Dayal (India)			
	Maintain the territorial integrity and political independence of the Congo	Mekki Abbas (Sudan)			
	Prevent the occurrence of civil war and secure the removal from the Congo of all foreign military				

Chapter Three

NAMIBIA

In December 1988, the governments of Angola, Cuba, and South Africa signed a peace agreement in New York to end 23 years of war and open the way for Namibia's independence. Namibia had been under the control of South Africa since World War I. In 1920, the League of Nations had granted South Africa a mandate over the territory. After the League of Nations dissolved, the South African government refused to turn over its defunct mandate to the United Nations and proposed instead that the territory be incorporated into South Africa. In 1971, the International Court of Justice ruled that the South African presence in Namibia was illegal. The United Nations Security Council reaffirmed South Africa's occupation as illegal, stated that the United Nations had legal authority over the country, and declared it "imperative that free elections under the supervision and control of the United Nations be held for the whole of Namibia."[1] This was followed in 1978 by UN Security Council Resolution 435, which established the United Nations Transition Assistance Group (UNTAG) to oversee elections and supervise Namibia's transition to independence.[2]

South Africa prevented UNTAG from deploying for over a decade. The most significant reason for the delay was the "linkage" that South Africa and the United States established between the withdrawal of South African troops from Namibia and the removal of Cuban troops from neighboring Angola.[3] The issue was finally resolved in the 1988 peace agreement in New York. The United Nations Angola Verification Mission would deploy to Angola to monitor Cuba's withdrawal, and UNTAG would deploy to Namibia. On April 1, 1989, UNTAG forces finally entered Namibia to supervise the election process and the transition to independence. The UN Secretary-General appointed Martti Ahtisaari to head the mission.

---

[1] UN Security Council Resolution 385, S/RES/385, January 30, 1976.

[2] UN Security Council Resolution 435, S/RES/435, September 29, 1978.

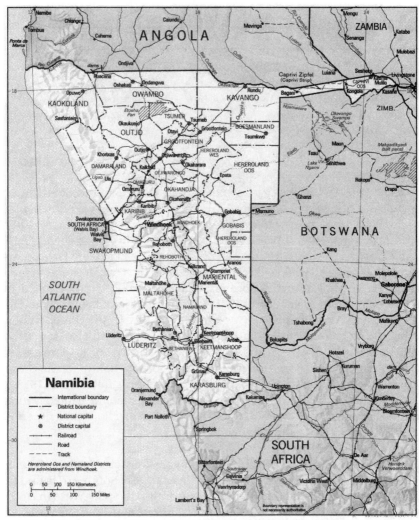

RAND *MG304-3.1*

Figure 3.1—Map of Namibia

CHALLENGES

United Nations responsibilities included ensuring that the fragile peace endured, assisting in the return of refugees, supervising national elections, and helping establish a democratic political system in a country with no history of democracy.

Security

There were three South African–controlled security forces in Namibia: the South West African Territorial Force, the South West African Police, and the South African Defense Force. In 1989, the South West African Territorial Force, which was created by South Africa to establish order in the Namibian territory, included approximately 22,000 troops. It was controlled by the Administrator General of the territory, who was appointed by the South African government. The force included six infantry battalions, a rapid reaction force, and a counterinsurgency unit. In addition, there were several thousand paramilitary soldiers from the South West African Police. These included a guard force to protect key tribal figures, a task force to conduct counterinsurgency operations, and 2,000 soldiers from the mobile counterinsurgency unit Koevoet.[4] Members of Koevoet were notorious for their brutal behavior and were linked to numerous human rights abuses in Namibia.[5] More than 10,000 soldiers from the South African Defense Force were also deployed to Namibia.[6]

The opposition group, the South West African People's Organization (SWAPO), fielded at least 9,000 soldiers with armored personnel carriers, rocket-propelled grenades, and surface-to-air missiles.[7] SWAPO was organizationally and militarily weak, and the 23-year war was rather one-sided

---

[3] Robert S. Jaster, *The 1988 Peace Accords and the Future of South-Western Africa*, Adelphi Paper 353, London: Brassey's, 1990; Laurent C. W. Kaela, *The Question of Namibia*, New York: St. Martin's Press, 1996; Vivienne Jabri, *Mediating Conflict: Decision-making and Western Intervention in Namibia*, New York: Manchester University Press, 1990.

[4] IISS, *The Military Balance, 1988–1989*, London: The International Institute for Strategic Studies, 1988, p. 141; Lionel Cliffe, *The Transition to Independence in Namibia*, Boulder, Colo.: Lynne Rienner Publishers, 1994, pp. 24–25.

[5] Jaster (1990), p. 41.

[6] Cliffe (1994), p. 92.

[7] IISS (1998), p. 141.

in favor of South Africa.[8] Before UNTAG's arrival, many of SWAPO's most capable leaders had either been jailed or exiled. Most SWAPO units were deployed to Angola and Zambia; few were actually located in Namibia. UN-TAG was thus faced with the difficult challenge of monitoring SWAPO guerrillas who were located in neighboring Angola.

Humanitarian

The war displaced about 69,000 Namibians; most went to refugee camps or SWAPO bases in Angola and Zambia. Many had lived in exile for decades, and their return was an important component of the settlement plan. Families had been torn apart and needed to be reunited. The United Nations faced a number of challenges with the resettlement program. One of the most acute was the health of refugees; most had come from Angola and Zambia, where there were high levels of HIV. The South African government proposed that all returnees have an AIDS test, but this would have been difficult to implement. Another challenge was finding space for returning refugees. Little territory was available for resettlement in Windhoek and the Ovambo area, where many of the refugees had originally come from. Refugees were also concerned about attacks from the South West African Police—especially Koevoet forces.[9] Finally, refugees needed transportation back to Namibia, and the transit centers provided little in the way of basic shelter or facilities.

Civil Administration

Civil administration challenges in Namibia proved minimal, and the United Nations had few responsibilities in this area. During the transition period, Administrator General Louis Pienaar, who had been installed by South African President P. W. Botha, continued to exercise administrative control over Namibia. His responsibilities included conducting the electoral pro-

---

[8] Official South African figures accounted for only 715 deaths of security force members. This included military and police units from South Africa and Namibia. According to South African statistics, Angolan and PLAN (People's Liberation Army of Namibia) forces lost 11,291 troops. Susan Brown, "Diplomacy by Other Means," in Leys and Saul (1995), p. 37.

[9] Roger Hearn, *UN Peacekeeping in Action: The Namibian Experience*, New York: Nova Science Publishers, 1999, p. 171.

cess for the November 1989 elections and controlling the police. The United Nations did not assume administrative control of Namibia or even of the elections.[10]

Democratization

Namibia had no democratic history and had been occupied by foreign powers for much of its history. In 1884, Britain laid claim to Walvis Bay, the best natural harbor on Namibia's coast, and several rocky islets in the south. At the same time, Germany declared a protectorate over the rest of Namibia. Most of the area remained a German colony until the beginning of World War I, when South Africa invaded the territory and defeated German forces. South Africa then installed a white-minority regime that ruled through intimidation and violence and discriminated against the majority black population. The promotion of political reconciliation was one of UNTAG's most difficult tasks: Decades of armed conflict and discrimination had created deep distrust between the sides. SWAPO was the major opposition party and became the bearer of Namibian nationalism. It functioned both as a guerrilla organization by conducting armed attacks against South African forces and a nationalist movement by advocating independence.[11]

Economic Reconstruction

There were fewer economic challenges in Namibia than in most other UN nation-building operations. Roads and railroads were in good condition. Namibia had rich natural resources, including some of the world's largest deposits of uranium and diamonds. But the United Nations did face several potential challenges. Namibia's economy was highly dependent on trade and financial flows with South Africa. Income distribution was also highly skewed. A majority of Namibia's 1.5 million people were poor, with limited access to health, education, and other social services. Consequently, economic reconstruction efforts focused on alleviating these large economic and social disparities through sustained economic growth.[12]

[10] See, for example, Jacob S. Kreilkamp, "UN Postconflict Reconstruction," *International Law and Politics*, Vol. 35, No. 3, 2003, pp. 623–626.

[11] On SWAPO, see Leys and Saul (1995).

[12] Donald L. Sparks and December Green, *Namibia: The Nation After Independence*, Boulder, Colo.: Westview Press, 1992, p. 73.

THE UN AND INTERNATIONAL ROLES

UNTAG was the first UN peacekeeping effort to combine international military and civilian operations. Its nation-building mandate was minimal, however. UNTAG personnel concentrated on overseeing the dismantlement of South Africa's security apparatus and assisting with the 1989 elections. Angola, Cuba, and South Africa also played an important role through the Joint Commission, which the Soviet Union and the United States attended as observers. The Joint Commission helped broker the peace settlement in December 1988 and assisted in resolving several crises during Namibia's transition to independence. In April 1989, for example, the Joint Commission played a pivotal role in negotiating a settlement and preventing a spiral of violence following the outbreak of fighting between SWAPO guerrillas and South African forces.

Military

UNTAG deployed 4,500 lightly armed peacekeepers and 1,500 lightly armed civilian police under a Chapter VI mandate.[13] It had the following tasks:

- Monitor the cease-fire.

- Confine the armed forces of both sides to bases.

- Monitor the withdrawal of the South African Defense Force and the dismantlement of the South West African Territorial Force.

- Supervise the South West African Police in maintaining law and order.

- Oversee border surveillance.

To accomplish these objectives, UNTAG had a contingent of several hundred military observers and monitors; three main infantry battalions provided by Finland, Kenya, and Malaysia; and a number of logistics and sup-

---

[13] Chapter VI of the Charter of the United Nations describes the UN Security Council's power to investigate and mediate disputes. It contrasts with Chapter VII, which outlines the Security Council's power to authorize sanctions and use military force to resolve disputes.

port units. The monitors were stationed in Angola at SWAPO camps and in Namibia at bases for the South African Defense Force and the South West African Territorial Force. Finland's battalion was deployed in the northeast section of Namibia; Malaysia's battalion in the northwest; and Kenya's battalion in the center and south. The logistics and support units came from a number of countries: a signals unit from the United Kingdom; an engineering squadron from Australia; an administrative company from Denmark; supply, transport, and maintenance units from Canada and Poland; a helicopter squadron from Italy; and a squadron of light transport aircraft from Spain. The Soviet Union and the United States provided air transport for the initial UNTAG deployment.[14]

UN civil police monitored the South West African Police, provided support during the elections, and helped UNTAG's military forces monitor the cease-fire. They had no arrest powers and were lightly armed. The UN police were commanded by an Irish Police Commissioner, Stephen Fanning, who provided advice to the Special Representative on all police-related issues. Fanning had a northern and southern regional commander, who helped coordinate police affairs at the regional level. UNTAG further divided Namibia into six—later seven—police districts. UNTAG deployed the first group of 500 civilian police officers in May 1989; the second group of 500 arrived between late June and late August; and the third group of 500 arrived for the elections between mid-September and the end of October. Almost all remained in Namibia until independence, although some stayed longer under bilateral agreements.[15]

Civil and Economic

When UNTAG entered Namibia in April 1989, it did not take control of the country. Administrative control remained with the South West African Administrator General, who acted under the supervision of the UN Special Representative. The United Nations' civilian mission consisted of the Spe-

---

[14] United Nations Department of Public Information, *The Blue Helmets: A Review of United Nations Peace-Keeping*, 3rd ed New York: United Nations, 1996, p. 214.

[15] Annika S. Hansen, *From Congo to Kosovo: Civilian Police in Peace Operations*, Adelphi Paper 343, New York: Oxford University Press, 2002, pp. 9, 19; James L. Woods, "Mozambique: The CIVPOL Operation," in Oakley et al. (1998), pp. 156, 160.

cial Representative's Office, an Independent Jurist, the Office of the United Nations High Commissioner for Refugees (UNHCR), the Electoral Division, and the Administration Division. Its primary tasks included the following:

- Supervise democratic elections.

- Oversee the return of refugees.

- Provide advice on the release of political prisoners and detainees.

The Special Representative's office was tasked with overall coordination of the UNTAG mission. This responsibility included liaison with the Administrator General's office, local administration, political parties, special interest and community groups, and governmental and nongovernmental observer missions. It deployed 42 political officers to ten regions throughout the country. The Independent Jurist was responsible for helping resolve disputes regarding the release of political prisoners and detainees. The UNHCR office assisted with the return and reintegration of refugees and internally displaced persons. UNHCR's objective was to return refugees before the elections to allow them to vote. The Electoral Division advised the Special Representative on all aspects of the November 1989 election, although the Administrator General was responsible for actually conducting the electoral process. The Administrative Division was responsible for all of UNTAG's administrative and logistics support.

WHAT HAPPENED

UNTAG's mission to Namibia was largely successful. In spite of several obstacles and delays, there was minimal violence. UNTAG helped dismantle the South African security apparatus; democratic elections took place as planned in 1989; and Namibia became independent in 1990.

Security

The United Nations' security efforts had a rocky start. On Special Representative Ahtisaari's first full day in Namibia, he faced what turned out to be the biggest crisis of the mission. SWAPO guerrillas had crossed into Namibia from Angola and engaged units of the South West African Police in some of the heaviest fighting of the civil war. Because of deployment delays, the United Nations had fewer than 1,000 of its 4,500 military forces in Namibia, and none had been deployed to the north. The delay was caused by a disagreement among UN member states about the size and funding of UNTAG's military component. The United States, with support from Britain, France, the USSR, and China, proposed cutting UNTAG's military force in half to reduce UN peacekeeping expenditures. This triggered a bitter debate in the UN General Assembly and the Security Council, which delayed UNTAG's deployment.[16] Since the United Nations had few vehicles and communications equipment, it could not deploy forces quickly enough. South African Foreign Minister Pik Botha warned the UN Secretary-General that if UNTAG was unable to contain the violence, his government would deploy additional forces. He also threatened to ask UNTAG forces to leave: "Unless the UN Secretary-General makes his position clear on this flagrant violation ... the South African government will be left with no choice but to request the UN Transition Assistance Group to depart from Namibia until SWAPO comes to its senses."[17]

With no means to intervene militarily and limited intelligence on the fighting, Ahtisaari was unable to prevent South African military forces—including the counterinsurgency unit Koevoet—from intervening. The fighting continued for ten days and threatened to derail the peace process. The South West African Administrator General suspended the peace plan and announced that he was prepared to indefinitely postpone the elections. It took high-level intervention by officials from Angola, Cuba, South Africa, the United States, and the Soviet Union to recommit all sides to the peace process. SWAPO fighters were guaranteed safe passage to UNTAG-monitored assembly points and then escorted back to Angola.[18] By mid-May, SWAPO forces had returned to their bases in Angola, South African forces were again confined to their bases in Namibia, and the peace process was back on track.

UNTAG was largely successful in dismantling the South African security apparatus. The South African Defense Force had reduced its presence to 1,500 by June 1989 and then completely withdrew in November. The South

---

[16] Jaster (1990), pp. 35–36.

[17] Peter Godwin and David Hughes, "Thatcher Helps Keep Namibia's Peace," *The Times (London)*, April 2, 1989, p. 1; William Claiborne, "Namibian Agreement Threatened," *Washington Post*, April 2, 1989, p. A1. British Prime Minister Margaret Thatcher, who happened to be in Namibia at the time, exerted additional pressure on the United Nations to permit South Africa to send support units. Margaret Thatcher, *The Downing Street Years*, New York: Harper-Collins Publishers, 1993, pp. 528–529.

[18] The text of the agreement, referred to as the Mount Etjo Declaration, is located in the Note by the Secretary-General, S/20579, April 17, 1989, pp. 5–8. Also see Cliffe (1994), p. 91.

West African Territorial Force, which had initially included 21,661 troops, was fully demobilized by June. UNTAG did not assist in the construction of the country's new military, the Namibian Defense Force. This force was formed at independence and included personnel from the demobilized South West African Territory Force and SWAPO's guerrilla force. The South West African Police was the only South African–controlled security force permitted to remain in Namibia. UNTAG monitors were instructed not to directly interfere in police operations but to conduct joint patrols, provide advice, and submit reports about offenses to their superiors. The United Nations did not help rebuild a Namibian police force as it did later in El Salvador or East Timor.

UNTAG civil police encountered three major problems after deployment. First, South West African Police forces were not always cooperative in allowing UN civilian police to accompany them on patrols.[19] Second, UNTAG police had difficulty deploying in the north, since they lacked mine-resistant vehicles. Third, UNTAG had difficulty dismantling some of the paramilitary forces, which continued to harass and intimidate the Namibian population. For instance, although Koevoet was officially disbanded in May, some members were integrated into the South West African Police force and continued patrolling in armored vehicles. As the UN Secretary-General argued:

> Many of the ex-Koevoet personnel continue to operate in the same manner as they had before the disbandment of Koevoet. This included the use of the armored personnel carriers known as "Casspirs" mounted with heavy machine guns. UNTAG received many complaints of intimidation and other unacceptable conduct by ex-Koevoet personnel and UNTAG police monitors were on a number of occasions themselves witnesses of such behavior.[20]

The Administrator General had dismantled Koevoet by the end of October 1989.[21] In addition, some senior South African Defense Force soldiers were reassigned to the Administrator General's office; UNTAG had to exert significant pressure to reduce their numbers.

---

[19] Hansen (2002), pp. 18–19.

[20] Report of the Secretary General to the Security Council, S/20883, October 6, 1989.

Finally, UNTAG's task of border surveillance was largely successful, with the notable exception of SWAPO's April 1989 infiltration into Namibia. UNTAG military observers established checkpoints at all border crossings between South Africa and Namibia and conducted regular patrols. Similar arrangements were established around the Walvis Bay enclave, where South Africa maintained a significant military presence. UNTAG also conducted daily patrols along Namibia's northern border with Angola. Despite repeated allegations by South African security sources that armed SWAPO units were poised for an invasion, UNTAG's Angola-based monitors found little evidence to that effect. Angola, Cuba, South Africa, the United States, and the Soviet Union established a Joint Intelligence Committee to assist UNTAG by investigating allegations of SWAPO activity along the Angola-Namibian border.

Humanitarian

Between June and September 1989, 42,000 of an estimated 69,000 refugees returned from camps in Angola and Zambia. There was widespread concern about violence from the South African–controlled security forces, which led to a temporary overcrowding of camps, but no cases of violence were reported. Refugees came through UNHCR-operated camps at six designated entry points and were provided with a month's food rations and resettlement aid. UNTAG military forces assisted in both constructing and protecting returnee centers. The United Nations World Food Program provided additional aid. The Council of Churches sponsored secondary reception centers for the elderly, orphans, and pregnant women. The centers also accepted refugees unable or unwilling to return to their previous communities.

Civil Administration

The United Nations did not have major civil administration responsibilities. It was deeply involved in supervising the repeal of discriminatory laws and the release of political prisoners. A total of 56 pieces of legislation was repealed or altered, including some of the most egregious legal instruments of colonial repression and apartheid. There was some controversy over a law referred to as AG-8, which provided for a system of ethnic administration

---

[21] Report of the Secretary General on the Implementation of Security Council Resolution 643 (1989) Concerning the Question of Namibia, S/20943, November 3, 1989.

in Namibia. Despite UN efforts, the Administrator General did not repeal AG-8 during the transition period. He argued that its repeal would entail a complete reconstruction of local administration and that the country possessed neither the resources nor the time to do this on the eve of elections.

The peace agreement stated that Namibian exiles should be permitted to return without risk of arrest, detention, intimidation, or imprisonment so they could participate in the electoral process. Provision was made for the peaceful return of former SWAPO forces under UN supervision through designated entry points. The Administrator General released 25 prisoners, and SWAPO released 284 prisoners. Some claimed that SWAPO was still keeping prisoners at its camps in Angola. UNTAG compiled a list of approximately 1,100 names, but a mission to Angola and Zambia could not verify any remaining detainees. UNTAG was unable to convince the International Committee of the Red Cross to join the verification mission as an independent third party and suffered from accusations that it was in favor of SWAPO. During the election campaign, SWAPO's opponents used this issue extensively for political purposes.

Democratization

UNTAG oversaw democratic elections that were internationally accepted as free and fair.[22] It supervised most aspects of the electoral process, which was actually conducted by the South African Administrator General. The most significant components of the process included the drafting of electoral laws, registration of voters, voter education, and the election itself. UNTAG officials oversaw each of the 70 voter registration centers and 100 mobile registration units, as well as the central register. Nearly 1,800 UN personnel were directly involved in supervising the elections at a total of 358 polling stations. An additional 1,023 UNTAG police monitors were also assigned to establish security at polling stations.

UNTAG officials encountered some challenges during the election process. South West African Police forces actively disrupted voter registration centers and used violence against SWAPO supporters in the Ovambo area.[23] Supporters of SWAPO and its strongest competitor, the Democratic Turn-

---

[22] National Democratic Institute for International Affairs, *Nation Building: The U.N. and Namibia*, Washington, D.C.: National Democratic Institute for International Affairs, 1990, p. 5.

[23] Hearn (1999), pp. 80–83.

halle Alliance, attacked each other at political rallies.[24] But the elections were held as scheduled over a five-day period from November 6 to November 10, 1989. SWAPO won the elections with 57 percent of the vote and received 41 of 72 seats in the Constituent Assembly. The Democratic Turnhalle Alliance received 28.6 percent of the vote and 21 seats in the assembly. Over the next three months, the Constituent Assembly debated and approved the draft constitution, written by South African constitutional experts.

On March 21, 1990, Namibia gained independence. At a midnight ceremony attended by UN Secretary-General Javier Perez de Cuellar, South African President Frederik W. de Klerk, and numerous international leaders, the South African flag was lowered and Namibia's new blue, red, green, and gold flag was slowly raised. President Sam Nujoma was sworn in by the UN Secretary-General as Namibia's first president. The Constituent Assembly became Namibia's National Assembly, and SWAPO's chairman of the Constituent Assembly, Hage Geingob, was elected as the country's prime minister. Namibia's transition to democracy strengthened over the 1990s. President Nujoma was reelected in 1994 and elected for a third five-year term in 1999 with 77 percent of the vote. There were some instances of government harassment of opposition candidates, as well as unequal access to media coverage and campaign financing. But Namibia's 1999 elections were judged largely free and fair. Namibia has remained democratic since 1999, and Namibians enjoy a free press, freedom of assembly, and universal suffrage.

Economic Reconstruction

Economic reconstruction was not part of UNTAG's core mission. Nevertheless, before the end of its mission, UNTAG's regional offices prepared a comprehensive guide to the local social, economic, and political structures. This guide was used by the UN Development Program and other development agencies for future international support.[25] Namibia's economy grew rapidly after independence. Its gross domestic product (GDP) grew at an average of 5 percent between 1990 and 1993 and then slowed to an average of 3 percent between 1994 and 2001. Namibia's economy has remained closely linked to South Africa's through extensive trade and financial flows, as well as such institutional relationships as the Southern African Customs Union

---

[24] Sparks and Green (1992), pp. 52–53.

[25] United Nations Department of Public Information (1996), p. 210.

and the Common Monetary Area. Namibia introduced its own currency, the Namibian dollar, but the South African rand has also continued as legal tender. Income distribution has remained one of the most unequal in the world. Namibia's per capita GDP was approximately $1,800 by the end of the decade, but the total expenditures of the richest 7,000 people (0.5 percent of the population) equaled the total expenditures of the poorest 800,000 people (57 percent of the population).[26]

LESSONS LEARNED

The United Nations operations in Namibia took place in near-ideal conditions and produced near-ideal results. The conditions included

- a favorable international climate

- compliant, helpful neighbors

- a competent indigenous government

- reasonably disciplined local security forces

- a clear end state accepted by all the principal parties.

Namibia was an early beneficiary of the end of the Cold War, which resulted in the withdrawal of Cuban troops from neighboring Angola, a reduction in external support for SWAPO, and the beginnings of political change in South Africa. South Africa's willingness to cooperate in Namibia's transition to democracy and independence, along with the presence of a competent South African–run administration and reasonably disciplined security forces, relieved the United Nations of the need to administer or secure the territory. This allowed the United Nations to concentrate on disarming the two sides and organizing elections, which were conducted by competent local authorities under UN oversight.

The existence of a well-defined end state—independence—and an agreed road map for achieving it contributed decisively to the success of the mission. The UN mission was well led, adequately manned,

[26] IMF, *Namibia: Recent Economic Developments*, Washington, D.C.: International Monetary Fund, December 1997; World Bank, *Namibia: Country Brief*, Washington, D.C.: World Bank, 2004a.

and sufficiently resourced. The April 1989 crisis on the Angolan-Namibian border that Ahtisaari encountered on his first day as UN special representative illustrates the danger of tardy deployment of UN peacekeeping forces. In this case, the absence of UN forces came close to torpedoing the entire effort. Namibia provided a positive launch for the spate of post–Cold War nation-building missions that followed it over the succeeding decade. But the comparative ease with which the United Nations was able to complete this mission proved deceptive. Only in El Salvador was the United Nations again to find conditions for a nation-building mission quite so favorable.

Table 3.1
UN Operation in Namibia—Key Facts

Population (1989): 1,338,777; Area: 318,252 Square Miles; Capital: Windhoek

Operation	Mandate	Special Representative	Peak Military Size	Peak Police Size	Civilian Components
UNTAG (1989–1990)	Resolution 632:	Martti Ahtisaari (Finland)	4,493 in all ranks	1,500 civilian police	1,000 international personnel for elections oversight
	Ensure the independence of Namibia through free and fair elections		Major Contributors: Finland, Kenya, Malaysia		
	Ensure end of hostilities				
	Confine troops to bases and ultimate withdrawal from Namibia of foreign forces				
	Repeal discriminatory laws				
	Release political prisoners				
	Oversee return of Namibian refugees				
	Maintain law and order				

Chapter Four

EL SALVADOR

In a solemn ceremony in Mexico City's Chapultepec Castle, representatives of El Salvador's government and the Farabundo Martí National Liberation Front (FMLN) signed a peace settlement in January 1992. The agreement ended 12 years of civil conflict that left approximately 75,000 people dead.[1] As elsewhere in Central America, the war in El Salvador had evolved into a proxy conflict between the United States and the Soviet Union. The Reagan Administration viewed El Salvador as a place to "draw the line" against communist aggression and provided over $6 billion in economic and military assistance to El Salvador's government over the course of the war.[2]

The end of the Cold War created a window of opportunity for peace negotiations. The Soviet Union's withdrawal of support for Marxist movements in Latin America eliminated an important source of supply of arms and logistical support to the FMLN.[3] The United States put significant pressure on El

---

[1] On the number of people killed during El Salvador's civil war see David H. McCormick, "From Peacekeeping to Peacebuilding," in Michael W. Doyle, Ian Johnstone, and Robert C. Orr, *Keeping the Peace: Multidimensional UN Operations in Cambodia and El Salvador,* New York: Cambridge University Press, 1997, p. 282.

[2] Benjamin C. Schwarz, *American Counterinsurgency Doctrine and El Salvador: The Frustrations of Reform and the Illusions of Nation Building,* Santa Monica, Calif.: RAND Corporation, 1991, p. 2. Also see Michael Childress, *The Effectiveness of U.S. Training Efforts in Internal Defense and Development: The Cases of El Salvador and Honduras,* Santa Monica, Calif.: RAND Corporation, R-4042-USDP, 1995; U.S. Department of State, *Communist Interference in El Salvador: Documents Demonstrating Communist Support of the Salvadoran Insurgency,* Washington, D.C., February 1981.

[3] The FMLN also received economic and military assistance from Cuba and the Sandinistas in Nicaragua. United Nations Institute for Disarmament Research (UNIDR), *Managing Arms in Peace Processes: Nicaragua and El Salvador,* Geneva: United Nations, 1997, p. 124. Also see Mark Levine, "Peacemaking in El Salvador," in Doyle et al. (1997), pp. 230–231; Gerardo L. Munck and Dexter Boniface, "Political Processes and Identity Formation in El Salvador: From Armed Left to Democratic Left," in Ronaldo Munck and Purnaka L. de Silva, *Postmodern Insurgencies: Political Violence, Identity Formation and Peacemaking in Comparative Perspective,* New York: St. Martin's Press, 2000, pp. 38–53.

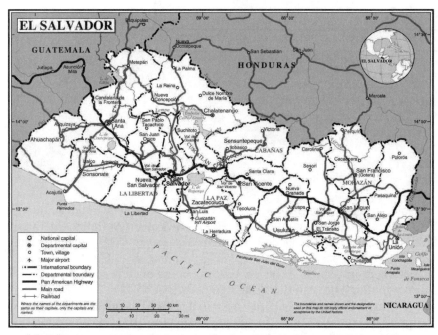

SOURCE: United Nations Cartographic Section, El Salvador, no. 3903 Rev. 3, May 2004. Available online at http://www.un.org/Depts/Cartographic/english/htmain.htm.
RAND *MG304-4.1*

Figure 4.1—Map of El Salvador

Salvador to negotiate a peace settlement, threatening to withdraw aid while offering to contribute financial assistance if a settlement was reached.[4] As a first step toward such an accord, the parties signed the Geneva Agreement in April 1990. This agreement established a framework for ending the civil war through political negotiations and stated that democratization and respect for human rights were important goals of the negotiations.[5] Over the next year and a half, the parties signed interim agreements in San José, Costa Rica; Mexico City; and New York outlining reforms of the armed forces, police, judicial system, constitution, and electoral system.

---

[4] Edelberto Torres-Rivas, "Insurrection and Civil War in El Salvador," in Doyle et al. (1997), pp. 209–226.

[5] Letter dated 8 October 1991 from El Salvador Transmitting the Text of the Geneva Agreement signed on 4 April 1990 by the Government of El Salvador and the FMLN, A/46/551-S/21328, October 9, 1991.

In January 1992, the FMLN and the Salvadoran government agreed to a final settlement under which the United Nations would verify the cease-fire and assist in reconstruction. After a preliminary deployment in July 1991, the UN Security Council authorized the United Nations Observer Mission in El Salvador (ONUSAL) in January 1992 to oversee the transition to a peaceful and democratic government in El Salvador.

CHALLENGES

After more than a decade of civil war in El Salvador, the United Nations faced difficult challenges. It had to supervise the demobilization and demilitarization of the FMLN, reform the government's armed forces, improve the observance of human rights in a country with one of the most appalling records in Latin America, and oversee democratic elections.

Security

Perhaps the most significant security challenge facing the United Nations was curbing the involvement of El Salvador's military in its domestic affairs. In addition to the Army, Navy, and Air Force, El Salvador's military controlled the National Guard, Treasury Police, National Police, National Intelligence Directorate, and paramilitary civil defense forces.[6] Since the outbreak of civil war in 1981, these forces had functioned as political police and had ruthlessly suppressed dissent throughout the country. Targets included FMLN guerrillas, labor and peasant organizations, church officials, religious workers, political opponents, the media, and human rights monitors.[7] Under the Chapultepec Agreement, the Salvadoran government committed to demobilize those forces and improve its human rights record.

Disarming and demobilizing the FMLN also posed a notable security challenge. FMLN guerrillas were capable of conducting major combat operations throughout El Salvador. Just three years earlier, they had captured sec-

---

[6] El Salvador's security forces included 40,000 Army, 1,200 Navy, 2,400 Air Force, 4,000 National Guard, 6,000 National Police, 2,000 Treasury Police, and 24,000 Civil Defense forces. International Institute for Strategic Studies (IISS), *The Military Balance, 1991–1992,* London: Oxford University Press, 1992, p. 198.

[7] America's Watch, *El Salvador's Decade of Terror: Human Rights Since the Assassination of Archbishop Romero,* New Haven, Conn.: Yale University Press, 1991, pp. 17–63.

tions of San Salvador, the capital city, during a major offensive.[8] The FMLN had approximately 7,000 combatants and operated in all 14 provinces of the country.[9] It enjoyed strong popular support in certain areas of the country, a de facto sanctuary in Salvadoran territory and border areas disputed by El Salvador and Honduras, and some international financial, logistical, and political support.

A final concern was common crime. The demobilization of thousands of government soldiers, police, and FMLN guerrillas in a country with high rates of unemployment exacerbated an already serious crime problem.

Humanitarian

El Salvador's civil war displaced over 500,000 persons, of whom 50,000 became refugees. More than a million Salvadorans emigrated legally or illegally to the United States.[10] Salvadorans began leaving the country en masse in April 1980 following the assassination of Catholic Archbishop Oscar Romero. In the mid-1980s, churches and popular organizations helped some displaced persons repopulate rural areas of the country emptied by the violence. Even following the peace agreement, however, the continued existence of right wing death squads and lingering violence in rural areas deterred many from returning to their previous homes. Other aspects of the humanitarian situation were also grim. Only 37 percent of Salvadorans had access to medical care, life expectancy was a mere 59 years, and 50 percent of children were malnourished.[11]

Civil Administration

Both the Salvadoran government and the FMLN committed numerous human rights abuses during the civil war. According to one report, government forces committed roughly 85 percent of the abuses, right wing death squads were responsible for 10 percent, and the FMLN committed 5 percent.[12] Dur-

---

[8] America's Watch (1991), pp. 64–70; United Nations Department of Public Information, *The United Nations and El Salvador, 1990–1995,* New York, United Nations, 1995b, p. 8.

[9] IISS (1992), p. 198.

[10] Timothy A. Wilkins, "The El Salvador Peace Accords: Using International and Domestic Law Norms to Build Peace," in Doyle et al. (1997), p. 274; Torres-Rivas (1997), p. 226.

[11] America's Watch (1991), p. 1.

[12] Leigh Binford, *The El Mozote Massacre: Anthropology and Human Rights,* Tucson, Ariz.: University of Arizona Press, 1996, p. 63.

ing 1991 and 1992, debates about post-conflict justice raged within El Salvador and among external actors, such as the United Nations and the United States. Should a war crimes tribunal or truth commission be established? If so, should it be composed of international personnel, prominent Salvadorans, or a mixture? A related challenge for the United Nations was improving El Salvador's poorly functioning justice system. The Supreme Court held an overwhelming amount of judicial power, the selection of Supreme Court justices was highly politicized, and the justice system was not independent from the executive or legislative branches.[13] "The judicial system was so debilitated that it became imprisoned by intimidation and vulnerable to corruption," concluded El Salvador's Truth Commission. "Given that the justice system has never enjoyed true institutional independence from the legislative and executive branches, its inefficiency only increased until it became, either because of inaction or an unfortunate attitude of subservience, a contributing factor to the tragedy that the country has suffered."[14]

Democratization

El Salvador had some experience with democracy prior to the Chapultepec Agreement. From 1871 until the 1930s, it enjoyed some democratic rule that transformed the country's economy, political structure, and society. That ended in 1931, when General Maximiliano Hernandez Martínez brutally suppressed an uprising in indigenous areas that was inspired by the revolution in Mexico and communist movements elsewhere. He then seized power in a military coup. From the 1930s to the 1970s, a succession of authoritarian, military-dominated governments ruled the country. Elections were held, but the results were foreordained: The official military candidates of the Party of Democratic Revolutionary Unification won. The military maintained indirect control over the legislative branch, although some opportunity for political opposition existed. All pretenses of democracy ended in 1979, however, when military officers overthrew the elected government in a coup, sparking the civil war.

---

[13] William Stanley and Robert Loosle, "El Salvador: The Civilian Police Component of Peace Operations," in Robert B. Oakley et al. (1998), pp. 135–137; Ian Johnstone, "Rights and Reconciliation in El Salvador," in Doyle et al. (1997), pp. 332–335; David Holiday and William Stanley, "Building the Peace: Preliminary Lessons from El Salvador," *Journal of International Affairs,* Vol. 46, No. 2, Winter 1993, pp. 423–424.

[14] "From Madness to Hope: The 12-Year War in El Salvador," *Report of the Commission on the Truth for El Salvador,* S/25500, April 1, 1993.

Economic Reconstruction

The Salvadoran Planning Ministry estimated that by the end of the civil war $1.5 billion in infrastructure had been destroyed, in addition to the $1.6 billion that had already been spent on replacing infrastructure.[15] The government spent money on the military that might otherwise have been spent on investment or social programs. GDP, which had grown at an average of 4.3 percent in the period before the civil war, declined at an average annual rate of 1.4 percent between 1978 and 1990. Per capita income fell by more than 15 percent between 1981 and 1990. The percentage of El Salvador's population living in poverty rose from 51 percent in 1980 to 56 percent in 1990, with the rural population most affected. The country ranked 110th out of 173 countries in the United Nations Development Program's human development rankings.[16] El Salvador emerged from the civil war heavily dependent on international assistance. Over the course of the 1980s, it received approximately $7.3 billion in U.S. aid, plus $315 million in development assistance and direct foreign investment from Europe, Canada, and Japan. External assistance, including remittances from Salvadorans working abroad, exceeded the value of El Salvador's exports during this period.[17]

THE UN AND INTERNATIONAL ROLES

Three consecutive UN Secretary-General Special Representatives oversaw the UN operation in El Salvador: Iqbal Riza (May 1991 to March 1993), Augusto Ramirez-Ocampo (March 1993 to March 1994), and Enrique ter Horst (March 1994 to April 1996). The United States played a significant role throughout the reconstruction process. It pressured the Salvadoran government to negotiate a peace settlement in good faith, contributed substantial economic aid and security training, and encouraged the military to accept unprecedented reforms and purge human rights violators.[18] Other promi-

---

[15] Alexander Segovia, "The War Economy of the 1980s," in James K. Boyce, ed., *Economic Policy for Building Peace: The Lessons of El Salvador,* Boulder, Colo.: Lynne Rienner, 1996, p. 31; John Eriksson, Alcira Kreimer, and Margaret Arnold, *El Salvador: Post-Conflict Reconstruction,* Washington, D.C.: World Bank, 2000, p. 18.

[16] Manuel Pastor and Michael E. Conroy, "Distributional Implication," in Boyce (1996), p. 157; Jenny Pearce, "From Civil War to 'Civil Society': Has the End of the Cold War Brought Peace to Central America?" *International Affairs,* Vol. 74, No. 3, 1998, pp. 591–592; Graciana del Castillo, "Post-Conflict Reconstruction and the Challenge to International Organizations: The Case of El Salvador," *World Development,* Vol. 29, No. 12, 2001, p. 1972.

[17] The figure for U.S. assistance includes remittances sent by its citizens in the United States. C. Vilas, *Between Earthquakes and Volcanoes: Market, State, and the Revolutions in Central America,* New York: Monthly Review Press, 1995, p. 161.

[18] Levine (1997), pp. 251–252.

nent international actors included Spain, Colombia, Mexico, and Venezuela, referred to as the "Four Friends" by the UN Secretary-General. These governments helped broker the peace settlement; placed pressure on El Salvador's military to adopt reforms; and contributed police, soldiers, and civilian observers to ONUSAL.

Military and Police

ONUSAL had no formal authority to enforce compliance with the Chapultepec Agreement. Its primary responsibilities in the military realm were to

- supervise the cessation of armed conflict and separation of forces

- oversee the creation of an Ad Hoc Commission to investigate human rights abuses by military offices and to evaluate their performance

- verify the demobilization and abolishment of the National Guard, Treasury Police, and National Intelligence Directorate

- monitor and evaluate the National Police and oversee its eventual demobilization

- monitor, evaluate, and assist in the creation of a new National Civil Police

- verify the concentration and demobilization of FMLN forces in agreed cantonments, destruction of all weapons, and reintegration of FMLN ex-combatants into Salvadoran society.

ONUSAL contained separate Military and Police Divisions. At peak strength, it deployed 4,948 military observers and 315 police observers.[19] Both divisions reported directly to the UN Secretary-General's Special Representative. The Military Division had four regional offices. A colonel managed each office, assisted by a staff of three to five officers, who were in charge of operations, intelligence, and logistics.[20] As soon as the parties had signed the Chapultepec Agreement, the United Nations immediately transferred more than 100 military observers from its mission in neighboring Nicara-

---

[19] United Nations, *El Salvador ONUSAL: Facts and Figures,* New York: United Nations, 1995.

[20] UNIDR (1997), pp. 170–171.

gua to help monitor the cease-fire. The Military Division verified the inventory of both sides' weapons and personnel, authorized and accompanied force movements, and received and investigated complaints of violations.[21] It also coordinated the clearing of 425 minefields.[22] The U.S. government played an important role by training, advising, and assisting the Salvadoran military during its restructuring phase.[23]

Civilian police from Spain, France, and Italy largely staffed the police division. These police observers lacked arrest authority and were unarmed. They depended on the Salvadoran police to make arrests. The main function of the civilian police was to oversee the elimination of the military-controlled National Police over a 24-month period and to supervise the creation of a National Civil Police under civilian command.[24] During this period, ONUSAL police observers were expected to accompany officers and members of the National Police in the performance of their duties and establish a UN presence in the National Police central and regional headquarters.[25] The ONUSAL Police Division was also responsible for overseeing the abolishment of the National Guard, Treasury Police, and National Intelligence Directorate, all of which operated under military command.

Civil and Economic
ONUSAL did not play a major role in economic reconstruction. Instead, the World Bank and other international financial organizations were responsible for assisting El Salvador with economic adjustment, stabilization, and investment. ONUSAL's primary nonsecurity objectives included the following:

- Monitor, investigate, and prepare periodic reports on the human rights situation

---

[21] "Chapultepec Agreement, Chapter VII," in United Nations Department of Public Information (1995b), pp. 210–213.

[22] United Nations Department of Public Information (1996), p. 429.

[23] McCormick (1997), p. 297.

[24] Wilkins (1997), pp. 273–274.

[25] *Report of the Secretary-General on the Monitoring of Agreements by ONUSAL,* January 10, 1992, p. 188; Chapultepec Agreement, Chapter II (7)(B)(e) in United Nations (1995b), p. 203; Stanley and Loosle (1998), pp. 110–112.

- Monitor and assist the organization and implementation of the March 1994 presidential, legislative, mayoral, and municipal council elections

- Help reform the judicial system.

- Transfer land to former FMLN combatants, government soldiers, and squatters who had occupied land in the conflict areas during the war.

To accomplish these objectives, ONUSAL created a Human Rights Division and an Electoral Division, and deployed 900 electoral observers and 30 human rights observers.[26] The Human Rights Division was established in May 1991, before the Chapultepec Agreement. Like the Military and Police Divisions, it reported directly to the UN Secretary-General's Special Representative. It assigned between four and eight human rights officers to each regional office and produced a total of 13 reports on the human rights situation for the UN Secretary-General.[27] In late 1993, ONUSAL established the Electoral Division to support the 1994 presidential and legislative elections. El Salvador's Supreme Electoral Tribunal directly oversaw the electoral process; ONUSAL assisted with voter registration, monitored the election campaign (including counting votes), and observed any second rounds of elections that were necessary.[28]

WHAT HAPPENED

ONUSAL successfully oversaw the maintenance of peace after a violent civil war, verified the demobilization and political integration of the FMLN, monitored the reform of the armed forces, and promoted a successful transition to democracy. But it encountered significant difficulties in reforming the police and justice system and made only limited progress in redressing major human rights violations.

---

[26] United Nations Department of Public Information (1996), p. 443.

[27] Tommie Sue Montgomery, "Getting to Peace in El Salvador: The Roles of the United Nations Secretariat and ONUSAL," *Journal of Interamerican Studies and World Affairs*, Vol. 37, No. 4, Winter 1995, p. 148.

[28] Report of the Secretary-General on the United Nations Observer Mission in El Salvador, S/1994/179, February 16, 1994, p. 1.

Security

ONUSAL's Military Division successfully oversaw and verified the dissolution of the FMLN's military structure, destruction of its weapons and equipment, and its transition from a combatant force to a political party. ONUSAL encountered several problems along the way. It verified that the FMLN had destroyed or handed over all weapons in December 1992 when it formally announced the end of armed conflict.[29] But the accidental explosion of an undisclosed arms cache in May 1993 and the discovery of large quantities of weapons indicated that the FMLN had not handed in all its weapons.[30] Over the succeeding months, the FMLN informed ONUSAL of another 114 arms caches in El Salvador, Nicaragua, and Honduras. These contained ammunition, rockets, grenades, and surface-to-air missiles. In total, the FMLN destroyed 10,230 weapons, 140 rockets, 9,228 grenades, 5,107 kilograms of explosives, 74 surface-to-air missiles, and over 4 million rounds of ammunition.[31]

ONUSAL was less successful in reintegrating former combatants into Salvadoran society. The Chapultepec Agreement provided for the transfer of land to former FMLN combatants, members of the armed forces, and squatters who had occupied land in the conflict areas during the war.[32] A maximum of 7,500 former FMLN combatants, 15,000 former military soldiers, and 25,000 landholders in the zone of conflict were to be reintegrated.[33] They were to be given credit to purchase land, agricultural training, basic household goods, agricultural tools, housing, and technical assistance. The available land would come from territory that landowners abandoned or were forced off of during the civil war. The National Commission for the Consolidation of Peace (COPAZ) was responsible for administering the land transfer program. But the agreement's vagueness on several issues created numerous problems. It said nothing, for example, about the size of the plots to which the beneficiaries were entitled, the amount of government credit available to beneficiaries, and the practical arrangements under which the land was

---

[29] Report of the Secretary-General Concerning the Formal End of the Armed Conflict in El Salvador, S/25006, December 12, 1992, in United Nations Department of Public Information (1995b), pp. 282–285.

[30] S/25006; Report of the Secretary-General on the United Nations Observer Mission in El Salvador, S/1995/220, March 24, 1995, p. 2.

[31] UNIDR (1997), pp. 137–138.

[32] Chapultepec Agreement, Chapter V, in United Nations Department of Public Information (1995b), pp. 206–209.

[33] United Nations Department of Public Information (1995b), p. 29.

to be transferred.[34] Even worse, COPAZ was completely ineffective at mediating land disputes. By the end of 1994, land titles had been issued to only 40 percent of potential beneficiaries. Setbacks continued over the next several years for a number of reasons: coordination problems among Salvadoran government agencies, payment delays, legal problems, and the refusal of some owners to sell their land.[35] In short, ONUSAL's attempt to reintegrate ex-combatants was much less successful than its attempt to disarm and demobilize them.

Efforts by ONUSAL and the United States to reform the armed forces had mixed success. Under ONUSAL supervision, the government demobilized the Civil Defense patrols and reduced the size of the army from 40,000 to 28,000 men. U.S. military advisors trained, advised, and assisted with restructuring. They helped develop a new training and doctrine command and provided technical advice on the reorganization of El Salvador's Military College.[36] Instead of abolishing the National Guard and Treasury Police, as stipulated in the Chapultepec Agreement, the government incorporated those organizations structurally intact into the army and renamed them the Military Police and National Border Guard. They retained largely the same missions. The government claimed to have abolished the National Intelligence Directorate, but there was evidence that it still existed "hidden beneath levels of bureaucracy."[37] With barely 100 military observers by early 1993, ONUSAL lacked adequate personnel to verify and the authority to compel the abolishment of these key internal security services.[38]

The United Nations and the El Salvadoran government established the Ad Hoc Commission to investigate and evaluate military officers based on three criteria: (1) observance of the law, especially respect for human rights; (2) professional competence; and (3) ability to function within a newly peaceful and democratic society.[39] The Ad Hoc Commission comprised three Salvadoran civilians chosen by the UN Secretary-General and two military observers chosen by El Salvador's president. It issued a report on Septem-

---

[34] Wilkins, (1997), pp. 275–277.

[35] Graciana del Castillo, "The Arms-for-Land Deal in El Salvador," in Doyle (1997), pp. 342–365.

[36] McCormick (1997), p. 297.

[37] McCormick (1997), p. 297. Also see United Nations Department of Public Information (1996), p. 441; S/1995/220, p. 3.

[38] On the number of military observers, see S/1995/220, p. 19.

[39] Chapultepec Agreement, Chapter I, in United Nations Department of Public Information (1995b), pp. 195–196.

ber 22, 1992, following a review of 232 of the most senior military officers. The report recommended the discharge of the entire senior military establishment, including officers who had played an integral role in the peace process. El Salvador President Alfredo Cristiani initially refused to remove all of the named officers. After pressure from the UN Secretary-General, the United States, and the "Four Friends," Cristiani ultimately acceded to the recommendation, although he transferred some officers to embassies abroad and allowed others to retire.[40]

The United Nations encountered significant problems in monitoring and assisting the National Police's performance.[41] ONUSAL established its Police Division in February 1992 under the command of Uruguayan General Homero Vaz Bresque. UN police observers accompanied National Police patrols and monitored their performance. Most of El Salvador's police deeply resented the United Nations for phasing out the force; many refused to cooperate with ONUSAL monitors.[42] Some Salvadoran police engaged in torture, excessive use of force, threats, and arbitrary detentions and executions during the UN mission.[43] Others, including the chief of its Investigative Department, were involved in criminal activities.[44] One UN report concluded:

> There exist solid grounds for asserting that the broad network of organized crime that flails the country, in which, the evidence shows, there is active participation of members of the armed forces of El Salvador and the National Police, cannot be divorced from many acts of politically motivated violence.[45]

---

[40] Letter dated 7 January 1993 from the Secretary-General to the President of the Security Council Concerning Implementation of the Provisions of the Peace Agreements Relating to the Purification of the Armed Forces, S/25078, January 9, 1993, in United Nations Department of Public Information (1995b), pp. 286–287; Johnstone (1997), pp. 316–318.

[41] McCormick (1997), pp. 288–291.

[42] Report of the Secretary-General on the United Nations Observer Mission in El Salvador, S/1994/561, May 11, 1994, p. 5.

[43] S/1994/385; S/1994/47; S/1994/561; S/1994/989.

[44] Report of the Secretary-General on the United Nations Observer Mission in El Salvador, S/1994/1000, August 26, 1994, pp. 1–3.

[45] Report issued on 28 July 1994 by the Joint Group for the Investigation of Politically Motivated Illegal Armed Groups, S/1994/989, 22 October 1994, in United Nations Department of Public Information (1995b), p. 570.

The government continued to operate the old National Police Academy and trained new agents for some time, but eventually demobilized the National Police in December 1994.[46]

Efforts to create a new National Civil Police force to replace the old National Police force also encountered difficulties. One of the government's first steps was to set up a National Public Security Academy to train police officers. Five representatives from Spain and the United States, along with a seven-person team from El Salvador, assisted with its establishment. They helped develop and implement lesson plans, establish disciplinary codes, find a building, and put together a budget.[47] The U.S. Department of Justice's International Criminal Investigative Training Assistance Program provided the bulk of the foreign instructors for the National Public Security Academy and advised the academy's directors and National Civil Police senior staff on the recruitment and selection process, curriculum, finances, and discipline.[48]

The new police force was unable to effectively combat rising crime. The demobilization of thousands of former soldiers, policemen, and guerrillas in a country with high unemployment contributed to the severe crime problem.[49] The homicide rate reached 140 murders per 100,000 inhabitants in 1997, the highest in the world behind South Africa.[50] A World Bank survey of business enterprises in 1996 found that expenditures on security had risen by 85 percent since 1990, with an increase of almost 300 percent among small firms.[51] Crime was consistently ranked as the most important problem facing the country between 1993 and 1999 in surveys conducted by the Central American University's Public Opinion Institute.[52] Criminal

---

[46] Stanley and Loosle (1998), p. 129.

[47] McCormick (1997), pp. 298–299.

[48] Report of the Secretary-General on the United Nations Observer Mission in El Salvador, S/1994/561, May 11, 1994, p. 6.

[49] Report Issued on 28 July 1994 by the Joint Group for the Investigation of Politically Motivated Illegal Armed Groups, S/1994/989, 22 October 1994, in United Nations Department of Public Information (1995b), pp. 568–574; Stanley and Loosle (1998), p. 117.

[50] Glenn Garvin, "Civil War Over, but Violence Goes On," *Miami Herald,* August 4, 1997, p. A1. On public opinion and security, also see publications from the Instituto Universitario de Opinión Pública in San Salvador such as *Evaluación del país a finales de 1998* (San Salvador: El Instituto Universitario de Opinión Pública, Universidad Centroamericana, 1999).

[51] World Bank, *El Salvador: Meeting the Challenge of Globalization* (Washington, D.C.: World Bank, 1996a), p. 80.

[52] Charles T. Call, "Democratization, War, and State-Building: Constructing the Rule of Law in El Salvador," *Journal of Latin American Studies,* Vol. 35, No. 4 (2003), p. 839.

organizations ranged from heavily armed rural gangs that robbed and terrorized communities and highway travelers to highly sophisticated kidnapping and car-theft rings. National Civil Police officers were often ineffective at quelling riots, as demonstrated in November 1994 when the government called in soldiers to support the police during a protest by bus owners.[53] The National Civil Police sometimes failed to cooperate with the judiciary and often refused to punish or prosecute its own personnel when they were involved in illegal activities or human rights violations.[54]

In sum, the United Nations lacked sufficient numbers of military and police observers, time, and authority to fully achieve many of its objectives.[55] A limited number of countries were willing and able to send police and military contingents, and both the government and the FMLN rejected several potential contributors.[56] But ONUSAL and its follow-on, the United Nations Mission in El Salvador (MINUSAL) helped maintain peace, supervise the demobilization and disarmament of the FMLN, and verify the reduction in numbers and types of El Salvador's armed forces. Three ONUSAL civilian police observers and two local civilian staff were killed in the process.[57]

Humanitarian

Refugees and internally displaced persons began returning home from Honduras, Nicaragua, Mexico, and other countries in significant numbers in 1992. The Office of the United Nations High Commissioner for Refugees (UNHCR) and a number of nongovernmental organizations assisted in the return of refugees. The combined effects of political instability and economic devastation in El Salvador made continued UNHCR presence and oversight essential. Many Salvadorans who fled to the United States remained there. The U.S. government granted the refugees Temporary Protected Status from 1990 through June 1992 and then granted them Deferred Enforced Depar-

---

[53] Report of the Secretary-General on the United Nations Observer Mission in El Salvador, S/1995/220, March 24, 1994, p. 5.

[54] Report of the Secretary-General on the United Nations Observer Mission in El Salvador, S/1994/561, May 11, 1994, p. 10.

[55] Iqbal Riza, former Special Representative of the Secretary General to El Salvador, has argued that more military personnel and police would have been useful. However, getting the UN Security Council to agree to greater numbers would have been politically infeasible. Conversation with Iqbal Riza, New York, April 29, 2004.

[56] Stanley and Loosle (1998), p. 111.

[57] On ONUSAL deaths see *El Salvador ONUSAL: Facts and Figures,* New York: United Nations, 1995.

ture. When ONUSAL departed from El Salvador in 1996, 190,128 asylum applications from Salvadorans were pending before the U.S. Immigration and Naturalization Service.[58]

ONUSAL, the FMLN, the armed forces, and the United Nations Children's Fund (UNICEF) coordinated the removal of land mines. They established the Mine Awareness and Accident Prevention Project to centralize and analyze information about the location and types of land mines and ordnance in El Salvador. Cooperation was critical. The FMLN and Salvadoran armed forces possessed maps with the precise location of the minefields laid during the war, and provided them to International Danger Disaster Assistance (IDAS), a Belgian company contracted to clear the mines. Between March 1993 and January 1994, IDAS combed over 202 square kilometers of territory, cleared 425 minefields, and disposed of 9,500 antipersonnel mines. UNICEF also established a program to educate children about the dangers of land mines.[59]

Civil Administration

The United Nations was responsible for assisting with post-conflict justice and encouraging reforms of the justice system. It helped establish two post-conflict justice bodies. The first was the Truth Commission, which was tasked with "investigating serious acts of violence that have occurred since 1980 and whose impact on society urgently requires that the public should know the truth."[60] It was responsible for investigating human rights abuses committed by both the government and the FMLN, documenting the abuses, and making recommendations to the government. The Truth Commission was staffed by three prominent foreigners: a former Colombian president, a former Venezuelan foreign minister, and an American jurist then serving as president of the Inter-American Court for Human Rights. The commission concluded by recommending the following:

- Dismissal of all persons named in the report from the armed forces, civil service, and judiciary

[58] U.S. Committee for Refugees, *Country Report: El Salvador,* Washington, D.C., 1997.

[59] Report of the Secretary-General on the United Nations Observer Mission in El Salvador, S/1994/561, May 11, 1994; UNIDR (1997), p. 135; United Nations Department of Public Information (1995b), p. 31.

[60] Letter dated 8 October 1991 from El Salvador Transmitting the Text of the Mexico Agreement and Annexes Signed on 27 April 1991 by the Government of El Salvador and the FMLN, A/46/553-S/23130, October 9, 1991, in United Nations Department of Public Information (1995b), p. 168.

- Disqualification of all persons named in the report from public office for ten years

- Resignation of all justices of the Supreme Court

- Implementation of major Supreme Court reforms

- Adoption of new legislation to guarantee due process in the criminal justice system, including measures to improve the effectiveness of habeas corpus.[61]

The Salvadoran government responded negatively to the report. The Supreme Court justices stated they had no intention of resigning. President Cristiani argued that the Truth Commission had overstepped its mandate and that the report did "not respond to the wishes of the Salvadorans who [sought] to forgive and forget everything having to do with that very sorrowful past."[62] In contrast with its firm backing for the results of the Ad Hoc Commission, the United Nations refrained from forcefully pushing for implementation of many of the Truth Commissions recommendations, including those for the resignation of the Supreme Court justices and the disqualification from public office of all those named in the report.

The second body formed by the United Nations was the Joint Group for the Investigation of Politically Motivated Illegal Armed Groups. It was established by ONUSAL and the Salvadoran government to investigate the infamous "death squads."[63] The Joint Group was composed of El Salvador's human rights ombudsman, the director of ONUSAL's Human Rights Division, and two individuals named by President Cristiani. It issued its report in July 1994. Relying heavily on declassified U.S. government documents, the report concluded that there were unambiguous connections between the death squads and the Salvadoran public security forces during the civil war. It also noted that the squads still existed after 1991, operating under the protection of some members of the armed forces and National Police, and stated that the justice system "continued to provide the margin of impunity

[61] "From Madness to Hope." Also see Report of the Secretary-General Containing an Analysis of the Recommendations of the Commission on the Truth, S/25812/Add.3, May 25, 1993, in United Nations Department of Public Information (1995b), pp. 447–454.

[62] Quoted in Johnstone (1997), p. 321.

[63] "From Madness to Hope." (1993). Also see Johnstone (1997), pp. 323–325.

these structures require."[64] The Joint Group's main recommendation was to create a special unit within the Criminal Investigation Division of the National Civil Police to continue the investigations. Little else happened as a result. No one was dismissed or prosecuted for involvement in the death squads.

Efforts by ONUSAL's Human Rights Division and the Truth Commission to reform El Salvador's justice system were largely unsuccessful. ONUSAL organized a number of seminars for judges and offered training in the development of a new democratic doctrine for Supreme Court of Justice judges and magistrates.[65] The Human Rights Division and Truth Commission also offered a series of recommendations on enhancing the independence and effectiveness of the justice system and improving the impartiality and competence of judges.[66] But these efforts had little impact.[67] In 1995, only 4.9 percent of El Salvadorans had confidence in the judiciary.[68] The poor performance of the judiciary was an obstacle to police reform and to effective management of the crime problem. The prison population grew dramatically during ONUSAL's tenure because there was an increase in arrests and long delays in bringing suspects to trial.[69]

Democratization
The United Nations monitored and supported the conduct of four simultaneous elections in March 1994—for president, parliament, municipal councils, and the Central American Parliament. All the elections were managed by El Salvador's Supreme Electoral Tribunal.

ONUSAL's Electoral Division assisted in voter registration, monitored the election campaign, and provided assistance in drawing up the voter roles. During the voter registration period, ONUSAL offered technical and logistical support to the Supreme Electoral Tribunal, which possessed outdated

[64] Report of the Joint Group for the Investigation of Politically Motivated Illegal Armed Groups, S/1994/989, October 22, 1994, p. 29.

[65] United Nations Department of Public Information (1996), p. 436.

[66] "From Madness to Hope" (1993).

[67] Johnstone (1997), pp. 332–333.

[68] Spence, Jack, et al., *Chapúltepec: Five Years Later: El Salvador's Political Reality and Uncertain Future,* Cambridge, Mass.: Hemispheric Initiatives, 1997, p. 10.

[69] Lawyers' Committee for Human Rights, *El Salvador's Negotiated Revolution: Prospects for Legal Reform* (New York: Lawyers' Committee for Human Rights, 1993); Stanley and Loosle (1998), pp. 135–137.

computer equipment and faced transportation and communication problems.[70] Monitoring teams made more than 2,350 visits to towns throughout the country to assist in voter registration.[71] Observer teams attended more than 800 political events and monitored political advertising through the mass media. On election day, ONUSAL deployed almost 900 international observers to observe conduct at the polls and the counting of the ballots; each of the 355 policing centers in El Salvador was monitored. Following the recommendation of the United Nations, polling stations marked voters with indelible ink to prevent multiple voting by the same individual.[72] A team of 40 specialized observers was also deployed to the Supreme Electoral Tribunal to monitor the official count.[73]

The campaign period was marred by a several murders of politicians and activists from both the FMLN and ARENA, the governing political party.[74] There were some voting irregularities and organizational problems on election day. But the elections were ultimately successful. There were no serious security problems and no ballot rigging. ARENA received 49 percent of the vote and 39 seats in the Legislative Assembly, the FMLN coalition received 25 percent and 22 seats, and the Christian Democratic Party 5 percent and 18 seats. No candidate in the presidential election obtained an absolute majority. A second round of voting was held on April 24, 1994, between the two candidates with the highest number of votes. Armando Calderón Sol, the ARENA candidate, won with 68 percent.

Over the ensuing decade, El Salvador regularly held free and fair democratic elections. Newspapers, books, magazines, films, and plays were not censored. Academic freedom was respected. The FMLN reinvented itself as a political party and became an increasingly powerful political force. It increased its seats in the National Assembly in 1997, became the largest party in the Assembly in 2000, and retained that position in 2003 with 35 percent of the popular vote.[75]

---

[70] Report of the Secretary-General on the United Nations Observer Mission in El Salvador, S/1994/179, February 16, 1994, p. 3.

[71] Report of the Secretary-General on the United Nations Observer Mission in El Salvador, S/1994/304, March 16, 1994, p. 2; United Nations Department of Public Information (1996), p. 438.

[72] S/1994/179, p. 6; S/1994/304, p. 4.

[73] Report of the Secretary-General on the United Nations Observer Mission in El Salvador, S/1994/375, March 31, 1994, p. 3.

[74] S/1994/179, pp. 7–8.

[75] Pearce (1998), p. 605.

Economic Reconstruction

The World Bank and International Monetary Fund (IMF) took the lead in El Salvador's economic reconstruction. The World Bank expanded its involvement in El Salvador with the election of the Cristiani government in 1989. By the time of the Chapultepec Agreement, the Bank had approved a structural adjustment loan and a social sector rehabilitation project, organized a series of consultative group meetings, and offered aid to the government for its National Reconstruction Plan.[76] The IMF also began negotiations with El Salvador's government in 1989. In January 1992, the IMF's executive board approved a 14-month stand-by arrangement for $42 million. International financial organizations and governments held a series of consultative group meetings in May 1991, March 1992, April 1993, and June 1995. Donors were much more willing to finance projects that targeted infrastructure and environmental reform rather than security or political projects, such as the creation of the National Civil Police, promotion of democratic institutions, or reintegration of former combatants into society.[77]

El Salvador's post-conflict economic recovery was impressive. Gross domestic product approached its preconflict 1978 peak in 1992, and the economy grew at an average annual rate of 5.6 percent between 1991 and 1996. The government also brought inflation under control. Inflation fell from 32 percent in 1986 and 24 percent in 1990, to below 10 percent by 1996. Government revenues and national savings increased relative to gross domestic product, and the share of private investment in GDP climbed to 15 percent from 6 percent a decade earlier. The balance of payments strengthened from a deficit of 0.4 percent of GDP between 1989 and 1992 to a surplus of over 2 percent between 1993 and 1997.[78] El Salvador's economic growth benefited from inflows of foreign exchange from private remittances, which came from Salvadoran émigrés and refugees living abroad, especially in the United States. By 1993 remittance inflows were double the volume of external assistance and exceeded total export earnings. They helped the government finance the trade gap, maintain a stable exchange rate, control inflation, and cushion the impact of structural adjustment on the poor.[79]

---

[76] Eriksson, Kreimer, and Arnold (2000), p. viii.

[77] Castillo, "Post-Conflict (2001), p. 1976.

[78] Alexander Segovia, "Macroeconomic Performance and Policies since 1989," in Boyce (1996), p. 57; Eriksson, Kreimer, and Arnold (2002), p. 24; Castillo (2001), p. 1976.

[79] Segovia (1996), p. 57.

LESSONS LEARNED

UN operations in El Salvador only marginally met this volume's definition of nation-building because armed force was employed only briefly during the assembly and disarmament of FMLN units. Otherwise, all UN military and police were unarmed and implementation depended upon the voluntary compliance of the parties. Nevertheless, El Salvador occupies an important place in any history of nation-building because of its significant accomplishments; the positive benchmarks it set for subsequent, more demanding missions; and its pioneering efforts in such areas as disarmament, demobilization, and reintegration. Among the lessons learned:

- Direct UN participation in presettlement negotiations can facilitate a transition to democracy.

- The integration of insurgent groups into a democratic political process is critical to ensure a lasting peace.

- Delaying the reintegration of ex-combatants into society and demobilizing police and other security forces into a country with high unemployment can increase crime.

- The deployment of international civilian police can help decrease organized and other forms of crime.

- Rebuilding internal security needs to address all components of the justice system: police, judges, prosecutors, the rule of law, and detention facilities.

Numerous governments supported the UN efforts in El Salvador with men, money, and political pressure on the parties to resolve their differences and carry out their commitments. U.S. influence with El Salvador's government and U.S.-led programs to train the new police force were particularly important.

The United Nations played a central role in negotiating a peace settlement. Secretary-General Javier Pérez de Cuéllar and other UN officials directly participated in the negotiations, from the first agreement signed in San José in 1990 to the final peace settlement at Chapultepec Castle in 1992. This greatly facilitated the reconstruction process for at least two reasons. First, it allowed the United Nations to influence the terms of the agreement, including its own role in post-conflict reconstruction. Second, it enabled the United Nations to develop a close relationship with both the Salvadoran government and the FMLN.

Perhaps the most challenging aspect of the UN mission was overseeing the demobilization, demilitarization, and reintegration of the FMLN. When the peace agreement was signed, the FMLN enjoyed strong popular support in El Salvador, could still conduct combat operations in most of the country, and maintained some international support. Despite initial setbacks, such as the December 1992 exposure of undisclosed weapons caches, FMLN guerrillas eventually demobilized and demilitarized. The FMLN success-fully transitioned from an insurgent organization that had participated in a bloody civil war to a competitive political party. FMLN leaders deserve par-ticular credit for having the courage and foresight to lay down their arms in favor of participation in the democratic political process.

The reintegration of ex-combatants was less successful. Delays in reinte-grating former FMLN and government combatants into society, along with a lack of funding for the land program, left thousands of unemployed fight-ers in El Salvador. Poor economic conditions and high unemployment in the immediate post-conflict period made finding jobs particularly chal-lenging. Consequently, crime rates soared. The homicide rate one year after the United Nations departed was one of the highest in the world. Former soldiers, police, and guerrillas were all involved in organized crime, and the newly formed National Civil Police could not stabilize the country. The emergence of organized crime is a problem in most nation-building opera-tions. But a rapid and well-funded reintegration program for former com-batants might have reduced the problem in El Salvador.

The deployment of international civilian police might have also helped ame-liorate the crime problem. ONUSAL deployed a maximum of 315 unarmed police observers and no armed international civilian police. The deploy-ment of UN civilian police would have been especially helpful in improving the effectiveness of National Civil Police officers, minimizing police partici-pation in organized crime, and combating crime. The international com-munity spent less time, money, and personnel in rebuilding the justice sys-tem than it did in constructing and training the National Civil Police force. ONUSAL organized a handful of seminars for judges and magistrates. The Human Rights Division and the Truth Commission also offered some rec-ommendations to improve the independence and effectiveness of the jus-tice system. The poor performance of the judiciary was an obstacle to police reform and to effective management of the crime problem. The increase in arrests, combined with long delays in bringing suspects to trial, contributed to the dramatic growth in the prison population during ONUSAL's tenure.

Table 4.1
UN Operation in El Salvador—Key Facts

Population (1991): 5,185,604: Area: 8,123 square miles; Capital: San Salvador

Operation	Mandate	Special Representative	Peak Military Size	Peak Police Size	Civilian Components
ONUSAL (1991–1995)	Resolution 693: Verify cessation of the conflict Verify implementation of all agreements between El Salvador government and FMLN Resolution 832: Monitor electoral process	Iqbal Riza (Pakistan) Augusto Ramírez-Ocampo (Colombia) Enrique ter Horst (Venezuela)	4,948 military observers Major Contributors: Spain, Colombia, Mexico, and Venezuela	315 civilian police	Monitor and guarantee respect for human rights Promote democratization, including rehabilitate justice system
MINUSAL (1995–1996)	No new resolution: Verify implementation of outstanding points of the agreements and provide a continuing flow of information	Chief military observer: Ricardo Virgil (Peru)	No military component	No police component	Complete ONUSAL verification responsibilities

Chapter Five

CAMBODIA

In the 1960s, Cambodia became increasingly caught up in the Vietnam War. Cambodian territory was used as a North Vietnamese transit route and a Viet Cong sanctuary, provoking American bombing and ground incursions. Prince Norodom Sihanouk, who had been neutral in the war, was overthrown in 1970 and succeeded by a pro-American regime under General Lon Nol. The Lon Nol regime, in turn, was overthrown in 1975 by the communist Khmer Rouge headed by Pol Pot. Following the fall of South Vietnam in 1976, the Khmer Rouge launched a genocidal campaign of collectivization in Cambodia in which 1.7 million of its citizens died, over 20 percent of the population. Following a period of border clashes between Khmer Rouge and Vietnamese forces and Khmer Rouge attacks on ethnic Vietnamese in Cambodia, Vietnam invaded Cambodia in December 1978. It defeated the Khmer Rouge and, for the ensuing decade, occupied Cambodia with some 250,000 troops. The Khmer Rouge retreated to the jungles and mountains and waged a guerrilla war. Throughout this period, China backed the Khmer Rouge; Russia backed Vietnam. In 1989, as the end of the Cold War approached, the five permanent members of the UN Security Council convened peace negotiations among the Cambodian factions in Paris.

In October 1991, these talks produced the *Agreements on a Comprehensive Peace Settlement of the Cambodian Conflict.* This accord gave the United Nations a prominent role in overseeing the transition to a democratic government and administering the country. The UN Security Council established the United Nations Advance Mission in Cambodia (UNAMIC) in October 1991 to help the Cambodian parties maintain the ceasefire and initiate mine-awareness training. It then established the United Nations Transitional Authority in Cambodia (UNTAC) in February 1992 to administer Cambodia during this transitional period; the UN Secretary-General appointed Yasushi Akashi to head the mission.

SOURCE: United Nations Cartographic Section, Cambodia, no. 3860 Rev. 4, January 2004. Available online at http://www.un.org/Depts/Cartographic/english/htmain.htm.

RAND MG304-5.1

Figure 5.2—Map of Cambodia

CHALLENGES

The Paris agreements launched the United Nations on its first full- scale post–Cold War nation-building operation. Cambodia was a significantly more challenging environment than the coincident mission in El Salvador, which had been authorized only a few weeks earlier.

Security

The Cambodian parties had agreed to a peaceful resolution of the conflict as part of the Paris agreements, but it was unclear whether they were willing to abide by the agreements in practice. Vietnam had withdrawn most of its 100,000 troops by September 1989, but the indigenous factions possessed large numbers of weapons and a legacy of military assistance from the former Soviet Union, China, the United States, and Vietnam. The United

Nations estimated that in late 1991 roughly 200,000 full-time Cambodian government and Khmer Rouge soldiers were scattered around the country in some 650 separate locations; there were an additional 250,000 militia members. These forces possessed 350,000 weapons.[1] The Cambodian government's military controlled between 80 and 90 percent of the country, but it could not enforce security and order in all areas.

The Khmer Rouge presented a particular threat to UNTAC forces. In 1991, the Khmer Rouge, led by Pol Pot and Khieu Samphan, controlled about 15 percent of the country along the Thai-Cambodian border and fielded up to 45,000 soldiers.[2] It financed its activities by mining gemstones in Battambang, selling them to Thai entrepreneurs, and charging royalties on the local timber trade.[3] Although Khmer Rouge representatives signed the Paris agreements, skeptics speculated that their real motive was to exploit the peace to overthrow the Cambodian government and retake control of Phnom Penh.[4] The agreements authorized an intrusive role by the United Nations and direct control over important areas of government, such as national defense, public security, and foreign affairs. Khmer Rouge leaders may have believed that UNTAC's activities would weaken the government enough to allow them to seize power. An estimated 6 to 10 million land mines littered the Cambodian countryside. Because of injuries from mines, Cambodia had the highest percentage of physically disabled citizens in the world.[5] Removing the mines would be a labor- and time-intensive process.

Humanitarian

The December 1978 Vietnamese invasion and food shortages in 1979 displaced large numbers of Cambodians, including routed Khmer Rouge soldiers. Cambodians fled to the country's western border, where at first the Thai government refused to admit them. Most were fearful of turning back.

---

[1] United Nations Department of Public Information, *The Blue Helmets: A Review of United Nations Peace-Keeping,* 3rd Edition, New York: United Nations, 1996, p. 456.

[2] Trevor Findlay, *Cambodia: The Legacy and Lessons of UNTAC,* New York: Oxford University Press, 1999, p. 4; Michael W. Doyle, *UN Peacekeeping in Cambodia: UNTAC's Civil Mandate,* Boulder, Colo.: Lynne Rienner Publishers, 1995, p. 17.

[3] Global Witness, *Forests, Famine, and War: The Key to Cambodia's Future,* London: Global Witness, 1995.

[4] Doyle, "War and Peace in Cambodia," in Doyle et al. (1997), pp. 194–197.

[5] Human Rights Watch, *Landmines in Cambodia: The Coward's War,* New York: Human Rights Watch, September 1991, p. 1; Cheryl M. Lee Kim and Mark Metrikas, "Holding a Fragile Peace: The Military and Civilian Components of UNTAC," in Doyle et al. (1997), pp. 111–112.

In October 1979, Thailand agreed to establish "holding centers" inside its borders with assistance from international donors, although it referred to them as "illegal immigrants" rather than refugees, a term that creates a special status under international law.[6] By the time the Paris agreements were signed, the United Nations and a host of nongovernmental organizations (NGOs), such as Médecins Sans Frontières and the International Committee of the Red Cross, had acquired over a decade of experience working with Cambodia's refugees and internally displaced persons. There were nearly 370,000 Cambodian refugees. Approximately 350,000 lived in camps in the Thai border region and were assisted by the United Nations Border Relief Operations. There were also another 150,000 to 200,000 internally displaced persons.[7] UNTAC was responsible for assisting in their safe return and providing financial assistance.

Civil Administration

Cambodia was the first of the post–Cold War nation-building missions in which the United Nations assumed at least nominal responsibility for governing the country and assisting with democratic transformation. As the decade progressed, the United Nations gradually became more accustomed to organizing and running such transitional administrations in Somalia, Kosovo, Eastern Slavonia, and East Timor. In 1992, however, the United Nations took on this function with considerable trepidation, both on legal grounds (the UN Charter seemed to forbid it) and practical ones.

The difficulties of organizing a transitional administration in Cambodia were both reduced and complicated by the existence of an indigenous government that was already exercising control over much of the country. The Paris settlement assumed the government would continue to function under UN oversight. This left the United Nations with the delicate task of trying to exercise intrusive control over an existing sovereign, centralized, communist bureaucracy while preparing the country for democratic elec-

---

[6] Macalister Brown and Joseph Jermiah Zasloff, *Cambodia Confounds the Peacemakers, 1979–1998,* Ithaca, N.Y.: Cornell University Press, 1999, p. 121; Linda Mason and Roger Brown, *Race, Rivalry, and Politics: Managing Cambodian Relief,* South Bend, Ind.: University of Notre Dame Press, 1983.

[7] Roughly 350,000 Cambodians were defined as "displaced persons" rather than refugees and were not eligible for refugee status under international legal standards. Nishkala Suntharalingam, "The Cambodian Settlement Agreements," in Doyle et al. (1997), p. 99; Valerie O. Sutter, *The Indochinese Refugee Dilemma,* Baton Rouge, La.: Louisiana State University Press, 1990, pp. 75–81.

tions. Despite its prior agreement, the Cambodian government proved predictably resistant to UN oversight, particularly in sensitive areas such as security and the budget.[8]

Cambodia lacked a viable judicial system. The few courts that did exist deferred to the wishes of the executive branch in cases in which the executive took an interest. The Supreme Court was not required to provide a reason for reversing a provincial court's action, and in many cases a judge who did not follow instructions from the minister of justice was punished.[9] As Gerald Helman and Steven Ratner concluded, "Twenty years of civil war, invasions, outside arms supplies, gross violations of human rights, massive dislocation of its population, and destruction of its infrastructure have rendered the country incapable of governing itself."[10]

UNTAC also was faced with the issue of how to deal with war crimes and crimes against humanity. The Khmer Rouge and its leader, Pol Pot, had never been held accountable for killing an estimated 1.7 million Cambodians between 1975 and 1979. The Khmer Rouge enjoyed a 3:1 numerical advantage over the United Nations in military forces, however, and the United Nations Security Council had not authorized UNTAC to use armed force except in self-defense.

Democratization

The Paris peace settlement provided for the development of a liberal democratic constitution for Cambodia. The country had limited experience with such a system. In 1946, France had allowed national balloting for a constituent assembly, the first elections in Cambodia's history. The victorious Democrat Party drafted a constitution modeled on that of the French Fourth Republic. The resultant democratic experiment was short-lived. In 1952, King Sihanouk staged a coup d'état, dismissed the Democrat Party cabinet, and governed the country by decree. "I am the natural ruler of the country . . . and my authority has never been questioned," Sihanouk claimed.[11] His gov-

---

[8] Michael W. Doyle, "Authority and Elections in Cambodia," in Doyle (1997), p. 140.

[9] Brown and Zasloff (1999), p. 113.

[10] Gerald B. Helman and Steven R. Ratner, "Saving Failed States," *Foreign Policy*, No. 89, Winter 1992–93, p. 14.

[11] David P. Chandler, *The Tragedy of Cambodian History: Politics, War and Revolution Since 1945*, New Haven, Conn.: Yale University Press, 1991, p. 66. Also see David P. Chandler, "Three Visions of Politics in Cambodia," in Doyle (1997), pp. 25–52.

ernment then proceeded to harass, intimidate, imprison, and kill political opponents. The Democrat Party was formally dissolved in 1957.

By 1992, there were four major factions in Cambodia. The most powerful was the State of Cambodia, headed by Hun Sen. Its political party, the Cambodian People's Party, enjoyed a significant advantage over other parties because of its ties to the government. Three factions opposed the Cambodian People's Party: The United National Front for an Independent, Neutral, Peaceful, and Cooperative Cambodia (FUNCINPEC), led by Prince Norodom Sihanouk, had received assistance and political support from the United States, Britain, France, Australia, and Japan. The Party of Democratic Kampuchea, better known as the Khmer Rouge, had been receiving financial and military aid from China. The Khmer People's Liberation Front was led by Son Sann and backed by the United States. UNTAC's major objective was to ensure that the four factions cooperated during the transition period, recognized the results of the upcoming elections, and did not return to civil war.

Economic Reconstruction

By 1992, Cambodia had become one of the poorest countries in the world. Agriculture employed 80 percent of the labor force and generated about half of gross domestic product. Industry contributed 19 percent of GDP.[12] Agricultural and industrial production, exports, and numerous social indicators had not recovered to the prewar levels of the 1960s. The country's physical infrastructure had been largely destroyed by more than two decades of war. There was almost no telecommunications system. Diseases such as malaria and tuberculosis were widespread; the average life expectancy was less than 50 years.[13]

The Cambodian government was also in the midst of a fiscal crisis. Most assistance from the Soviet Union or Soviet bloc states had dried up; the government was unable to cover the shortfall through increased tax collection. By 1992, the budget gap was running 4.5 percent of GDP. The government's decision to cover the deficit by printing money resulted in an increase in

---

[12] Brown and Zasloff (1999), pp. 124–126.

[13] Elisabeth Uphoff Kato, "Quick Impacts, Slow Rehabilitation in Cambodia," in Doyle (1997), p. 187.

inflation from less than 10 percent before 1988 to 150 percent in 1991.[14] Foreign investors were deterred by the unstable political situation. The result was a "jungle economy" in which Cambodian government and business officials attempted to grab whatever they could before the political situation either stabilized or collapsed.[15]

THE UN AND INTERNATIONAL ROLES

UN Secretary-General Boutros Boutros-Ghali appointed Yasushi Akashi as his special representative to Cambodia on January 9, 1992. On February 28, the UN Security Council, acting at the invitation of the signatories to the Paris agreements, formally established the UN Transitional Authority in Cambodia. UNTAC was organized into seven distinct components: military, civilian police, human rights, elections, civil administration, repatriation, and rehabilitation.

As with El Salvador, the Cambodian settlement was an early product of post–Cold War collaboration among major and regional powers. Many of these countries, having promoted the peace negotiations, went on to assist the United Nations in carrying out its mandate. The United States helped organize elections. Its National Democratic Institute and the International Republican Institute trained Cambodian parties on such issues as political party organization and campaign management. China, which had played a pivotal role in prodding the Khmer Rouge to participate in the peace negotiations, helped restrain Khmer Rouge guerrillas during the transition period. Australia, which had pushed for a significant UN role during the negotiations, provided technical assistance to the Cambodian military, and contributed soldiers to UNTAC—including its force commander, Lieutenant-General John Sanderson. Japan provided financial assistance and dispatched unarmed peacekeeping troops for the first time in its history. France, which had also helped negotiate the peace settlement, went on to provide a military contingent to UNTAC and train Cambodia's armed forces.

---

[14] World Bank, *Cambodia: Agenda for Rehabilitation and Reconstruction,* Washington, D.C.: World Bank, June 1992, p. 40.

[15] Kato (1997), pp. 187–188.

Military and Police

UNTAC deployed 15,991 troops and 3,359 civilian police.[16] The force was large compared to the UN peacekeeping operations that had preceded it, except for the Congo. But with a ratio of two UNTAC soldiers per thousand Cambodians, the military force was modest in light of the country's size, the expansive UN task set by the Paris accords, and the resultant Security Council mandate. UNTAC's military component was expected to

- supervise the relocation of Cambodian forces to designated cantonment areas, and oversee their disarmament and demobilization

- locate and confiscate weapons caches and military supplies throughout the country

- assist with mine clearing

- verify the withdrawal of all foreign forces and their equipment from Cambodia[17]

- provide security around polling stations during elections.[18]

To accomplish these objectives, UNTAC deployed approximately 10,000 soldiers, an engineering element, an air support group with fixed-wing and helicopter aircraft, and a naval component with patrol boats and landing craft. UNTAC divided Cambodia into nine sectors, with its force headquarters in Phnom Penh. The Paris agreements also gave the Secretary-General's Special Representative authority to establish a civilian police component. The main objectives of UNTAC civilian police were to supervise the local police and ensure that law and public order were maintained effectively and impartially.[19] To do this, UNTAC deployed 3,359 civilian police.[20]

---

[16] United Nations Transitional Authority in Cambodia (UNTAC), UNTAC, *Facts and Figures,* New York: United Nations, 1993.

[17] *Agreement on a Comprehensive Political Settlement of the Cambodia Conflict,* Annex 1, Section C.

[18] The objective to provide security for elections was added in 1992. Operation Order No. 2 for the Joint Military Component of UNTAC, issued December 9, 1992.

[19] United Nations Department of Public Information (1996), p. 457.

[20] UNTAC, *Facts and Figures,* New York: United Nations, 1993.

Civil and Economic

In addition to the police and the military, UNTAC comprised five other components: human rights, elections, civil administration, repatriation, and rehabilitation. The human rights component investigated allegations of abuse and conducted an education campaign. The Paris agreements entrusted UNTAC with organizing and conducting elections. This process involved adopting an electoral law; developing an information campaign directed at the public; designing and implementing a registration system for voters, political parties, and candidates; ensuring free and fair access to the media; and investigating complaints of electoral irregularities.[21]

UNTAC's civil administration component was tasked with supervising and controlling five areas of governance: foreign affairs, national defense, finance, public security, and information. The Secretary-General designated UNHCR as the lead agency to oversee the return and repatriation of Cambodian refugees and internally displaced persons. UNHCR was to identify and provide agricultural and settlement land for the returnees and provide them reintegration assistance. UNTAC's rehabilitation component addressed basic humanitarian needs, including food, health, and housing.

One of the most unusual features of the Paris agreements was the creation of the Supreme National Council. Article 78 of the UN Charter precludes the United Nations from adopting a trusteeship role over a member state. But a special arrangement was made in which Cambodian national sovereignty would be vested in the Supreme National Council during the transition period.[22] The council included representatives of the four main factions: Cambodian People's Party (CPP), FUNCINPEC, the Khmer Rouge, and the Khmer People's Liberation Front. The Paris agreements provided that this council should serve as the "unique legitimate body and source of authority in which, throughout the transitional period, the sovereignty, independence, and unity of Cambodia are enshrined."[23] Its members represented Cambodia abroad during the transitional period and occupied Cambodia's seat at the United Nations. However, the Supreme National Council had no legal governing powers, although it could advise UNTAC on policy matters.

[21] *Agreement on a Comprehensive Political Settlement of the Cambodia Conflict,* Annex 1, Section D.

[22] Article 78 states: "The trusteeship system shall not apply to territories which have become Members of the United Nations, relationship among which shall be based on respect for the principle of sovereign equality." *Charter of the United Nations,* June 26, 1945, Article 78.

[23] *Agreement on a Comprehensive Political Settlement of the Cambodia Conflict,* Section III, Article 3.

WHAT HAPPENED

The United Nations verified the departure of foreign forces and organized successful democratic elections. The Khmer Rouge was neither disarmed nor integrated into the political system, but it was effectively marginalized.

Security

In September 1992, UN Secretary-General Boutros Boutros-Ghali announced that UNTAC had successfully marshaled 52,292 Cambodian troops into cantons and confiscated 50,000 weapons.[24] At that point, UNTAC still had not accounted for some 150,000 troops, 250,000 militia members, and 300,000 weapons. UNTAC's most difficult challenge was dealing with the Khmer Rouge, which barred UNTAC controllers from entering Khmer Rouge-controlled territory and never adhered to the cease-fire.[25] On June 10, 1992, the Khmer Rouge announced that it was not obliged to comply with UNTAC's requirements until all foreign military forces were withdrawn from Cambodia. Its leaders argued that Vietnamese soldiers were still located in Cambodia in disguise, and it accused UNTAC of favoring the Cambodian People's Party over the Supreme National Council.[26]

When the Khmer Rouge refused to put its forces in cantons, the CPP and other factions refused to continue demobilizing and disarming. Khmer Rouge forces repeatedly breached the cease-fire. Skirmishes ensued between Khmer Rouge and government forces, UNTAC civilian and military personnel were killed, and the Khmer Rouge attacked ethnic Vietnamese living in Cambodia.[27] The UN Security Council "strongly deplored" the vio-

---

[24] These included 42,368 troops from the Cambodian People's Armed Forces; 3,445 from the National Army of Independent Kampuchea; and 6,479 from the Khmer People's National Liberation Armed Forces. "Second Progress Report of the Secretary-General on the United Nations Transitional Authority in Cambodia," S/24578, September 21, 1992.

[25] Perhaps the clearest example of the Khmer Rouge's refusal to cooperate with the United Nations was in May 1992. When Special Representative Akashi and General Sanderson tried to enter the PDK-controlled zone near Pailin in western Cambodia, Khmer Rouge soldiers barred their entry. Brown and Zasloff (1999), p. 138. On UNTAC's difficulties with the Khmer Rouge, also see Ben Kiernan, "The Failures of the Paris Agreements on Cambodia, 1991–93," in Clark (1994), p. 8.

[26] Kim and Metrikas (1997), pp. 116–117.

[27] Brown and Zasloff (1999), pp. 137–139; Kim and Metrikas (1997), pp. 121–122.

lence in Cambodia and the Khmer Rouge's refusal to cooperate. But UNTAC did not possess the capabilities or mandate to compel compliance with the Paris agreements.[28]

UNTAC military and police forces faced challenges in providing adequate security around polling stations and otherwise creating a safe environment for the May 1993 elections. In March, April, and May 1992, Cambodian government soldiers and police attacked, ransacked, and burned opposition political offices and harassed and killed opposition party members.[29] Judy Thompson, who served as the UN's deputy electoral official, acknowledged that "voter intimidation is widespread."[30] Security conditions on the eve of the elections were precarious. The Khmer Rouge shelled the town of Stoung in the central province of Kompong Thom hours before voting began on May 23. Secretary-General Boutros-Ghali acknowledged that initial expectations of a safe environment for elections were too optimistic: "UNTAC will be conducting the most impartial election that is possible in conditions that are not susceptible to its full control."[31] The conclusion of the elections did not result in immediate peace. During the dry season in early 1994, the newly formed Cambodian government launched a military offensive against Khmer Rouge strongholds in western Cambodia.

The majority of UNTAC's 3,600 unarmed civilian police trained local Cambodian police in patrolling, traffic control, criminal investigations, riot control, and human rights. They also provided special instruction to police officers and judges in implementing the new penal code adopted by the Supreme National Council. However, the civilian police component of UNTAC was given overly ambitious goals and was never able to effectively oversee and control the Cambodian police. UN police performance was hampered by slow deployment, a poor-quality staff, and a system of justice controlled by the existing Cambodian executive. The United Nations set minimum standards for its civilian police component, including police experience, medical standards, driving skills, and the ability to speak French or Eng-

---

[28] UN Security Council Resolution 766, S/RES/766, October 13, 1992. As Gerard Porcell, chief of UNTAC's Civil Administration Component, noted: "We don't have the will to apply the peace accords. This absence of firmness with the Khmer Rouge was a sort of signal for the other parties who saw there the proof of UNTAC's weakness towards the group that from the start eschewed all cooperation." Quoted in Ben Kiernan (1994), p. 14.

[29] Brown and Zasloff (1999), pp. 146–147.

[30] Peter Goodspeed, "UN Flirting With Disaster," *Toronto Star,* February 28, 1993, p. 13. Also see Doyle, "Authority and Elections in Cambodia," in Doyle (1997), pp. 153–156.

[31] Report of the Secretary-General in Pursuance of Paragraph 6 of Security Council Resolution 810, S/25784, May 15, 1993.

SOURCE: United Nations Cartographic Section, UNTAC Sectors of Cantonment and Demobilization, No. 3736, January 2004. Available online at http://www.un.org/Depts/Cartographic/english/htmain.htm.

RAND MG304-5.2

Figure 5.2—UNTAC Forces in Cambodia

lish. But many contingents failed to meet these standards.[32] Some police monitors lacked basic community policing skills and were involved in corrupt behavior such as smuggling.[33] UN civilian police conducted hundreds of criminal investigations, but prosecution was difficult in the absence of a functioning justice system.[34]

UNTAC efforts to verify the withdrawal of foreign forces and clear minefields were successful. UNTAC officials investigated Khmer Rouge accusations that Vietnamese forces remained in Cambodia but found no evidence that this was true. By August 1993, UNTAC's Mine Clearance Training Unit had cleared more than 4 million square meters of land and removed 37,000

---

[32] Klaas Roos, *UNTAC Evaluation Report, UN CIVPOL* (Phnom Penh, Cambodia: UNTAC, August 1993), p. 8.

[33] Brown and Zasloff (1999), p. 110.

[34] Kim and Metrikas (1997), pp. 125–126, 130–132.

mines. It also trained over 2,230 Cambodians in mine-clearing techniques, many of whom were employed by such nongovernmental organizations as Halo Trust, Norwegian People's Aid, and Mine Action Group.[35] The sheer number of antipersonnel land mines ensured that demining would continue long after UNTAC left. The Cambodian Mine Action Center, which was established by the Supreme National Council in 1992, continued mine clearance following UNTAC's departure in 1993.

The civilian police component completed its withdrawal on October 15, 1993, and the military component had withdrawn by November 15. UNTAC faced severe challenges during its tenure in Cambodia. On the one hand, it prevented the return of civil war, facilitated the end of Chinese support for the Khmer Rouge, and verified the removal of Vietnamese soldiers. On the other hand, it did not disarm or canton most soldiers or militia or effectively supervise the local police. In the course of its operations, UNTAC suffered 83 total casualties, including 46 soldiers and 16 police, of which 25 were fatal.[36]

Humanitarian

The UNHCR facilitated the return of 361,462 refugees between March 30, 1992 and April 30, 1993.[37] UNHCR managed the refugee operation and contracted with NGOs to build the transit stations; UNTAC provided security along the roads. Each refugee received a kit with essentials for setting up a new household and food for 400 days. In addition, UNHCR gave 88 percent of the refugees a cash grant, 8 percent land and wood for building, and 3 percent land to farm.[38] The refugees were free to choose where to return and to change their minds once they were back in Cambodia.

The United Nations was less successful in introducing human rights reforms. The Paris agreements tasked UNTAC with "fostering an environment in which respect for human rights would be ensured," and, in reference to the Khmer Rouge genocide in the 1970s, with preventing a return to "the

[35] "Further Report of the Secretary General Pursuant to Paragraph 7 of Resolution 840," S/26260, August 26, 1993; Kim and Metrikas, (1997), pp. 111–112; United Nations Department of Public Information (1996), pp. 476–477.

[36] *UNTAC Facts and Figures* (1993).

[37] UNTAC Daily Press Briefing, April 30, 1993; Brian Williams, "Returning Home: The Repatriation of Cambodian Refugees," in Doyle (1997), pp. 165–185.

[38] UNTAC Daily Press Briefing, April 30, 1993.

policies and practices of the past."[39] UNTAC sent one human rights officer to each of Cambodia's 21 provinces to monitor human rights and investigate violations, but serious human rights violations continued.[40] Ethnic Vietnamese residents of Cambodia were killed by ethnic Cambodians, especially Khmer Rouge; the government continued to abuse prisoners; and incidents of politically motivated murder, assault, and intimidation increased in the months leading up to the May 1993 elections.[41] According to UNTAC estimates, the Khmer Rouge committed over 90 percent of the ethnic killings directed against Vietnamese, whereas the State of Cambodia was responsible for most of the political assassinations.[42] UNTAC did not have a mandate to use force to halt human rights abuses; such abuses continued over the next decade, although they were not at the levels of Cambodia's recent past.

Civil Administration

UNTAC's modest personnel resources never came close to matching its expansive mandate to administer Cambodia. Barely 200 UN civil administrators were supposed to control or supervise 140,000 State of Cambodia civil servants.[43] As usual, the deployment of civil staff lagged significantly behind that of the military component. UN civil administrators were not fully deployed to Cambodia until October 1992, one year after the Paris agreements had been signed and only one year before the end of UNTAC's mandate, in September 1993.

The United Nations had few precedents for planning UNTAC's administrative functions. The UN General Assembly's partition plan for Palestine called for the creation of a *corpus separatum* for Jerusalem under a special international regime administered by a Trusteeship Council. But the Arab states and Israel ultimately rejected the plan.[44] Another distant precedent was the UN Temporary Executive Authority that governed the western half

---

[39] *Agreement on a Comprehensive Political Settlement of the Cambodia Conflict,* Annex 1, Section E.

[40] Ibid.

[41] Human Rights Watch, *An Exchange on Human Rights and Peace-Keeping in Cambodia,* New York: Human Rights Watch, September 1993.

[42] UNTAC, "Human Rights Component Final Report," Appendix 3; Doyle, *UN Peacekeeping in Cambodia,* pp. 45–47.

[43] Brown and Zasloff (1997), p. 103.

[44] Simon Chesterman, *You, the People: The United Nations, Transitional Administration, and State-Building,* New York: Oxford University Press, 2004.

of New Guinea during its transition from Dutch to Indonesian rule in 1962 and 1963.

In Cambodia, the Paris agreements gave UNTAC control over foreign affairs, national defense, finance, public security, and information. As the UN Secretary-General explained in his Second Progress Report, UNTAC's primary role was to monitor and supervise existing administrative structures at national and provincial levels, rather than act itself as an "administrative bureaucracy."[45] Such supervision required access to all documentation on decisionmaking, personnel policies, and material questions within each existing administrative structure; exercising veto power on all decisions pertaining to personnel and finance; and proposing improvements. To fulfill this mandate, UNTAC inserted staff directly into Cambodia's civil administration and held weekly meetings with decisionmakers.[46] UNTAC's efforts to get an effective handle on Cambodian government actions was, however, largely unsuccessful. UN administrators encountered widespread resistance in providing information or obeying orders at national and local levels of government. UNTAC employed too few personnel to supervise such a large bureaucracy. Delays in recruiting a full staff and the early departure deadline left UNTAC little time to accomplish its objectives.

Much of the central government's administration disintegrated after the Paris agreements, and control slipped into the hands of provincial governors and generals. UNTAC was unable to monitor and supervise these officials, especially as the "controlling" ministries in Phnom Penh were unable themselves to exercise effective control. Where a central apparatus in Phnom Penh still functioned, Cambodian officials maneuvered around UNTAC by creating concealed parallel structures, communicating via back channels and informal networks. As Michael Doyle argued:

> When the factions wished to be controlled, they allowed themselves to be "controlled." But usually, the actual chain of policy bypassed UNTAC control, as the UNTAC officer was kept busy controlling an official without function and the real budgetary (or other) mechanism flowed elsewhere, diverted out of UNTAC's sight.[47]

---

[45] S/24578.

[46] Doyle, "Authority and Elections in Cambodia," in Doyle (1997), p. 137.

[47] Ibid., p. 144.

A Cambodian government document captured in March 1993 instructed local officials to maintain "the initiative with regard to the storage of documents to prevent control of them by UNTAC."[48] Government officials increasingly used mobile telephones for informal transmissions to circumvent UNTAC monitoring. A unit of the Public Security Ministry was transferred to the Ministry of Culture, which was free from UNTAC scrutiny.[49] The Khmer Rouge, for its part, prevented all UNTAC officials from deploying to territory it controlled.

UNTAC's foreign affairs component created a new passport and visa system that was endorsed by the Supreme National Council. It was unsuccessful, however, in preventing smuggling or forestalling corruption in the issuance of passports—the government merely issued its own entry visas. UNTAC's public security component helped improve conditions in prisons and conducted information sessions on the Supreme National Council's new penal code for police and judges, but otherwise it had little impact. UNTAC's finance component was somewhat successful in managing the issuance of currency, controlling the expenditures and revenues of the state budget, and enforcing customs controls. Beneath the surface, however, the finances of the government were intermeshed with those of the CPP.

International civil servants working in UNTAC's defense component inventoried the Cambodian army's fixed assets, including equipment, vehicles and weapons, and oversaw sales, rentals, and exchanges of land by the Defense Ministry. They also discovered "a high level of political activity by the CPP within the armed forces of the Phnom Penh authorities," but were unable to stop it.[50] UNTAC's information component was among the most successful. It published media guidelines, lifted legal restrictions on the media, encouraged the operation of a free and responsible press, launched a Media Association of all Cambodian journalists, and made available its own television and radio facilities to the 20 political parties participating in the 1993 elections.[51]

---

[48] Ibid., p. 144.

[49] Brown and Zasloff (1999).

[50] S/24578.

[51] United Nations Department of Public Information (1996), pp. 479–480.

Democratization

UNTAC had seven months to organize national elections. The United Nations began preparations in October 1992 and held national elections from May 23 to May 28, 1993. UNTAC first prepared a draft electoral law, drawing on the United Nation's experience in Namibia in 1989 and 1990. UNTAC outlined procedures for administering the election, listed requirements for the registration of political parties and voters, allocated legislative seats according to provinces, provided instructions for polling and tabulating the election results, and prescribed a code of conduct for all participants.[52] UNTAC surmounted several significant logistical hurdles: It acquired computers to make voter lists and print registration cards; and it provided initial training to 50,000 Cambodians recruited as election officials.

UNTAC's Advance Election Planning Unit implemented a voter registration campaign between October 1992 and January 1993. The Khmer Rouge refused to participate in elections and stated that it could not guarantee the security of election officials on its territory. UNTAC nevertheless managed to penetrate some Khmer Rouge–controlled areas and even to register Khmer Rouge soldiers and their commanders.[53] UNTAC eventually registered 4.6 million potential voters representing nearly all of the estimated eligible voters to whom it had territorial access.[54] Its computer system could store as many as 5.2 million voter registration records, and it prepared laminated voter identity cards that included a color photograph and fingerprint of each Cambodian voter. Two American organizations—the National Democratic Institute and the International Republican Institute—provided training on party organization and campaign management to all registered political parties.[55]

The formal political campaign began in April 1993. UNTAC conducted training for 900 international polling station officers from 44 countries, and recruited and trained 50,000 Cambodian electoral staff.[56] It also helped organize political rallies and transported candidates and equipment to remote areas.[57] Most Cambodians possessed little knowledge of what democratic

---

[52] *United Nations Electoral Law for the Conduct of a Free and Fair Election of a Constituent Assembly for Cambodia,* March 31, 1992.

[53] Findlay (1999), p. 55; Brown and Zasloff (1999), pp. 135–136.

[54] United Nations Department of Public Information (1995a), p. 29.

[55] International Republican Institute, *IRI in Cambodia* Washington, D.C., 2004; National Democratic Institute for International Affairs, *Cambodia,* Washington, D.C., 2004.

[56] Brown and Zasloff p. 150.

[57] United Nations Department of Public Information (1995a), pp. 38–40.

elections entailed because Cambodia's last experience with democracy had been in the 1950s. To educate the public, UNTAC distributed posters and banners, deployed mobile information units to the countryside, arranged for public rallies and debates among the candidates, and broadcast information on the radio and television. UNTAC tried to reassure voters that the ballots would be secret and they could freely select the party of their choice. Radio UNTAC gave each political party weekly time to broadcast its messages, as well as the ability to respond if unfairly attacked by opponents.[58] The CPP maintained a distinct advantage, however, because it owned the Cambodian media and used public officials for campaigning.[59]

UNTAC went to great lengths to ensure the secrecy of the ballots. Since most voters were illiterate, they made their selection by checking the symbols for party affiliation. Ballots from several villages were intermixed before counting in order to disguise the pattern of local voting and reduce the risk of reprisal. The United National Front for an Independent, Neutral, Peaceful, and Cooperative Cambodia (FUNCINPEC), led by Prince Norodom Sihanouk, took first place in the election with 45 percent of the vote and 58 seats in the Constituent Assembly. It was followed by the CPP with 38 percent and 51 seats, the Buddhist Liberal Democratic Party with 4 percent and 10 seats, and Molinaka with 1 percent and 1 seat. Local elections were not held until February 3, 2002.

Following the May 1993 election, the CPP made numerous allegations of electoral irregularities, demanded that UNTAC hold new elections in seven provinces, and announced that it would not recognize the results of the elections. Some members in the three eastern provinces of Kompong Cham, Prey Veng, and Svay Rieng threatened to secede. Hun Sen used local security forces, the support of state and provincial administrations, and his control over the army to persuade FUNCINPEC to include the CPP in a coalition government. Backed by Cambodia's security forces, the CPP harassed and intimidated FUNCINPEC members, opposition groups, and the press before finally ousting Prince Ranariddh (son of King Norodom Sihanouk) in a bloody coup in 1997.

Cambodia's 1998 parliamentary elections were neither free nor fair because of violence, restrictions on press coverage and campaign opportunities, and CPP manipulation of the rules for allocating parliamentary seats among parties. The CPP's landslide victory in Cambodia's February 2002 local elec-

---

[58] United Nations Department of Public Information (1996), pp. 469–470.

[59] Doyle, "Authority and Elections in Cambodia," in Doyle (1997), pp. 153–156.

tions further strengthened Prime Minister Sen's hand. The vote followed a violent campaign that included several election-related killings, threats, vandalism, and other acts of intimidation against opposition parties.

Economic Reconstruction

International support for post-conflict reconstruction contributed to economic growth. To quell inflation, the Cambodian government negotiated an agreement with the International Monetary Fund in which it promised to stop printing money and to place cash limits on wage and salary payments under UNTAC supervision. The government abided by the agreement despite pressure to resume the issuance of currency. Inflation slowed in 1993, the exchange rate stabilized, and consumer prices increased at a slower rate. The resultant budget crunch precluded government pay raises to keep pace with inflation. As a result, by early 1993 average civil service salaries had fallen to less than 25 percent of their previous year's value. In addition, many civil servants were paid irregularly. Heightened corruption and absenteeism weakened the government's control over the provinces.[60]

UNTAC established a Technical Advisory Committee composed of delegates from all four factions and chaired by UNTAC's rehabilitation component. It reviewed and coordinated aid proposals before passing them to the Supreme National Council for approval. At a June 1992 conference in Tokyo, donor countries pledged a total of $880 million in infrastructure restoration, resettlement, and other reconstruction projects. However, pledged funds were not disbursed quickly. Disagreements among the political factions slowed the disbursement of aid. In March 1993, FUNCINPEC vetoed a $75 million emergency rehabilitation loan from the World Bank because it believed the loan would favor the rival Cambodian People's Party.[61] Donor hesitancy to commit money in an unstable political environment slowed and skewed the flow of aid.

Despite such problems, Cambodia made significant progress in stabilizing the economy and restoring economic growth after several decades of war. Macroeconomic developments were impressive. GDP increased at an average annual rate of 6 percent between 1991 and 1995; inflation decreased to 3.5 percent in 1995 from an average of 140 percent per year between 1990 and 1992; and budgetary revenue as a share of GDP doubled from 1991 to

---

[60] Kato (1997), pp. 194–197.

[61] Ibid., pp. 190–194.

1995. The Cambodian government also introduced customs reform and new tax measures, created a two-tier banking system with a central bank, and eliminated most nontariff barriers to trade.[62] Economic growth has continued. Political violence in 1997 triggered a short-term economic downturn as GDP growth declined to 2.1 percent in 1998, but Cambodia recovered quickly and annual GDP growth averaged 7 percent over the next three years. The government's fiscal and monetary discipline, financial support from the international community, and rapid development of the garment industry contributed to the country's high economic growth rates.[63]

LESSONS LEARNED

The United Nations was ill prepared to assume its large, unprecedented responsibilities for overseeing implementation of the Paris accords on Cambodia. But it nevertheless achieved the most essential elements of its mandate: the organization of elections and the transfer of power to an internationally recognized and broadly representative government. In the decade since the United Nations' departure, democracy has not thrived, but neither has civil war resumed. The Khmer Rouge has remained marginalized as a force in Cambodian society, foreign forces have not returned, the economy has grown rapidly, and some level of open public debate and civil society has been sustained. Thrust into its largest nation-building operation since the Congo 30 years earlier, the United Nations gained valuable experience in Cambodia that would be applied elsewhere over the coming decade. Lessons included the following:

- The United Nations must be prepared to actually govern as well as help secure and assist states in post-conflict transition.

- Transitional governance requires a cadre of trained administrators available at reasonably short notice.

- There must be a reasonable correlation between the assets committed to UN operations and the objectives set for them.

---

[62] World Bank, *Cambodia: Progress in Recovery and Reform,* Report No. 16591-KH, Washington, D.C.: World Bank, June 1997. Also see World Bank, *Cambodia Rehabilitation Program: Implementation and Outlook,* Report No. 13965-KH, Washington, D.C.: World Bank, February 1995.

[63] International Monetary Fund, *Cambodia: Selected Issues and Statistical Appendix,* IMF Country Report No. 03/59, Washington, D.C., International Monetary Fund, March 2003.

- Unarmed and unempowered international police can have only limited impact on local policing practices.

- Democratization often requires long-term engagement.

- Elections in a post-conflict society may sometimes be better treated as a guide to power sharing rather than a means of determining winners and losers.

Cambodia represented the first occasion in which the United Nations assumed responsibility for actually administering a state emerging from conflict. In this case, however, the United Nations did not actually gain control of the country's administration. The existing government devised means to maintain its control and authority. In light of the United Nations' extremely limited capacity to run the Cambodian government at the time, this was not surprising. In later cases, such as Kosovo or East Timor, the absence of local government institutions forced the United Nations to take real, comprehensive responsibility for administering the territory. Cambodia demonstrated the difficulty of quickly fielding experienced civil administrators in significant numbers to a distant, dangerous locale, highlighting a recurrent problem that the United Nations has made only modest progress in addressing.

The assets committed to nation-building, in terms of manpower, money, and time, must stand in some proportion to tasks and expectations. In this case, UNTAC had neither the forces nor the mandate to enforce compliance with the Paris accords. The gap between available resources and the task at hand partially explains why UNTAC failed to disarm and demobilize the Khmer Rouge and ensure the participation of voters in elections in areas under Khmer Rouge control. UNTAC deserves credit for pursuing elections in the rest of the country and for securing a high rate of participation.

International police with no arms or arrest authority have only limited capacity to oversee and control indigenous police forces because they can neither compel obedience nor lead by example. A more robust international police force would have been more effective.

UNTAC's mandate was limited in time as well as function. The United Nations was successful in organizing an inclusive electoral process that led to the installation of a broadly representative government. But there was little likelihood that an engagement as brief as UNTAC's—less than two years—would be sufficient to implant enduring democratic reforms in a country and a region without such a tradition. The 1993 election produced a plurality for Sihanouk's FUNCINPEC party. In an established democracy, this might have provided an adequate basis for effective governance. In a society as divided as Cambodia's, the best such a narrowly contested result could be expected to provide was a guide to power sharing among the principal factions. Even this result was not sustained after UN peacekeepers left the county.

UN intervention in Cambodia provided the context for disengagement of regional and global powers, marginalization of the Khmer Rouge, democratic elections, and the emergence of an internationally recognized government of a broadly representative nature. It also created the conditions for economic growth. Given the United Nations' comparatively brief and limited commitment, these were not negligible achievements.

Table 5.1
UN Operation in Cambodia—Key Facts

Population (1991): 9,621,504; Area: 69,899 square miles; Capital: Phnom Penh

Operation	Mandate	Special Representative	Peak Military Size	Peak Police Size	Civilian Components
UNAMIC (1991–1992)	Resolution 717: Assist the four Cambodian parties maintain ceasefire Initiate mine-awareness training of civilian populations Resolution 728: Implement training program for Cambodians in mine-detection and mine-clearance	A.H.S. Ataul Karim (Bangladesh)	1,090 military personnel Major Contributors: Australia, China, France, India, New Zealand, Pakistan, Russia	No police component	Mine Awareness Unit
UNTAC (1992–1993)	Resolution 745: Monitor human rights Organize and conduct free and fair elections Military arrangements Maintain law and order Assist with repatriation and resettlement of refugees and displaced persons Rehabilitate essential infrastructure	Yasushi Akashi (Japan)	Military component: 15,991 Major Contributors: France, Japan, Australia	3,395	50,000 Cambodians served as electoral staff and some 900 international polling station officers were seconded from governments Administrative control of government functions Return and repatriation of refugees Human rights reforms

Chapter Six

MOZAMBIQUE

In October 1992, the president of Mozambique and the leader of the resistance movement, the *Resistencia Nacional Mozambicana* (RENAMO), signed a peace agreement in Rome. The agreement ended a civil war that had begun shortly after Mozambique gained independence from Portugal in 1975, 17 years earlier. That war had pitted a pro-Soviet Marxist Leninist government against RENAMO, a local resistance movement supported by the governments of Southern Rhodesia and South Africa. With the end of the Cold War and the transition to majority rule in Zimbabwe and South Africa, both the government of Mozambique and RENAMO lost their external sources of support. Religious organizations and neighboring governments pressured both to start peace negotiations. In 1990, the Roman Catholic lay society of Sant'Egidio succeeded in putting the two sides in contact with each other.[1] After two years of negotiations facilitated by Sant'Egidio, the Mozambique government and RENAMO agreed to a General Peace Agreement in October 1992. This accord provided for a cease-fire, disarmament and demobilization, and multiparty elections.

The United Nations was asked by the parties to monitor implementation of the agreement and assist in elections. Secretary-General Boutros-Ghali dispatched an interim Special Representative to Mozambique in October 1992, and on December 16 the Security Council established the United Nations Operation in Mozambique (ONUMOZ) to conduct these tasks.[2]

---

[1] Chris Alden, *Mozambique and the Construction of the New African State: From Negotiations to Nation Building*, New York: Palgrave, 2001, pp. 11–12.

[2] United Nations Security Council Resolution 797, S/RES, 797, December 16, 1992.

SOURCE: United Nations Cartographic Section, Mozambique, no. 3706 Rev. 5, June 2004. Available online at http://www.un.org/Depts/Cartographic/english/htmain.htm.

RAND MG304-6.1

Figure 6.1—Map of Mozambique

CHALLENGES

The major challenges facing the United Nations included assisting the return of 2 million refugees and 3 million internally displaced persons, disarming and demobilizing both combatant forces, reanimating a devastated economy, and holding elections in a society with no democratic experience.

Security

Although RENAMO and the Mozambique government had agreed to a peaceful resolution of the civil war, the United Nations faced the difficult task of ensuring that they abided by the Rome peace agreement. This was an enormous challenge, especially since earlier attempts at peace had failed to end the war. In 1984, South Africa attempted to mediate a peace agreement between the Mozambique government and RENAMO, but the negotiations collapsed.[3] RENAMO intensified its campaign, targeting and destroying government installations, factories and workshops, schools, and infrastructure. RENAMO eventually gained control over much of the country as increasing numbers of Mozambicans grew disaffected with government policies or were intimidated by a wide range of RENAMO terror tactics.

Another significant challenge was the proliferation of weapons in Mozambique. There were about 6 million AK-47s, including 1.5 million that the government had distributed to the civilian population during the civil war.[4] In addition, during the war government troops, RENAMO rebels, and foreign forces had planted several million mines on arable land and near power lines, roads, bridges, railroads, airports, and even schools. The mines endangered subsistence farmers and made it difficult to access RENAMO-occupied areas. The most heavily mined areas were near the Zimbabwean border and in the provinces of Sofala, Maputo, Manica, and Inhambane.[5] Both sides also had little control over many of their soldiers. Government soldiers had frequently deserted their units. Based on random inspections of barracks, up to two-thirds of soldiers on the government's payroll were

---

[3] United Nations Department of Public Information, *The United Nations and Mozambique*, New York: United Nations, 1995, pp. 10–13.

[4] Christopher Smith, "The International Trade in Small Arms," *Jane's Intelligence Review*, Vol. 7, No. 9 (1995), p. 427. Online at http://www4.janes.com (accessed on April 15, 2004).

[5] Human Rights Watch, *Land Mines in Mozambique*, New York, 1994, p. 28.

absent at any one time.[6] Only about half of RENAMO's approximately 20,000 troops remained attached to formal military units.

Humanitarian

Over the course of the civil war, 2 million refugees had fled to neighboring countries and 3 million Mozambicans were internally displaced. When the fighting ended, many returned to rural areas that had little in the way of dwellings or roads. These returnees required food and resettlement aid because RENAMO had denied humanitarian aid organizations access to areas under its control. In addition, the civil war destroyed much of the country's infrastructure, and the fighting left numerous civilians either killed or wounded. Both sides recruited and utilized child soldiers during the war. To make matters worse, Mozambique experienced a series of floods and droughts that devastated agricultural output.

Democratization

Mozambique had no experience with democracy. From 1885 until 1975, it had been a Portuguese colony.[7] Following independence in 1975, the Front for the Liberation of Mozambique secured control over the country and established a one-party system based on the principles of Marxism-Leninism. Samora Machel became Mozambique's first president. In 1986, President Machel was killed in an airplane crash and Joaquim Chissano, the foreign minister, succeeded him. In 1990, the government adopted a new constitution that eliminated references to Marxism-Leninism, established Mozambique as a multiparty democracy, and guaranteed freedom of expression. Perhaps the biggest challenge to creating a democracy was transforming RENAMO from a rebel movement into a political party. Few RENAMO leaders were ardent democrats. Yet, if peace was to be established, the government would need to accept RENAMO as a legitimate political competitor and be willing to accept the outcome of elections.

---

[6] Eric Berman, *Managing Arms in Peace Processes: Mozambique*, Disarmament and Conflict Resolution Project, United Nations Institute for Disarmament Research, Geneva: United Nations Publications, 1996, p. 46.

[7] Allen Isaacman and Barbara Isaacman, *Mozambique: From Colonialism to Revolution, 1900–1982*, Boulder, Colo.: Westview Press, 1983), p. 3, as cited in Berman (1996), p. 9.

Economic Reconstruction

Entrepreneurs, managers, and technicians had fled the country during the civil war. Their exodus resulted in a sharp drop in GDP. Initially, the government's attempts to restore output and spur exports were complicated by its commitment to a socialist economy. Investment was wasted on large-scale projects that the country lacked the capacity to manage. Efforts to nationalize banks and businesses and to set up collective farms led to a collapse in output in the industrial and agricultural sectors. Between 1981 and 1985, Mozambique's GDP dropped from $2.1 billion to $1.2 billion. Sizable parts of Mozambique's infrastructure were destroyed during the war.[8] The economy remained highly dependent on neighboring countries—especially South Africa—and on international assistance and expertise.

THE UN AND INTERNATIONAL ROLES

The United Nations became involved in the peace negotiations as an observer only four months before the signing of the General Peace Agreement.[9] After the agreement was signed, the United Nations' role expanded rapidly. Its broad responsibilities, including chairmanship of the principal commissions set up to implement the accord, were agreed upon literally at the last minute.

Military and Police

ONUMOZ's primary military responsibilities were to

- monitor and verify the demobilization, disarmament, and reintegration of the armies and irregular armed groups on both sides

- monitor the withdrawal of foreign forces

- authorize arrangements to protect vital infrastructure

- provide security for all supporting UN and other international operations

---

[8] Alden (2001), p. 7.

[9] Chissano's government tried as long as possible to keep the United Nations out of the process. RENAMO, on the other hand, regarded the United Nations as a means to legitimize its political role and to increase its leverage over the Government. See Berman (1996), p. 27.

- monitor Mozambique's police, protect election monitors, and report human rights abuses.

To achieve these objectives, the UN Security Council approved a force of about 7,000 troops and 354 military observers. The major units—five logistically self-sufficient infantry battalions—were assigned to protect the major transport corridors vital for the distribution of humanitarian aid. They were also expected to monitor and verify the complete withdrawal of foreign forces and provide security for United Nations and other international activities in support of the peace process.[10] Zimbabwean and other foreign troops, which had been securing the main communications corridors, were to withdraw. Two of the ONUMOZ battalions came from southern Africa: Botswana and Zambia. The other contingents came from Bangladesh, Italy, and Uruguay. India, Japan, Portugal, and Argentina contributed engineering companies, logistics companies, a headquarters company, movement control detachments, a signal battalion, medical units, and an aviation unit. Nineteen countries contributed personnel to the Military Observer Group.

The UN mission also included a civilian police unit. In June 1994, the UN Security Council approved an expansion of the civilian police mission, which increased from 128 to 1,087 police. The police were tasked with monitoring the Mozambican police, reporting human rights abuses, and protecting election monitors.

Civil and Economic

Because legislative and presidential elections were scheduled for one year after the peace agreement, ONUMOZ also provided technical assistance and monitored the entire election process. Its Electoral Division monitored and verified all aspects of the electoral process, which was organized by Mozambique's National Election Commission. ONUMOZ also coordinated and monitored humanitarian assistance, which was distributed by the numerous NGOs operating in the country. Donor assistance was coordinated by the UN Office for Humanitarian Assistance Coordination (UNOHAC), which was established at an international donors conference in December 1992. UNOHAC set up field offices in all 11 provinces.[11]

---

[10] Richard Synge, *Mozambique—UN Peacekeeping in Action 1992-94*, Washington, D.C.: United States Institute of Peace Press, 1997, pp. 92-94.

[11] Alden (2001), p. 45.

WHAT HAPPENED

ONUMOZ was largely successful in implementing the peace agreement. Because the immediate security and humanitarian needs were so great, ONUMOZ focused on restoring order and providing humanitarian assistance. Long-term economic development was not a priority.

Security

The UN Secretary-General's Special Representative, Aldo Ajello, arrived in Maputo on October 15, 1992, with a group of 25 military advisors. By November 3, Ajello, RENAMO, and the Mozambique government had established a Supervisory and Monitoring Commission to oversee the peace process. It was chaired by Ajello and composed of representatives from the government, RENAMO, Italy, Portugal, France, Britain, and the United States. At its first meeting, it set up three commissions to oversee demobilization, demilitarization, and reintegration: the Ceasefire Commission, Reintegration Commission, and the Commission for the Formation of the Mozambican Defense Force.

The deployment of UN military forces began slowly. The Mozambique government, which was uncomfortable with the larger-than-envisioned UN contingent, initially delayed signing a Status of Forces agreement. However, by April 15, 1993, Zimbabwean and Malawian forces withdrew from the transportation corridors and ONUMOZ troops moved into their positions. ONUMOZ forces were fully deployed by June 1993, eight months after the peace agreement was signed. They secured the major roads and transportation corridors by conducting regular land and aerial patrols. They also provided security to oil-pumping stations, airports, UN warehouses, ONUMOZ headquarters, and arms depots.

The disarmament, demobilization, and reintegration program was ONUMOZ's top priority. In light of the difficulties encountered in Angola, where the opposition group UNITA had rejected the UN-assisted election results and plunged the country back into civil war, ONUMOZ made clear that national elections would only be held *after* the two sides demobilized. Demobilization was largely successful, though it took longer than expected. The original timetable to complete demobilization in one year was not achieved because ONUMOZ forces did not deploy quickly enough. Consequently, UN Secretary-General Boutros-Ghali organized a special summit with Mozambique President Chissano and RENAMO President Afonso Dhlakama in October 1993 to set a more realistic timetable. They agreed to begin bringing their troops to cantonment areas in September 1993 and to complete demobilization by May 1994.[12]

The process of setting up cantonment areas for government and RENAMO troops also took much longer than planned. A significant number of nongovernmental organizations were involved in the demobilization process, leading to coordination problems and delays. The World Food Program, World Health Organization, Oxfam, Médecins Sans Frontières, and UNICEF provided food, health care, and other assistance to both sides in the cantonment areas.[13] RENAMO leaders wanted to retain some of their forces in case the country plunged back into civil war. They were also poorly prepared for the political process and introduced a number of obstacles that delayed demobilization. Despite such problems, by August 14, 1994, a total of 64,130 government and 22,637 RENAMO troops had been demobilized. Both sides kept several thousand troops out of the process to hedge against post-electoral crises.[14] But most soldiers were eager to go home because they were weary of the war and because the financial package offered by the United Nations was so attractive.

The disarmament process was less successful. In March 1994, ONUMOZ allowed both sides to move military equipment from cantonment areas that had more than 200 weapons to one of three regional arms depots, which were guarded by armed ONUMOZ infantry battalions. Both sides also possessed hidden arms depots. ONUMOZ collected almost 200,000 weapons, although many were dysfunctional and in poor condition. In addition, many of the weapons collected were poorly secured at the cantonment areas, where they were guarded by unarmed UN personnel.[15] Numerous weapons were stolen and ended up on the black market. The remaining weapons were given to the newly formed Mozambican Defense Force.[16]

The establishment of a new Mozambican Defense Force was a mixed success. On July 22, 1993, the Joint Commission for the Formation of the Mozambican Defense Force, under UN chairmanship, requested the assis-

---

[12] Alden (2001), p. 48.

[13] Berman (1996), pp. 61–63.

[14] Berman (1996), p. 55.

[15] Berman (1996), pp. 72–73.

[16] Smith (1995), p. 427.

tance of France, Portugal, and the United Kingdom in forming a new army. The commission sent 540 officers from the government and RENAMO to a training facility in Nyanga, Zimbabwe, where they received training as military instructors. These individuals then helped train new infantry soldiers at the three Mozambican Defense Force training centers. Because of delays with equipment and housing, new soldiers received only six weeks of training. Many of the new soldiers were dissatisfied with their training and their compensation. At the time of the elections, only 10,000 troops had been trained for the new army, and many had already deserted.

ONUMOZ civilian police were charged with supervising election security, monitoring the Mozambican police force, and reporting human rights abuses. The Mozambican police force had a reputation for corruption and excessive force. Most of the international police assigned to Mozambique did not have adequate training or experience. UN police were stationed at 83 field posts and at provincial capitals throughout the country. Although they helped contribute to a peaceful transition process, they were unarmed and did not have the authority to actively prevent human rights violations or hold perpetrators accountable. Consequently, they could do little to stop the Mozambique police when they committed abuses. ONUMOZ police reported 511 complaints through the National Police Commission to the Interior Ministry, but there was little government response.[17]

The United Nations also helped establish a National Mine Clearance Plan to clear an initial 4,000 kilometers of roads, develop a mine awareness program, and educate the population on the dangers of land mines. In May 1994, the United Nations Office for Coordination of Humanitarian Affairs assumed responsibility for assuring that mines were cleared expeditiously. Over the course of ONUMOZ's deployment, however, only a small fraction of land mines was cleared.[18] Bureaucratic infighting between UN agencies delayed the mine-clearing process. Frequent flooding dislodged mines and spread them into previously cleared areas. In 1996, the United Nations Accelerated Demining Program estimated that there were still between 2 million and 4 million land mines left in Mozambique.[19]

---

[17] Alden (2001), pp. 60–61.

[18] Mozambique, Internal Affairs, *Jane's Sentinel Security Assessment—Southern Africa,* January 14, 2004. Online at http://www4.janes.com (accessed on April 15, 2004).

[19] A.V. Smith, *Equipment for Post-Conflict Demining: A Study of Requirements in Mozambique,* Working Paper No. 48, Coventry, United Kingdom: Development Technology Unit, University of Warwick, January 1996; *Multi-Country Mine Action Study: Mozambique,* Maputo, Mozambique: United Nations Office for Coordination of Humanitarian Affairs, 1997; *Annual Report: Mine Action Programme, 2003* (Maputo: Mozambique Ministry of Foreign Affairs and Cooperation, February 2004).

Humanitarian

UNHCR was the lead agency for repatriating refugees. It established a three-year program that included restoring basic services in Mozambique, conducting a planning survey, carrying out a landmine education campaign, demining transportation routes, and giving assistance to the asylum countries. By April 1994, 1.5 million refugees and over 2 million internally displaced people had returned to their homes.[20] UNOHAC, international donors, and a number of NGOs effectively provided humanitarian assistance to the population.[21] When demobilized troops returned home, they became part of the humanitarian assistance program. An Information and Referral Service and Reintegration Support Scheme were set up to inform ex-combatants about available support and employment opportunities and to provide them with financial assistance for 18 months. Soldiers also received kits with agricultural tools, seeds, and food rations at the assembly areas.

Democratization

To prepare for the elections, the United Nations trained 1,600 civilians to educate the population about the elections and encourage participation. Approximately 5.2 million people registered to vote. The United Nations deployed 900 electoral observers to verify the polling and vote counting throughout the country. They were supplemented by another 1,400 international observers from such organizations as the European Union and the Organization of African Unity.

The elections, held in October 1994, were generally successful. RENAMO transformed itself from a rebel movement into a credible opposition political party. At the last minute, RENAMO President Dhlakama threatened to boycott the elections, alleging significant irregularities in the election process. He eventually agreed to hold the elections following pressure from the UN Security Council, the UN Secretary-General, and the presidents of South Africa, Zimbabwe, and several other countries in the region. Almost 90 percent of 6.1 million registered voters participated. Chissano was elected president with 53 percent of the vote. The ruling party, the Mozambique Liberation Front (FRELIMO), won 129 of 250 seats in the National Assembly; RENAMO won 112 seats.

The next presidential and legislative elections took place in December 1999. Chissano and the ruling FRELIMO party were reelected, despite a

[20] Alden (2001) p. 559.

[21] Synge (1997), p. 70.

strong showing by RENAMO. RENAMO continues to claim that there were widespread instances of election fraud. These charges and poor relations between the two parties have resulted in a highly polarized political environment. RENAMO deputies have repeatedly walked out of parliament to protest alleged government fraud, threatening to form a government of their own.

Economic Reconstruction

ONUMOZ's top priorities were to help stabilize the security situation, monitor the election process, and coordinate humanitarian assistance operations—not to oversee economic reconstruction. Both the World Bank and IMF were involved in reconstruction efforts. The IMF became involved in Mozambique in 1987 and focused on reducing macroeconomic imbalances, restoring economic growth, and establishing the foundations of a market-based economy. Beginning in 1993, the IMF encouraged the Mozambique government to further liberalize its foreign exchange and foreign trade systems, reduce fiscal imbalances, and diminish the role of the state in the economy through privatization.[22] Mozambique's economy has improved somewhat since reconstruction began in 1992, largely due to the end of civil war and the revival of agricultural production. Gross domestic product grew at an average annual rate of 9 percent from 1996 to 2001. However, with a per capita annual income of $230, Mozambique remains among the poorest countries in the world. Privatization has continued in such sectors as banking. But the transition from an economy run by the state to a market economy has been difficult.

LESSONS LEARNED

The UN operation in Mozambique focused on establishing order and stability after 15 years of civil war, providing emergency humanitarian assistance, and overseeing the country's first democratic elections. It was largely successful in accomplishing these objectives. Several important lessons can be drawn from the operation:

---

[22] IMF, *Republic of Mozambique: Ex Post Assessment of Mozambique's Performance Under Fund-Supported Programs,* Country Report No. 04/53, Washington, D.C.: International Monetary Fund, March 2004.

- As in numerous other UN operations, the cooperation of neighboring states and the support of more distant powers was essential to success.

- Demobilizing military forces *before* democratic elections can reduce the possibility of a return to violence.

- Disarming warring factions should involve destroying weapons and ammunition, not just recording them and placing them in government stockpiles.

- The incorporation of insurgent groups into a political process is important to ensure long-term stability and a transition to democracy.

Like many failed states, Mozambique was pulled apart by its neighbors. Only when these neighbors could be persuaded to collaborate to put the state back together could there be much hope of doing so. As in other UN operations, success depended on the willingness of neighboring states to withdraw their forces and cut off support for their belligerent proxies, as well as on more distant powers to provide resources and use their influence to support the mission.

One of ONUMOZ's priorities was the disarmament, demobilization, and reintegration into civilian life of government and RENAMO combatants. Another priority was holding democratic elections. The order in which these events took place was important. In Angola, the United Nations had sent a peacekeeping force to help maintain order for the September 1992 elections. When the well-armed UNITA faction lost the election, its leader, Jonas Savimbi, rejected the results as fraudulent, refused to participate in the runoff election, and resumed the war. In Mozambique, ONUMOZ decided to hold elections after demobilization was well under way. This turned out to be a wise decision. Demobilization was largely successful. By August 14, 1994, a total of 64,130 government and 22,637 RENAMO troops had been demobilized. Because so many soldiers had already been demobilized, the option for RENAMO of returning to the conflict after the October 1994 elections was much less attractive.

The disarmament process was less successful. Although the United Nations originally viewed disarming the factions as a prerequisite to holding elections, the process proceeded so slowly and was so incomplete that the United Nations abandoned this objective. Many of the weapons stored at the regional arms depots were poorly secured; both sides also kept hidden arms depots. ONUMOZ and the government destroyed few of the weapons. Most were transferred to the Mozambican Defense Force, but many ultimately made their way to the black market. Since the weapons and ammunition that ONUMOZ recorded were enough to arm the Mozambique military several times over, the United Nations should have destroyed more of the arms and munitions when it had the opportunity.

RENAMO's transition from a powerful insurgent group to an opposition political party was critical to the mission's success. RENAMO had grown from a tiny military force of a few dozen combatants in the mid-1970s to 20,000 soldiers by 1990.[23] Much of the credit for demobilizing this force and participating in elections goes to RENAMO leaders such as Dhlakama, who, under pressure from the United Nations and neighboring countries, did not follow in the footsteps of UNITA's Savimbi. Since the 1994 elections, RENAMO has continued to pose a credible electoral challenge to FRELIMO.

---

[23] IISS, *The Military Balance, 1992-1993,* London: International Institute for Strategic Studies, 1993

Table 6.1
UN Operation in Mozambique—Key Facts

Population (1992): 13,148,929; Area: 309,495 square miles; Capital: Maputo

Operation	Mandate	Special Representative	Peak Military Size	Peak Police Size	Civilian Components
ONUMOZ (1992–1994)	Resolution 797: Monitor cease-fire, the separation and concentration of forces, and demobilization Monitor the withdrawal of foreign forces Authorize security arrangements for vital infrastructure Provide technical assistance and monitor the entire electoral process Coordinate and monitor humanitarian assistance operations	Aldo Ajello (Italy)	6,576 in all ranks Major Contributors: Botswana, Zambia, Bangladesh, Italy, Uruguay, India, Japan, Portugal, Argentina	1,087 police observers	Electoral Division United Nations Office of the Humanitarian Affairs Coordinator (UNHAC)

Chapter Seven

EASTERN SLAVONIA

The end of the Cold War and the rise of such nationalist figures as Slobodan Milosevic triggered the collapse of Yugoslavia in the early 1990s. In June 1991, Slovenia and Croatia declared independence from Yugoslavia. Fighting immediately broke out between hastily assembled Croatian forces and the Yugoslav Army, which was heavily staffed by Serbs and paramilitary units from regions in Croatia with large Serb populations. In contrast to the rapid withdrawal of the Yugoslav Army from Slovenia, Serbian forces captured and held the Croatian territories of Krajina, Western Slavonia, and Eastern Slavonia, areas with either Serb majorities or substantial minority populations of Serbs.[1] The battle for Eastern Slavonia was especially bitter. Vukovar, the largest city in this region, is situated on the Danube River; it was bombarded by Serbian artillery from across the river in Serbia for over 100 days. By the time its Croat defenders capitulated, Vukovar had suffered the worst destruction of any European city since World War II.[2]

On February 21, 1992, the United Nations Security Council passed Resolution 743 establishing the United Nations Protection Force (UNPROFOR).[3] UNPROFOR had neither a peace enforcement nor a nation-building mission. Rather it was a UN peacekeeping mission of the Cold War variety, intended to separate combatants and, by its presence, to create the conditions of peace and security needed to negotiate a settlement of disputes between the former republics of Yugoslavia. Unfortunately, the combatants had not agreed

---

[1] Croatia: History, http://www.encyclopedia.com/html/section/Croatia_History.asp (accessed November 16, 2004).

[2] John G. McGinn, "After the Explosion: International Action in the Aftermath of Nationalist War," *National Securities Quarterly,* Volume 4, Issue 1, Winter 1998, p. 99.

[3] United Nations Department of Public Information, "Former Yugoslavia—UNPROFOR," United Nations, September 1996, at http://www.un.org/Depts/dpko/dpko/co_mission/unprof_b.htm (accessed November 23, 2004).

SOURCE: University of Texas, Perry-Castañeda Library Map Collection, University of Texas. Available online at http://www.lib.utexas.edu/maps/europe/croatia.jpg.

RAND MG304-7.1

Figure 7.1—Map of Croatia, Including Eastern Slavonia

on the separation, and the international community was not yet ready to impose a settlement.

In Croatia, UNPROFOR was deployed to the three areas occupied by Serbs. It was also deployed in Bosnia. The United Nations and efforts by the UN and the European Union (EU) to broker a peace settlement among the warring republics foundered. UNPROFOR, for its part, proved unable to halt widespread ethnic cleansing and associated human rights abuses.

On March 31, 1995, UNPROFOR was briefly replaced in Croatia by United Nations Confidence Restoration Operation for Croatia (UN-

CRO).[4] UNCRO proved short-lived. In May 1995, the American-trained Croatian Army launched offensives against Serbian-held regions. Western Slavonia fell in May; Krajina, in August. To prevent a possible war between Croatia and Yugoslavia, which was by then composed solely of Serbia and Montenegro, the five-nation Contact Group—comprising France, Germany, Russia, the United Kingdom, and the United States—induced the Croatian government and the Serbian leadership of Eastern Slavonia to sign a Basic or Erdut Agreement to peacefully integrate Eastern Slavonia into Croatia. This agreement, signed on November 12, 1995,[5] called for the United Nations to both administer and secure Eastern Slavonia for a one- to two-year period of transition from Serb to Croatian rule. Accordingly, the UN Security Council, in Resolution 1037, established the United Nations Transitional Authority in Eastern Slavonia, Baranja, and Western Sirmium (UNTAES).[6]

The agreement on Eastern Slavonia, although negotiated separately, occurred within the wider framework of a peace process that included Bosnia. A little more than a week after the Basic Agreement was signed, negotiations were concluded on the General Framework Agreement for Peace in Bosnia and Herzegovina, known as the Dayton Agreement, after the location where it was negotiated. It is also referred to as the Paris Agreement, the city where the agreement was signed. The Basic Agreement on Eastern Slavonia was in many ways a necessary precursor for Dayton. The primary goal of Croatian President Franjo Tudjman was to regain sovereignty over the entire territory of Croatia; Yugoslav President Slobodan Milosevic wished to prevent an exodus of Serb refugees from another region that he had formerly occupied. Once a satisfactory agreement was reached and signed concerning Eastern Slavonia, the Yugoslav and Croatian governments were better able to come to an agreement to end the Bosnian conflict as well.[7] The Milosevic government recognized that it had lost the conflicts in both Croatia and Bosnia. The Croatian government, cognizant of the heavy cost of the military conflict in Eastern Slavonia in 1991, preferred a negotiated settlement to a war that might lead to engagement with the Yugoslav Army.

---

[4] United Nations Department of Public Information, "United Nations Confidence Restoration Operation (UNCRO)," http://www.un.org/Depts/dpko/dpko/co_mission/uncro.htm (accessed November 23, 2004).

[5] United Nations, *The United Nations Transitional Administration in Eastern Slavonia, Baranja and Western Sirmium (UNTAES) January 1996–January 1998: Lessons Learned,* New York, July 1998, p. 3.

[6] United Nations Department of Public Information, "Croatia—UNTAES," http://www.un.org/Depts/DPKO/Missions/untaes_p.htm (accessed November 16, 2004).

[7] Discussion with Ambassador Jacques Paul Klein, September 21, 2004.

CHALLENGES

The situation in Eastern Slavonia reflected in miniature the wider devastation and displacement caused by nearly half a decade of civil war throughout much of Croatia and all of Bosnia.

Security

Between 8,000 and 12,000 ethnically Serb soldiers were stationed in Eastern Slavonia in January 1996, grouped into a number of units. The largest and best disciplined of these was the Army of the Republika Srpska Krajina. In addition, the 11th Slavonia Branja Corps and a number of paramilitary groups operated in the region, including the Scorpions, the Jumping Snakes, and the Tiger militia. The latter was commanded by the warlord Arkan.[8] These paramilitary groups terrorized local Croats and engaged in extortion and theft. Because some of the most violently abusive paramilitary groups in former Yugoslavia were holed up in Eastern Slavonia, UN officials considered disarming local militias and assuring the withdrawal of Serb troops their top priority.[9] They were concerned that the paramilitaries would attack UN forces and seek to continue to terrorize the local populations. The widespread availability of small arms and heavier weapons contributed to the climate of insecurity. Looters and organized criminal gangs had taken advantage of the chaotic situation to pillage homes and commercial establishments.

Croatia's reconquest of Western Slavonia and Krajina had been marked by an exodus of ethnic Serbs, a movement encouraged by Croatian forces. Reprisal killings, house burnings, and other forms of intimidation contributed to flight from these two regions. International actors and local Serbs wished to forestall similar developments in Eastern Slavonia. UNTAES was faced with the problem of protecting all nationalities during a period when Croatia did not yet have full control. It also sought to ensure that minority rights would be protected after Croatia attained full sovereignty.

Humanitarian

Because the Croatian army was dissuaded from invading Eastern Slavonia, Serbs did not flee the region as they had in Western Slavonia and Krajina.

---

[8] United Nations (1998), p. 16.

[9] United Nations (1998), p. 12.

However, the agreement to return the region to Croatian control after a period of UN oversight still triggered the movement of refugees. Many ethnic Serbs, uneasy about the transfer of authority to Croatia, contemplated moving to Serbia. Most of the Croatian population, as well as other ethnic groups that had fled Eastern Slavonia after it fell to Serbian forces in 1991, wished to go home. At the end of 1995, the Croatian government reported that there were 84,000 internally displaced Croatians from Eastern Slavonia in other parts of Croatia.[10] Once it became clear that Eastern Slavonia would be returned to Croatian control, some of these individuals began to return. Roughly 42,000 ethnic Serbs from Bosnia and other parts of Croatia had taken refuge in Eastern Slavonia during the war; many of them were newly arrived following the Croatian and Bosnian offensives of 1995. Ethnic Serb refugees from Bosnia and other areas of Croatia, who had settled in houses abandoned during the period of Serb control, faced eviction by Croatian returnees. The ebb and flow of refugees also made it difficult to supply adequate food.

Civil Administration

Eastern Slavonia had been ruled by an ethnic Serb administration primarily consisting of local inhabitants. This administration had staffed and provided authorization for the Serb Negotiating Delegation that signed the Basic Agreement, with the acquiescence of the Yugoslav government. The Croatians considered this administration illegitimate. The Serbs, however, were unwilling to accept a Croatian administration immediately. UNTAES's challenge was to provide an acceptable interim administration during a transition period of one to two years.

Democratization

To create a legitimate and representative local government for the region, elections were necessary. However, because of the large movements of refugees over the previous five years, both technical and legal issues hampered election organization. On the technical side, creating up-to-date voter lists and ensuring that those on the list were valid voters posed a major problem. Ethnic Serbs who had settled in Eastern Slavonia after fleeing other parts of former Yugoslavia now considered themselves residents of the region. Croats and members of other ethnic groups who had fled Eastern Slavonia

---

[10] Organization for Security and Cooperation in Europe (OSCE), "Report of the OSCE Mission to Croatia on Croatia's Progress in Meeting International Commitments Since September 1998," Vienna, Austria, January 26, 1999.

but planned to return also considered themselves residents. Identifying all such people and providing them with the means to vote were major tasks.

To compound matters, the Croatian government, headed by President Tudjman's Croatian Democratic Union (HDZ), was slow to implement the Erdut Agreement; it continued to encourage the exodus of Serbs from Croatia long after hostilities had ceased. The Croatian government also had a record of human rights abuse in the region second only to that of the regime in Belgrade. The HDZ government muzzled independent newspapers, whereas state-controlled television had a decidedly uncritical view of the government and its actions. At the time of the Basic Agreement, there were no organized local political parties in Eastern Slavonia. Because Serbs had occupied Eastern Slavonia, Croatian parties were not organized in the region. However, the region had never been incorporated into Serbia, so Serbian parties also did not have a strong presence. As in the rest of Yugoslavia, the tradition of democracy was weak. Elections had been held in the former Yugoslavia, but these had been dominated by the ruling League of Communists of Yugoslavia.

Economic Reconstruction

Eastern Slavonia, especially Vukovar, had never recovered from the siege of 1991. Once one of the wealthiest areas of former Yugoslavia, much of the infrastructure and industrial base of the region had been destroyed.[11] In 1995, industrial output was running at just 10 percent of its 1990 level. Few people were employed. The only industry that continued to function close to prewar levels was the oil sector: Eastern Slavonia's Djelatovci oil fields produced a substantial share of former Yugoslavia's oil output. A Serb paramilitary group, the Scorpions, occupied these fields when UNTAES took control of Eastern Slavonia.[12]

THE UN AND INTERNATIONAL ROLES

Prior to passage of Security Council Resolution 1037 setting up UNTAES, the principal parties involved, Croatia and the local Serbian authorities, had signed the Erdut, or Basic Agreement, stipulating what was to be accomplished. In this agreement, the Serbs recognized that Eastern

---

[11] McGinn (1998), pp. 99–101.

[12] McGinn (1998), p. 100.

Slavonia was part of Croatia and that it would return to Croatian control within a set period of time. The Croatian government recognized the minority rights of Serbs and other ethnic groups in the region and pledged to protect those rights and the local populations.

In contrast to the post-Dayton operations in Bosnia, UNTAES was under exclusive UN control. The Serbs insisted on UN leadership because they perceived other actors, such as NATO or the EU, as anti-Serb. UNTAES had both a military and a civilian component. Both operated under the supervision of the Secretary-General's Special Representative, Jacques Paul Klein, a former American diplomat who was also a major general in the U.S. Air Force Reserves. Klein became the Transitional Administrator.[13]

The mandate for UNTAES was short, comprehensive, and to the point. The goals of the operations were incorporated in both the Basic Agreement and Security Council Resolution 1037. The task force was charged with the following tasks:[14]

- Demilitarize the region within 30 days of deployment of the military component of UNTAES.

- Establish a temporary police force and monitor treatment of offenders and prisoners in the prison system.

- Assist in demining the region.

- Facilitate and monitor the voluntary and safe return of refugees and displaced persons.

- Monitor Croatian and Serbian compliance with the Basic Agreement. In particular, contribute to maintaining peace and security and assist in reconciling the populations in conflict.

- Run the civil administration and ensure the provision of public services.

- Organize local elections.

- Assist in coordinating plans for reconstruction and development.

---

[13] Ibid.

14 United Nations Security Council Resolution 1037.

UNTAES was also tasked with assisting the International Criminal Tribunal for the Former Yugoslavia in fulfilling the Tribunal's mission. This involved protecting investigators sent by the Tribunal and sites where atrocities may have occurred. UNTAES arrested Slavko Dokmanovic in June 1997, the first war criminal in the former Yugoslavia to be forcibly arrested.

Military and Police

Consistent with the approach taken by NATO in neighboring Bosnia, UN-TAES was given robust rules of engagement and a force sized accordingly. At its peak, the military element numbered 4,948 troops, a ratio of 34.2 soldiers per thousand inhabitants, the highest of any UN- or U.S.-led nation-building operation of the 1990s. Even so, the United Nations was initially apprehensive that this number would be too small. The force consisted of a contingent of 1,600 relatively lightly armed Belgian and Russian troops already in the country as part of UNPROFOR. For these troops, the usual problems of finding, transporting, and billeting troops to be part of a peace-keeping operation had already been solved. An additional 3,300 troops, the bulk of whom were from Pakistan and Jordan, arrived over the course of the spring. During this period, UNTAES was buttressed by the addition of 50 tanks, 204 armored vehicles, and six assault and six transport helicopters.[15] The military arm of UNTAES was fully staffed by June 1996. NATO commanders in Bosnia received explicit authorization from the North Atlantic Council to provide close-air support and, if circumstances made it necessary, to evacuate UNTAES personnel. The Transitional Administrator controlled all UN military. The chain of command was very clear.[16]

UNTAES was also given authorization to recruit unarmed international civilian police (CIVPOL) officers. These UN police monitored the existing police force, accompanying them on patrols. They also recruited new police from other ethnic groups and engaged in training the force. Despite not being armed and the lack of arrest authority, CIVPOL was effective in ensuring the peace: CIVPOL officers were present in all police stations, closely monitoring the activities of the local police and quickly calling them to account if local police failed to enforce the law.[17] Because the Transitional Administrator had executive authority in Eastern Slavonia, local police could be reprimanded or fired if CIVPOL reported that they were not performing their duties properly.

[15] United Nations (1998), p. 12.

[16] United Nations (1998), pp. 12, 16.

[17] United Nations (1998), pp. 14, 15.

Civil and Economic

The Transitional Administrator had broad executive powers: His authority superseded that of the Croatian government and local Serb authorities. However, UNTAES was established not to replace the local administration but to supervise it, monitor compliance with the Basic Agreement, and set up a Transitional Police Force. To provide and improve local services, UNTAES had to rely on the local administration, initially staffed and run by Serbs. The Transitional Administrator also believed that local Croat and Serb leaders had to cooperate if his mandate was to be achieved. To foster cooperation, UNTAES set up Joint Implementation Committees that included representatives from both the Serbian and Croat communities to address specific issues.[18]

In contrast to the military component, each civilian component of the operation had to be recruited individually, and an administrative structure had to be created from the ground up. A contingent of international civil servants, civilian police, and local support staff had to be hired, housed, and paid.

Because the Croatian government was to regain control over Eastern Slavonia at the end of UNTAES's mission, it was not inimical to channeling funds or facilitating the transfer of international assistance to the region—in sharp contrast to the Serbian government's attitude toward Kosovo when that region fell under UN/NATO oversight three years later. Nevertheless, despite Croatia's comparatively benign attitude, no mechanism was initially put in place to provide local government funding that, during the war, had been supplied by the government of Serbia in the form of payments for petroleum from the East Slavonian oil fields.

International financial institutions cooperated with the United Nations in pressuring the Croatian government to fulfill its commitments under the Basic Agreement. Both the International Monetary Fund and the World Bank agreed to tie their lending to Croatian government adherence to the Basic Agreement. If the Croatian government obstructed the attempts of Serbs or other non-Croat ethnic groups to register to vote or discriminated against them in property disputes, the IMF and the World Bank agreed to insist that these actions cease if lending were to continue.

In addition to support from the IMF and World Bank, UNTAES cooperated closely with other international agencies. The United Nations High Com-

---

[18] United Nations (1998), p. 10.

missioner for Refugees (UNHCR), the United Nations Children's Fund, the World Food Program (WFP), and the International Committee of the Red Cross (ICRC) all had mandates to operate throughout Croatia, including Eastern Slavonia. To the extent possible, UNTAES avoided interfering in areas for which other agencies were responsible. UNTAES also cooperated with the Organization for Security and Cooperation in Europe (OSCE) in the field of democratization, especially in organizing and running elections.

WHAT HAPPENED

UNTAES took up its responsibilities on January 15, 1996, and ended operations on January 15, 1998, following a 12-month extension of the original one-year mandate. A provision for such a 12-month extension had been included in the initial Security Council Resolution and the Basic Agreement.

UNTAES was a highly successful operation. All aspects of the mandate were fulfilled, although reconciliation proceeded haltingly and the Croatian government continued to discriminate against Serbs.

Security

To ensure that UNTAES had the necessary capabilities to deal aggressively with any recalcitrant elements, the Administrator waited until the authorized troop strength of 5,000 had been reached before triggering demilitarization. That process began on May 21, 1996. During the ensuing 30 days, ethnic Serb forces either handed over or removed to Serbia all heavy weaponry under their control, including 120 tanks, 120 artillery pieces, and 140 mortars. The Army of the Republika Srpska Krajina was disbanded.

UNTAES consulted closely with the commander of the Army of the Republika Srpska Krajina, General Dushan Loncar, before, during and after the period of disarmament. Not only did Loncar cooperate with demilitarization, he also agreed to stay in Eastern Slavonia after demilitarization, accompanied by 450 troops, to reassure local Serbs that they had not been abandoned. His cooperation was key to the success of the program. UNTAES fostered this cooperation by making concerted efforts to portray an image of balance. When Croatian police attempted to enter Eastern Slavonia in contravention to the Basic Agreement, UNTAES faced them down, forcing them to leave the region. This provided UNTAES with crucial credibility with the ethnic Serb community.[19]

Demilitarization of paramilitary forces was more difficult. The Scorpions, who had seized control of the Djelatovci oil fields, refused to disband. UNTAES deployed troops from the Jordanian battalion and Ukrainian assault helicopters to confront them. The Scorpions backed down, left their base, and effectively disbanded. As local Serbs gained more confidence and after UNTAES became convinced that Serbian formations would remain disbanded, the UN troop strength was cut to 2,433 in 1997.[20] Although clashes were infrequent, the operation experienced 11 fatalities: 9 military, 1 civilian, and 1 policeman. Of these, 3 casualties were due to combat.

To reduce the massive numbers of small arms held by households, UNTAES implemented a weapons buy-back program. Although not explicitly included within UNTAES's mandate, the Transitional Administrator interpreted his instructions to demilitarize the region and ensure civil law and order as including initiatives to reduce the numbers of weapons in the hands of the population. After some prodding, the Croatian government agreed to fund the program; the United Nations is forbidden by its own regulations from funding the purchase of weapons. The buy-back program was accompanied by a ban on the ownership of automatic weapons and a program to register those guns permitted under Croatian law.

The buy-back program, which was launched on October 2, 1996, and ended on August 19, 1997, was a success. UNTAES acquired thousands of rifles, anti-tank rocket launchers, and grenades, and millions of rounds of ammunition. Although local inhabitants continue to own weapons, guns are no longer carried openly on the streets. The program provided a carrot that made the introduction of gun registration and the handover of heavier weaponry much easier to achieve.

The existing police force was overwhelmingly Serb. By the end of its mandate, UNTAES had created a new multiethnic force, the Transitional Police Force (TPF), comprised of 811 Serb officers recruited by local Serb authorities and 815 Croat officers, recruited by the Croatian government.[21] Fifty-two officers from other ethnic groups fleshed out the force. These officers were initially trained at the American-funded International Law Enforce-

---

[19] Discussion with Ambassador Jacques Paul Klein, September 21, 2004.

20 Croatia-UNTAES, http://www.un.org/Depts/DPKO/Missions/untaes_b.htm (accessed November 16, 2004).

21 United Nations (1998), p. 14.

ment Academy in Hungary. Subsequently, training was provided in Eastern Slavonia by UN CIVPOL.

Smuggling and extortion aside, common crime was surprisingly low at the time UNTAES took over, but incidents of ethnically related attacks quickly rose. CIVPOL did not have arrest authority, but in their role as monitors and trainers, CIVPOL officers patrolled with the local police and held them to account if they did not respond to these incidents. Although TPF was reluctant to confront perpetrators, TPF officers accepted this duty under CIVPOL pressure.[22] However, they remained reluctant to face down crowds composed of their own ethnic compatriots unless pressed to do so by CIVPOL officers. To provide continued monitoring after the end of UNTAES's mandate, a force of 180 international police remained in Eastern Slavonia for an additional nine months.

Humanitarian

Most of the Croatian population had fled Eastern Slavonia once hostilities broke out in 1991. A reverse flow of roughly 42,000 Serbs from Bosnia and other parts of Croatia had taken refuge in Eastern Slavonia during this period; as noted previously, many of these arrived in 1995, fleeing from the Croatian and Bosnian offensives.

Refugee returns were one of the most difficult problems facing UNTAES. The government of Croatia did agree to adopt a two-way return policy: Serbs from other parts of Croatia were to be encouraged to return to their home regions; Croats who had fled Eastern Slavonia were to be encouraged to return home. On a practical level, local Croatian government officials—with the tacit backing of HDZ party and government leadership—hampered the return of Serbs to their home regions. For example, the Croatian government passed laws repossessing socially owned flats if absent owners had not reclaimed them by December 27, 1995, not long after the peak period of disruption following Croatia's recovery of Serb-controlled lands in 1995. However, homes occupied by Croatian refugees could not be repossessed unless the owner found lodging for current inhabitants. Returning Serbs also had much more difficulty obtaining government assistance to reconstruct their homes than did ethnic Croats. As a consequence of these policies, ethic Serbs from elsewhere in Croatia who had taken refuge in abandoned homes in Eastern Slavonia were loath to vacate them.

---

[22] United Nations (1998), p. 16.

Despite Security Council insistence, the Croatian government was reluctant to provide an amnesty to returning Serbs for crimes other than war crimes. Although it finally passed a law to this effect on May 31, 1996, the law was so ambiguous that it failed to achieve its objective. Ethnic Serbs were worried that the Croatian government had a secret list of Serbs to be charged as war criminals on which it would act once Eastern Slavonia passed from UNTAES to Croatian control.[23]

Because returnees were often moving to or from other parts of Croatia or other former Yugoslav republics, UNTAES had to work with governments and other organizations to facilitate returns. The United Nations, other international institutions, and foreign governments often took primary responsibility for pressuring the Croatian government to change policies that discriminated against returning Serbs. Within Eastern Slavonia, UNTAES used CIVPOL to discourage harassment and improve the performance of the local police. The local civil administration was involved in adjudicating local property disputes. Here, ethnic differences affected outcomes, often hindering the return of Croats to their former homes. Throughout this process, UNHCR worked closely with UNTAES and remained responsible for humanitarian relief.

In all post-conflict societies, reconciliation has been difficult and has taken considerable time. UNTAES attempted to foster reconciliation through public information campaigns, opening borders, improving transit and telecommunications, and encouraging commercial activities involving the various ethnic groups. One of UNTAES's most effective measures was the establishment of a large open-air market on the Osijek-Vukovar highway. UNTAES's Civil Affairs officers facilitated meetings between Croatian and Serb commissions on prisoners of war, although this task was eventually transferred to the Red Cross.

Although Serbs and Croats remained antagonistic and deeply divided, by the end of UNTAES's mandate, reports of harassment had begun to decline; Serbs were organizing politically and taking a more active role in Croatia's political life; and the Croatian national media had adopted a more conciliatory tone when discussing issues of importance to the Serb minority.[24] However, Serbs remained deeply suspicious of the Croatian government even after a comprehensive program of national reconciliation was finally adopted in October 1997.

---

[23] United Nations (1998), p. 18.

[24] United Nations (1998), p. 21.

The difficulty in reconciling the two sides resulted in the continued emigration of ethnic Serbs from the region. In 1999, the total Serbian population was only 51,000, down from a prewar total of 70,000 and a peak of 127,000 in 1995 when Serbs from Krajina and Western Slavonia sought refuge in the region.[25] A net 9,000 Serbs left the region in 1999 alone. Out-migration since 1999 has slowed and may have ceased on a net basis, but the Serbian population of Eastern Slavonia in 1999 was down by over one-quarter from the prewar total. In a number of instances, the elderly and middle-aged have returned to their homes, but they encourage their children to go to Serbia, especially Belgrade, for higher education because Serbia is seen as offering more long-term prospects for Serbian youth.[26]

Civil Administration

After the fall of Vukovar, ethnic Serbs staffed the local civil service. These individuals remained when UNTAES took over. Prior to UNTAES's mandate, the government of Yugoslavia had funded government services in Eastern Slavonia in the form of payments for crude oil from the Djelatovci fields. The Yugoslav government abruptly stopped purchasing crude oil from these fields in mid-April 1996, yet the Croatian government failed to pick up the slack in funding local government. Pension and local government salary payments were delayed. Because there was little other economic activity in the region, the remaining tax base was very small; the cutoff in oil exports worsened an already bleak economic situation.

Oil exports were eventually redirected to Croatia, and the Croatian government agreed to finance the local government. Eastern Slavonian pension, police, health, and education systems were integrated with Croatian institutions during the UNTAES mandate. However, it took until December 3, 1997, barely a month before UNTAES quit Eastern Slavonia, for the regional health authority to be integrated into Croatia's national system.

UNTAES set up 15 Joint Implementation Committees (JICs) to integrate Eastern Slavonian government institutions with their Croatian counterparts. Their performance was mixed. Although some JICs that dealt with

---

[25] U.S. Committee for Refugees (USCR), *World Refugee Survey, Country Report: Croatia*, 1996, 1997, 1998, 1999, 2000, Washington, D.C., http://www.refugees.org/ (accessed November 16, 2004).

[26] Letter from Christine Coleiro, September 13, 2004. Ms. Coleiro is the author of *Bringing Peace to the Land of Scorpions and Jumping Snakes: Legacy of the United Nations in Eastern Slavonia and Transitional Missions*, Clementsport, Nova Scotia: Canadian Peacekeeping Press Publications, 2002.

economic issues operated amicably, UNTAES faced more difficulties integrating other government services. Dissension on the Education and Culture JIC was especially strong; the Transitional Administrator had to dismiss the committee and make curriculum decisions on his own. Issues pertaining to ethnic rights, such as the use of language and the teaching of history and culture, were especially contentious. However, by putting Serbs and Croats in charge of the JICs and giving the JICs the authority to make decisions, UNTAES forced Serbs and Croats to cooperate and gave them joint ownership of the final decisions.[27]

Democratization

UNTAES succeeded in organizing elections in April 1997. The OSCE monitored the elections and judged them free and fair. Creating a consensus for the organization of these elections was difficult. Serb and Croat representatives on the JIC on elections differed sharply over who should be eligible to vote, the institutions to which people were to be elected, the legal framework governing the elections, and electoral boundaries. The difficulties involved in registering displaced people, the initial reluctance of the Serbs to participate, and problems with documentation resulted in a large backlog of voter registrations shortly before the election. UNTAES addressed this problem by relaxing the requirements for registering to vote and extending the voting period. On the day of the voting, materials arrived late to some polling stations, some voter lists were inaccurate, and some election regulations were changed at the last minute. While these difficulties were criticized for lessening the integrity of the voter list, all parties—Croats, Serbs, OSCE observers, and UNTAES—agreed that the results of the elections were fair and reflected the sentiment of the voters.[28] However, as elsewhere in the region, the results of the elections were not unambiguously favorable for reconciliation. Among Serb candidates, hardliners did well. These newly elected individuals replaced Serb officials who had come to cooperate with UNTAES and the Croatian administration. It took quite some time for the new Serbian leaders to conclude that it was in their interests to cooperate, a conclusion the former group of leaders had already reached. The change in leadership thus slowed the process of reconciliation and reintegration.[29]

Since those initial elections, Eastern Slavonia has regularly participated in local and national elections in Croatia. The elections in Eastern Slavonia

---

[27] Letter from Christine Coleiro, September 13, 2004.

[28] United Nations (1998), p. 21.

[29] Letter from Christine Coleiro, September 13, 2004.

have been judged free and fair. However, Croatian governments controlled by the HDZ party have only grudgingly agreed to provide special representation for minorities in Eastern Slavonia in the form of minority councils. Ethnic Serbs continue to receive inferior treatment compared with ethnic Croats when issues of compensation or repatriations are involved.[30]

Economic Reconstruction

In the immediate aftermath of UNTAES's assumption of control, economic conditions in Eastern Slavonia deteriorated. Government employees ceased receiving salaries when the government of Yugoslavia stopped providing financing; the Croatian government was slow to fill the gap. Demobilization resulted in an influx of large numbers of men onto the local labor market, which had little capacity to absorb them.

Eastern Slavonia nevertheless made substantial economic progress under UNTAES. Economic ties were rapidly reestablished with Croatia: Postal service was restarted, the telephone system was reconnected, and the Vukovar-Sid railway line and roads were demined and reopened. Demining, a crucial step for economic recovery, proceeded expeditiously. Demining also employed substantial numbers of demobilized soldiers. Opening borders with Croatia and Hungary and establishing normal trading relations with Yugoslavia contributed appreciably to economic growth. The replacement of the Yugoslav dinar with the Croatian kuna as of May 19, 1997, furthered the integration of the region into the Croatian economy.[31]

Although these policies and programs have contributed to economic recovery in the region, the economic situation in Eastern Slavonia still remains depressed relative both to the current Croatian average and to its prewar standing. Prior to 1991, the region was one of the better off in Yugoslavia. Agriculture, oil, trade, and industry, especially in Vukovar, had made the local population prosperous. Per capita incomes were higher and unemployment rates lower than elsewhere in Croatia outside of Zagreb. As of 2002, the local unemployment rate of 40 percent was almost double the Croatian average rate of 22 percent. Car ownership was 30 percent less than the national average.[32] Although the region is no longer flat on its back, per capita incomes

---

[30] OSCE, Mission to Croatia, "Background Report: Implementation of the Constitutional Law on the Rights of National Minorities and Related Legislation," Zagreb, Croatia, May 12, 2003, available through osce-croatia@oscecro.org.

[31] United Nations (1998), p. 26.

[32] Central Bureau of Statistics of the Republic of Croatia, *Statistical Information,* Zagreb, 2003, pp. 81, 83·

remain substantially below the national average. The slow recovery might be partially related to comparatively low levels of assistance: Eastern Slavonia received a total of $453 per capita between 1996 and 1998, about one-fourth of per capita levels given Bosnia and Kosovo.[33]

LESSONS LEARNED

UNTAES was the most successful of all post–Cold War UN- or U.S.-led nation-building missions. It was also the smallest and the best resourced (at least in military manpower), and it had the clearest desired end state. The Eastern Slavonia operation demonstrated the following:

- If properly supported by its member nations, the United Nations is fully capable of conducing a robust peace enforcement mission of at least modest dimensions.

- As with the larger NATO mission in Bosnia, the U.S. capacity for escalation dominance and the credible threat to employ that capacity provide the essential margin of deterrence.

- In one respect—its capacity to unify military and civil command within a single chain—the UN operation was more soundly organized than NATO- or U.S.-led missions. The prior experience of the Transitional Administrator, who had been both an Army general officer and a career diplomat, madde him particularly suited for this role.

- As in other nation-building operations, the cooperation of neighboring states, however difficult to achieve, is essential for success.

The Balkans proved a bitter testing ground for the international communities' post–Cold War nation-building skills. For nearly half a decade, the United States and its principal allies bickered ineffectually while Yugoslavia came apart, with attendant bloodshed, ethnic cleansing, and large-scale refugee flows. During this period the United Nations and the European Union were engaged to little effect. NATO stood aside—with even less effect. The U.S. decision in 1995 to risk its own troops on the ground changed

---

[33] Calculated from information on international donations provided in UNTAES, "Recent Developments: Economic Reconstruction," December 22, 1997, p. 10, http://www.un.org/Depts/DPKO/Missions/untaes_b.htm#FINANCING (accessed November 23, 2004). All figures deflated to 2000 dollars using U.S. GDP deflators.

the dynamic, galvanizing the Western alliance and bringing even a reluctant Russia to support a policy of robust peace enforcement and full-scale nation-building. UNTAES was the product of this new international resolve, as were the larger operations in Bosnia and, later in the decade, Kosovo.

NATO's success in stabilizing Bosnia is often compared unfavorably with the United Nations' earlier failure there. A more valid contrast is between the pre-1995 failure of all international institutions to halt the conflict in the former Yugoslavia, and the post-1995 success of those same organizations. As noted above, the key variable was Washington's willingness to back international diplomacy with American military force. Although the United States did not commit troops to UNTAES, the presence of a former American diplomat (and general officer) at its head, combined with the stated willingness of NATO forces in neighboring Bosnia to intervene on UNTAES's behalf, provided the capable and comparatively numerous UN force on the ground with an additional element of escalation dominance. This deterrent effect proved enough to secure compliance from local potential spoilers and cooperation from reluctant neighboring states.

The United States has traditionally separated the command for its military and civil agents, the two chains meeting only in the person of its president. This division has helped preserve American constitutional liberties and ensures that successive presidents act on the basis of civil as well as military advice. However, as an arrangement for conducting nation-building operations, where military force is used to promote political transformation, this separation has its disadvantages.

In its management of nation-building missions, NATO has followed the American pattern, assuming responsibilities only for military tasks, usually rather narrowly conceived, and leaving governance and the promotion of political and economic reform to other institutions, including the United Nations, the OSCE and the European Union. In Bosnia, Kosovo and Afghanistan, this division has led to less-than-optimal integration of international efforts.

The United Nations adopted a different model. Beginning with its first major nation-building operation in the Belgian Congo, the United Nations has emphasized civilian control of the military at the local level, this control effected by a representative of the Secretary-General. In Eastern Slavonia, as elsewhere, this arrangement has helped ensure better coordination between the security and political aspects of the operation.

Quality of command was as important as unity of command. The two Administrators who served in Eastern Slavonia were both given high marks by the United Nations assessment team, even though they had very different management styles. The two Belgian generals who commanded the UNTAES forces under the auspices of the Administrator were also highly regarded.[34] Unity of civilian and military command and more independence than customary from UN headquarters in New York permitted the Administrators to react quickly and to marshal the resources—military, political, and financial—needed to fulfill their mandate. However, this independence was not easily given. The Transitional Administrator frequently cited "operational security" as a rationale for not consulting with UN headquarters prior to taking action. This elicited some frustration in New York.[35] The Dayton Agreement was controversial at the time and has remained so. To secure peace, the international community had to deal with precisely the two countries, Croatia and rump Yugoslavia, and with the two men, Tudjman and Milosevic, most responsible for the war and the war crimes the international community was intervening to end. Worse still, those two governments and leaders then became the international community's principal partners in implementing the accords. Many objected to the apparent legitimization and boost in prestige thus afforded to both regimes. However, as a practical matter, there could be no peace in Bosnia or Eastern Slavonia without the active, if reluctant, collaboration of those in power in Belgrade and Zagreb.

This unpalatable lesson regarding the role of neighboring states was applied to good effect in stabilizing post-9/11 Afghanistan and largely neglected during the American intervention in Iraq.

---

[34] United Nations (1998), pp. 8–9.

[35] Discussion with Ambassador Jacques Paul Klein, September 21, 2004.

Table 7.1

UN Operations in Eastern Slavonia—Key Facts

Population (1996): 144,600; Area: 1,364 square miles

Operation	Mandate	Special Representative	Peak Military Size	Peak Police Size	Civilian Components
UNCRO (1995–1996)	Resolution 981: Monitor the crossing of military personnel, equipment, supplies, and weapons over specified international borders	Colonel Rodolfo Sergio Mujica	6,581 troops, 194 military observers Major Contributors: Canada, Czech Republic, Denmark, Kenya, Russia	296 civilian police	No civilian component
	Facilitate humanitarian assistance to Bosnia and Herzegovina				
	Monitor the demilitarization of the Prevlaka peninsula				

Table 7.1—Continued

Operation	Mandate	Special Representative	Peak Military Size	Peak Police Size	Civilian Components
UNTAES (1996–1998)	Resolution 1037: Supervise and facilitate the demilitarization of the region Monitor the voluntary and safe return of refugees and displaced persons Supervise local government administration Contribute to the maintenance of peace and security in the region Otherwise assist in implementation of the Basic Agreement	Ambassador Jacques Paul Klein (United States) William Walker (United States)	8,248 Major Contributors: Belgium, Russia, Pakistan, Jordan	457 civilian police	Civil affairs unit Legal unit Public information unit Political unit Administrative unit

Chapter Eight

SIERRA LEONE

On July 7, 1999, Ahmad Tejan Kabbah, President of Sierra Leone, and Foday Sankoh, leader of the Revolutionary United Front of Sierra Leone (RUF), met in the Togolese capital of Lomé to sign an agreement to end the eight-year RUF insurrection.[1] The conflict had begun in March 1991, when RUF fighters launched a war from the border with Liberia to overthrow Sierra Leone's government.

Numerous attempts to end the conflict had failed. The Economic Community of West African States (ECOWAS) dispatched its Military Observer Group (ECOMOG) to defend the government and help establish order, but it was not successful in accomplishing either objective. In November 1996, UN Special Envoy Berhanu Dinka helped negotiate a peace agreement between the Sierra Leone government and RUF in Abidjan. It was derailed by a military coup d'état six months later. In October 1997, the Economic Community of West African States helped negotiate another peace agreement in Conakry, Guinea. Fighting continued, however, as the RUF conducted a series of offensives, gaining control of more than half the country and briefly overrunning the capital city of Freetown.

The Lomé Agreement thus came on the heels of several failed peace attempts. On October 22, 1999, the Security Council authorized the establishment of the United Nations Mission in Sierra Leone (UNAMSIL) to oversee the disarmament, demobilization, and reintegration called for under the Lomé Agreement. UN Secretary-General Kofi Annan appointed Oluyemi Adeniji of Nigeria as his Special Representative, who assumed his functions in Sierra Leone on December 11, 1999.

---

[1] For an overview of Sierra Leone's civil war, see John Hirsch, *Sierra Leone, Diamonds and the Struggle for Democracy*, Boulder, Colo.: Lynne Rienner Publishers, Inc., 2001.

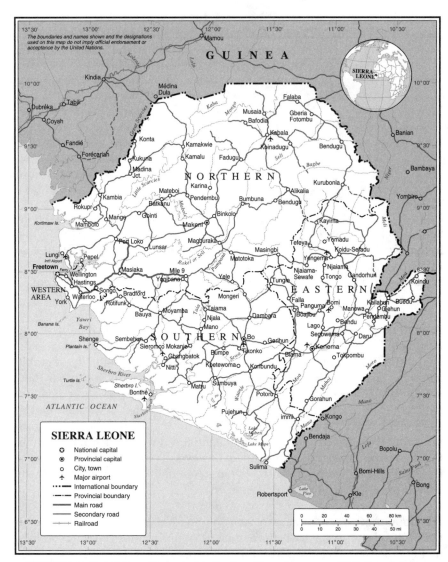

SOURCE: United Nations Cartographic Section, Sierra Leone, no. 3902 Rev. 5, January 2004. Available online at http://www.un.org/Depts/Cartographic/english/htmain.htm.

RAND *MG304-8.1*

Figure 8.1—Map of Sierra Leone

CHALLENGES

The government of Sierra Leone was weak and corrupt. Rebel forces controlled more than half the country. Their willingness to comply with the peace agreement was doubtful. Hunger and disease were rampant. Roads, schools, clinics, and other institutions were severely damaged.

Security

Despite the Lomé Agreement, Sierra Leone's security situation was still tense. The RUF fielded as many as 30,000 soldiers and controlled more than half the country. Among their number were rebellious elements from the Army of Sierra Leone that had previously overthrown President Kabbah soon after he won the wartime election of 1996. The Kabbah regime was correspondingly weak. The newly reconstituted Sierra Leone Army was wholly dependent on British assistance for equipment and training. The Sierra Leone Police had been severely shaken during the most recent RUF offensive, known ominously as "Operation No Living Thing." Hundreds of police officers had been killed and dozens of police stations destroyed in the course of the January 1999 assault on Freetown in January 1999 that left over 6,000 dead.[2] The remnants of the Sierra Leone Police were able to do little more than conduct the most rudimentary police functions—and only in Freetown.

Security in much of the country rested in the hands of pro-government militia, the Civil Defense Force (CDF), and ECOMOG troops. While the CDF was able to field up to 35,000 fighters from various tribes, it was notoriously difficult to control. Like the RUF, it perpetrated atrocities against civilians and prisoners. It also engaged in illegal diamond mining activities.[3] The CDF's relations with ECOMOG, which fielded approximately 10,000 men, mostly Nigerian, had become increasingly antagonistic. ECOMOG troops, while experienced, had weak logistical support and frequently lacked transport. ECOMOG commanders also faced considerable politi-

---

[2] For a dramatic description of "Operation No Living Thing," see Greg Campbell, *Blood Diamonds: Tracing the Deadly Path of the World's Most Precious Stones,* Boulder, Colo.: Westview Press, 2002, pp. 86–89. For a description of the brutality of the RUF troops, see "Sierra Leone: Getting Away with Murder, Mutilation and Rape, New Testimony from Sierra Leone," *Human Rights Watch Report,* Vol. 11, No. 3(A), July 1999.

[3] Amnesty International, *1999 Annual Report on Sierra Leone*: "The CDF were responsible for extra judicial executions and torture and ill-treatment of captured combatants and real or suspected supporters of the AFRC and RUF." http://www.amnesty.org/ailib/aireport/ar99/afr51.htm (accessed November 20, 2004). For a description of the CDF's organization, see "Sierra Leone: Time for a New Military Strategy," International Crisis Group (ICG) Africa Report, No. 28, Freetown/London/Brussels, April 11, 2001, p. 8.

cal uncertainty because the newly elected President of Nigeria, Olusegun Obasanjo, had made a campaign pledge to pull Nigerian forces out of Sierra Leone.[4]

The security situation in Sierra Leone was further complicated by the civil war in neighboring Liberia, where the RUF enjoyed refuge and from which Liberian rebels occasionally mounted attacks into Sierra Leone.

The Lomé Agreement was favorable to the RUF. Sankoh, who had been on death row in Freetown, was given a full pardon and a cabinet position. Because RUF forces already controlled the diamond trade, the Lomé Agreement actually awarded Sankoh the chairmanship of the committee that supervised Sierra Leone's mineral resources.[5] The agreement stipulated that more than 30,000 RUF guerrillas and 60,000 soldiers from the pro-government CDF were to be disarmed, demobilized, or reintegrated into the Sierra Leone Army. Sankoh, a former corporal in the Sierra Leone Army, had transformed the RUF from a fringe group of young quasi-Marxist, pan-Africanists into a "kleptocratic effort cloaked in revolutionary rhetoric" strong enough to defeat both the Sierra Leone Army and the mostly Nigerian ECOMOG force.[6]

The power of the RUF rested on four bases. First was the weakness of the Sierra Leone government, in which the culture of corruption was deeply entrenched. One consequence of this corruption was that the civilian control over the Army of Sierra Leone was weak.[7] The RUF benefited from economic dissatisfaction in Sierra Leone. During the years of civil war, the economy failed to grow; poverty was endemic. The masses of poorly educated teenagers furnished the RUF with a rich recruiting base and responded to

---

[4] R. A. Adeshina, *The Reverse of Victory, The Story of Nigerian Military Intervention in Sierra Leone*, Ibadan, Nigeria: Heinemann Educational Books Plc, 2002, pp. 153–164.

[5] ICG (2001).

[6] Dena Montague, "The Business of War and the Prospects for Peace in Sierra Leone," *The Brown Journal of World Affairs*, Vol. IX, Issue 1, Spring 2002, p. 231. For a detailed discussion of the RUF's origins and early development, see Ibrahim Abdullah, "Bush Path to Destruction: The Origin and Character of the Revolutionary United Front/Sierra Leone," *The Journal of Modern African Studies*, Vol. 36, No. 2, June 1998, pp. 203–235.

[7] Sahr John Kpundeh, "Limiting Administrative Corruption in Sierra Leone," *The Journal of Modern African Studies*, Vol. 32, No. 1, March 1994, pp. 139–157.

Sankoh's effective appeals for economic justice.[8] He characterized the capital of Freetown as "the end of a pipe sucking out the wealth of this well-endowed country and sending it overseas, leaving millions living in Iron Age conditions."[9]

Second, early in the civil war, the RUF seized and managed to hold on to the richest diamond fields in Sierra Leone. Easy lines of communication with Liberia and cooperation from Burkina Faso provided the RUF with secure routes to export diamonds from these fields. Revenues from diamond exports were used to pay for arms and ammunition from the international arms market. Charles Taylor, the warlord who was elected president of Liberia in 1997, went through guerrilla training with Sankoh in Libya. Later, they fought together in Liberia. This strong personal connection helped ensure that the diamonds-for-arms trade between Liberia and Sierra Leone proceeded unimpeded. This trade generated between $350 million and $450 million per year in revenue.[10]

Third, the RUF troops effectively terrorized the civilian population. They raped, pillaged, murdered, and mutilated civilians, routinely cutting off limbs. In the face of this brutality, RUF control over the diamond fields went unchallenged. The RUF enslaved local inhabitants to work in the diamond fields, conscripted children, and looted villages for supplies.

Finally, Sankoh proved an able negotiator. He employed diplomacy to secure well-timed pauses in the conflict, which allowed the RUF to rebuild its forces and replenish supplies using revenues from diamond exports before resuming the war with renewed vigor. Sankoh had signed and broken the Abidjan Peace Agreement in 1996 and the Conakry Peace Agreement in 1997. This opportunistic pattern allowed the RUF to exploit the weaknesses of the Sierra Leone government.

---

[8] For a discussion of the relationship between political corruption and economic decline in Sierra Leone, see Earl Conteh-Morgan and Mac Dixon-Fyle, *Sierra Leone at the End of the Twentieth Century: History, Politics and Society*, New York: Peter Lang Publishing, 1999, pp. 112–117. Also see David Fashole Luke and Stephen P. Riley, "The Politics of Economic Decline in Sierra Leone," *The Journal of Modern African Studies*, Vol. 27, No. 1, March 1989, pp. 133–141.

[9] Mark Malan and Sarah Meek, "Extension of Government Authority and National Recovery," in Institute for Security Studies (2003), p. 126. For Sankoh's formal justification of the RUF insurrection, see "Footpaths to Democracy," http://www.sierra-leone.org/footpaths.html (accessed November 24, 2004).

[10] Hirsch (2001), p. 25.

Humanitarian

The RUF offensive into Freetown in 1999 halted nearly all nongovernmental organizations (NGO) humanitarian operations in the RUF-controlled areas, triggering widespread hunger and outbreaks of disease, especially cholera. What little agricultural production that had existed was stopped. When personnel employed by NGOs succeeded in obtaining permission from RUF commanders to return on an ad hoc basis, they reported whole communities trying to live off of wild mangoes, rats, maggots, and frogs.[11] Children were especially hard hit, with rates of serious malnutrition often as high as 25 percent. The RUF routinely abducted children to make them soldiers, sometimes "initiating" them by forcing them to kill their parents. Child soldiers were induced to fight with drugs and threats of violence. The brutal RUF attacks on civilians exacerbated the refugee crisis. Approximately 500,000 people were internally displaced; more than 150,000 sought refuge in Freetown alone.[12] More than 400,000 refugees fled across the border to Guinea; 100,000 fled to Liberia. Refugee camps, even those within the relative safety of Freetown, were crowded and living conditions miserable.

After the Lomé Agreement was signed, thousands of child soldiers were demobilized. Many suffered from severe psychological trauma. The thousands of victims of rape and sexual slaves in the RUF and Armed Forces Revolutionary Council (AFRC) presented an equally grim situation that promises to haunt the country for years to come. The AFRC was a group of disaffected Sierra Leone Army (SLA) soldiers led by Major Johnny Paul Koroma, who overthrew the government of President Kabbah in May 1997. The amputee victims of the RUF presented another extraordinarily distressing humanitarian challenge: In a largely agricultural society where manual labor is often the only means of economic survival, amputees face a particularly bleak economic future.

Civil Administration

The government of Sierra Leone under President Kabbah functioned poorly. After Koroma overthrew President Kabbah in 1997, an AFRC/RUF junta looted the treasury and government offices. The treasury was empty when Kabbah returned to power in 1998, and it stayed that way. The Kabbah administration remained mired in Sierra Leone's culture of corruption. It also remained completely dependent on Great Britain and Nigeria for military

---

[11] "About 20,000 risk starvation to death in Leone," Reuters News Service, July 7, 1999.

[12] "EU Pledges 5.2 Million US Dollars for Refugees," Pan African News Agency, April 25, 1999.

support, and on international NGOs and UN agencies for the provision of basic humanitarian services. Some ministers were more preoccupied with arranging personal contracts and drawing money from the international community than with reestablishing basic government services.[13] The police force could do little more than direct traffic and man checkpoints; criminal investigation and training of new recruits were beyond its capabilities. Primary and secondary education had virtually stopped following the AFRC/RUF coup. When Kabbah returned to power in March 1998, only a handful of schools reopened. The destruction of facilities and looting of educational materials, coupled with the flight of teachers and administrative staff, resulted in fewer than 10 percent of primary age children attending school when the Lomé Agreement was signed in 1999.[14]

Democratization
Sierra Leone had held a democratic election in 1996, following the ouster of Valentine Strasser, who had come to power in a coup in 1992. Kabbah won. Although the election was viewed as fair, the new government faced the challenge of creating the capacity and providing incentives for officials to govern honestly and competently. Three years later, the Kabbah administration and the governing party had achieved a widespread reputation for corruption. Relations between the government and its armed forces were strained.

Economic Reconstruction
Sierra Leone's physical infrastructure, never well developed, deteriorated during its post-colonial years. The RUF rebellion resulted in widespread destruction of the remaining capital stock. Many towns, especially in the east near Liberia, were looted and destroyed during the course of the war. Freetown was devastated in early 1999, especially the western part of the town, which the RUF/AFRC units temporarily controlled. Some 65 to 80 percent of the homes in that area were destroyed, leaving approximately 250,000 inhabitants of Freetown homeless.[15] RUF forces also destroyed police stations, medical facilities, schools, and other public facilities. Over 64 pub-

---

[13] Hirsch (1991), p. 76.

[14] David Pratt, "Sierra Leone: The Forgotten Crisis," Report to the Minister of Foreign Affairs, the Honourable Lloyd Axworthy, P.C., M.P. from David Pratt, M.P., Nepean Carleton, Special envoy to Sierra Leone, April 23, 1999, p. 33, http://www.sierra-leone.org/pratt042399.html (accessed November 24, 2004).

[15] Pratt (1999).

lic schools were closed as a result of the fighting and vandalism in January 1999, in addition to more than 300 schools that had been destroyed since the AFRC coup of 1997.[16]

UN AND OTHER INTERNATIONAL ROLES

In the wake of the Conakry Peace Agreement, the UN Security Council authorized the establishment of the UN Observer Mission in Sierra Leone (UNOMSIL) in July 1998 to assist ECOMOG in implementing the agreement. Seventy UN military observers, a small medical unit, and civilian support staff were sent to help monitor the disarmament and demobilization of RUF and CDF units.[17] UNOMSIL also had a mandate to monitor ECOMOG's adherence to international norms and advise the government of Sierra Leone on rebuilding its police force. Most of UNOMSIL's staff were evacuated to Guinea following the collapse of the Conakry Agreement, where they remained during "Operation No Living Thing." After the Lomé Agreement, the Security Council authorized the establishment of the United Nations Mission in Sierra Leone (UNAMSIL) on October 22, 1999. It was a much larger mission with a maximum of 15,255 military personnel, including 256 military observers. The UN Secretary-General appointed Oluyemi Adeniji as his Special Representative.

Several great powers, especially the United Kingdom and the United States, played important roles in the events in Sierra Leone. The generous peace terms offered to the RUF in the Lomé Agreement were due in part to pressure from the Clinton and Blair administrations on Kabbah.[18] The Reverend Jesse Jackson, President Clinton's special envoy to West Africa, helped broker the Lomé Agreement, maintained contacts with Charles Taylor, and sought to redirect Sankoh's ambitions into political channels. The United Kingdom had supported an arms embargo against the AFRC/RUF regime.[19] Foreign Secretary Robin Cook joined the Clinton administration in pressing Kabbah to sign the Lomé Peace Agreement. While initially content to let regional forces assume responsibility for security in Sierra Leone, Prime Minister Blair proved ultimately willing to intervene militarily. The United

---

[16] Pratt (1999), p. 32.

[17] United Nations Security Council Resolution 1132, October 8, 1997.

[18] *A Review of Peace Operations: A Case for Change*, London: Conflict Security & Development Group, King's College, 2003, p.66.

[19] Robin Harris, "Blair's 'Ethical' Policy," *The National Interest* No. 1, Spring 2001, p. 27.

States, for its part, provided training and logistical support for ECOMOG, including airlifting Indian and Jordanian contingents.[20]

A number of neighboring countries also had considerable influence. In the early 1990s, the RUF had received support from Libya, Liberia, and, to a lesser extent, Burkina Faso.[21] Sankoh and other early RUF leaders had received their initial guerrilla training in Libya. As noted earlier, Sankoh developed a friendship there with future Liberian President Charles Taylor, under whom Liberia furnished the RUF with crucial logistical support in exchange for diamonds. This trade was a key source of financial support for the RUF. Diamond dealers in Monrovia, Liberia, handled the bulk of the RUF's "blood diamonds," channeling them into the legitimate international diamond market. Government forces also relied on the diamond trade for financial support. The Civil Defense Force paid for arms and ammunition from the sales of diamonds to merchants in Guinea.[22] Thus, what Liberia did for the RUF, Guinea did for government forces.

Nigeria, the leading contributor to ECOMOG, had actively supported the government of Sierra Leone since 1994, when the two countries signed a mutual defense agreement. Nigeria and other West African contributors to ECOMOG deployed a peacekeeping force that sought to oversee the disarmament promised by the RUF in the Abidjan and Conakry peace agreements. When these earlier efforts broke down, ECOMOG forces had become active combatants in support of Sierra Leone government forces.

Military and Police

The United Nations Mission in Sierra Leone was authorized to provide for the security and freedom of movement of UN personnel, monitor the ceasefire, support the delivery of humanitarian assistance, and help safeguard future political elections.[23] Its specific objectives were the following:

- Help the government of Sierra Leone implement the disarmament, demobilization, and reintegration plan.

---

[20] Hirsch (1991), p. 102.

[21] For an example of Burkina Faso's logistical support for the RUF, see Campbell (2002), pp. 66–69.

[22] Campbell (2002), p. 126.

[23] United Nations Security Council Resolution 1270, October 22, 1999, p. 3.

- Monitor adherence to the cease-fire.

- Provide security at key locations, such as Freetown, and government buildings, important intersections, and major airports.

- Coordinate with and assist the Sierra Leone law enforcement authorities in the discharge of their responsibilities.

- Guard weapons, ammunition, and other military equipment collected from ex-combatants, and assist in the disposal or destruction of those weapons.

UNAMSIL's military component had an initial authorized strength of 6,000 military personnel, including 260 military observers. Twelve thousand ECOMOG troops also remained in the country and assisted the United Nations in its military tasks. In addition, the United Nations deployed up to 170 civilian police to help rebuild the Sierra Leone Police by analyzing the training and development needs of the police.[24]

Civil and Economic

The civil element consisted of 300 international staff divided into sections responsible for political affairs, civil governance, police, policy planning, child protection, human rights, public information, and disarmament, demobilization, and reintegration.[25] At the top was the Special Representative of the Secretary-General, Oluyemi Adeniji of Nigeria.[26] The Child Protection Section was unique, a response to the abuse suffered by the child soldiers at the hands of both the RUF and CDF.

WHAT HAPPENED

Initially, the United Nations proved no more successful in dealing with the RUF and supporting the government of Sierra Leone than

[24] United Nations Security Council Resolution 1436, S/RES/1436, September 24, 2002, pp. 2–3.

[25] UNAMSIL's civil section was originally outlined as an augmentation of UNOMSIL prior organization. See Seventh Report of the Secretary-General on the United Nations Observer Mission in Sierra Leone, S/1999/836, July 30, 1999, p. 9.

[26] Mark Malan, Phenyo Rakate, and Angela McIntyre, *Peacekeeping in Sierra Leone: UNAMSIL Hits the Home Straight*, ISS Monograph 68, Pretoria, South Africa, ISS, January 2002, Chapter 4.

ECOMOG had been. Only after the mission was on the verge of collapse did the intervention of British forces and the personal engagement of the UN Secretary-General manage to turn incipient failure into partial success.

Security

Initial contributors of troops to UNAMSIL included Kenya, Zambia, Nepal, Croatia, India, Bangladesh, and several members of ECOWAS: Ghana, Guinea, and Nigeria. Most of these units came poorly equipped. The original UN force commander, Major General Vijay Jetley of India, complained,

> Most units ... have very little or no equipment with them. They have not been properly briefed in their country about the application of Chapter VII in this mission for certain contingencies. It is for [these] precise reasons that the troops do not have the mental ascendancy and thereby emboldened them to take on the United Nations in the matter in which they have done in the present crisis. Guinea, Kenya and Zambia [are cases] in point.[27]

Problems of troop quality and lack of preparation were compounded by serious tensions that erupted between Jetley and his boss and principal subordinate. Both were Nigerians: Special Representative Oluyemi Adeniji and Deputy Force Commander Brigadier-General Mohamed Garba. As the United Nations' military position deteriorated, Jetley accused both of actively promoting Nigerian interests and collaborating with the RUF at the expense of the peace process. He further accused Brigadier-General Garba of colluding with the RUF for a share in diamond profits.

UNAMSIL had neither the capacity nor the mandate to react forcefully when RUF units refused to relinquish control of territory, including the diamond fields, and demobilize in accordance with the Lomé Agreement. The United Nations' work with and reliance on ECOMOG troops, with whom the RUF had decidedly mixed relations, made its task more difficult. In addition, Secretary-General Annan encountered difficulties securing adequate financial support for demobilizing and reintegrating RUF troops. Of the $25 million Annan identified as necessary for that process, he initially collected less than one-third. Sankoh took advantage of the bitterness of RUF units

---

[27] Vijay Kumar Jetley, "Report on the Crisis in Sierra Leone," http://www.sierra-leone.org/jetley0500.html (accessed November 23, 2004).

over the seemingly false promises concerning payments for demobilization and reintegration to stall giving control over the diamond fields to UNAMSIL.

By early 2000, UNAMSIL had succeeded in disarming more than 10,000 men. Most were AFRC troops who turned in relatively few weapons. By mid-April, more than 24,000 troops were demobilized, but these had turned in only 10,000 arms.[28] In the meantime, RUF units grew increasingly hostile, even as President Obasanjo accelerated the removal of Nigerian troops assigned to ECOMOG. May 2000 was set as their final departure date.[29] The Security Council responded on February 7, 2000, with Resolution 1289, which expanded UNAMSIL's authorized strength to 11,000 soldiers and extended its mandate to include the use of force to ensure freedom of movement and protection of civilians. Nevertheless, by May 2000, UNAMSIL troop strength was only 9,200.

As noted, UNAMSIL's command structure was badly divided. The Nigerian government protested Lt. General Jetley's accusation that his Nigerian deputy, Brigadier General Garba, had colluded with RUF forces for a share of the diamond profits. This led to Jetley's resignation and withdrawal of the sizable Indian contingent. Equally damaging was Jordan's simultaneous withdraw of 1,800 troops in protest over the refusal of any Western nations to send troops to serve in UNAMSIL.

In May 2000, UNAMSIL units from Kenya and Zambia moved into the RUF-controlled diamond districts around Makeni and Magburaka. More than 500 men from these units, including a large portion of the Kenyan headquarters staff, were captured by RUF forces and held hostage. RUF commanders were particularly emboldened by their seizure of 13 Zambian armored personnel carriers, which they used in a new attack on Freetown.

Neither UNAMSIL nor the government of Sierra Leone was in a position to defend effectively against this renewed RUF threat. Only decisive action by the United Kingdom prevented a humiliating collapse. The Blair government dispatched a task force of seven warships and an airborne battalion to evacuate British nationals and stabilize the situation. These British forces operated outside the UN command structure. They proved ready to confront the RUF and to use deadly force. Their immediate objectives were to

---

[28] Of those troops, 4,949 came from the RUF, 10,055 from the AFRC, and 9,038 from the CDL. Cited in Stuart Gordon and James Higgs, "Peace: At What Price?" *Jane's Defense Weekly*, September 27, 2000.

[29] *A Review of Peace Operations* (2003), p. 67.

safeguard British citizens and help rescue the 500 UNAMSIL hostages.[30] Most of the hostages were released by July 2000 after intense negotiations. Once this mission was accomplished, the bulk of British forces departed in July, leaving behind a contingent of 400 soldiers to help train and equip the Sierra Leone Army. In September 2000, British Special Forces rescued members of their Short-Term Training Team members, who had been held hostage since August by an ARFC unit called the "West Side Boys." The operation led to the collapse of the West Side Boys.

These successful hostage rescue operations, along with UNAMSIL's reinforcement by Russian and Indian attack helicopters, led the RUF to gradually release other hostages. The United Nations, for its part, managed to transform UNAMSIL into an effective peace-enforcement mission. Secretary-General Annan secured agreement from ECOMOG governments to contribute an additional 3,000 troops to UNAMSIL and a commitment from the U.S. government to help train and equip these new units.

Secretary-General Annan also successfully pressed for an international ban on trade in diamonds from Liberia. This measure helped reduce funds to pay for logistical support to the RUF.[31] Annan also continued his efforts to transform UNAMSIL into an effective force capable of offensive action. He organized a strategic planning conference in August 2000, where he met with the military chiefs of staff of the UNAMSIL contributing nations. He persuaded the Security Council to strengthen UNAMSIL's mandate "to deter and, when necessary, decisively counter the threat of RUF attack by responding robustly to any hostile action or threat of imminent and direct use of force."[32] Subsequent resolutions authorized UNAMSIL to increase its force up to 17,500 troops, which it achieved by March 2002, and to acquire more sophisticated equipment.[33] Additional troops arrived from Pakistan, Nepal, and Ukraine, as did new U.S. trained and equipped units from Nigeria and Ghana.

---

[30] The May 2000 collapse of the Lomé Peace Agreement also provoked numerous denunciations of ambitious UN peacekeeping missions. For an example, see Frederick H. Fleitz, Jr., *Peacekeeping Fiascos of the 1990s: Causes, Solutions, and U.S. Interests*, Westport, Conn.: Praeger, 2002. Also see William Dowell and Douglas Waller, "When the Peace Cannot Be Kept," *Time*, Vol. 155 No. 21, May 22, 2000, pp. 54–55.

[31] United Nations Security Council Resolution 1306, July 5, 2000.

[32] United Nations Security Council Resolution 1313, August 4, 2000, p. 1.

[33] United Nations Security Council Resolution 1346, March 30, 2001.

By late summer 2000, the RUF was confronting UN and UK peacekeeping forces who routinely responded with deadly force. Sankoh had been arrested and imprisoned by the Sierra Leone government soon after the hostage crisis erupted. This did not dissuade the RUF from attacking a camp of Sierra Leone refugees in Guinea, which provoked the Guinean Armed Forces into counterattacking with helicopter gunships and artillery. The Guinean forces, in conjunction with simultaneous CDF and SLA offensives, inflicted significant casualties on the RUF, leading it to capitulate in the Abuja II Peace Agreement of May 2001. From May 2001 to January 2002, UNAMSIL was able to disarm most of the remaining RUF and CDF forces in Sierra Leone. By the beginning of 2002, 47,000 combatants had been demobilized and 30,000 weapons destroyed.[34]

Approximately 120 UN unarmed civilian police advisers helped support the reconstitution of government authority throughout the country. Together with the Commonwealth Community Safety and Security Project, which furnished long-term support and training to local police, the UN civilian police helped open new regional police training schools in Kenema and Bo.[35] The UN civilian police worked with NGOs to promote human rights training and awareness. The Inspector General of the Sierra Leone Police commended the UN civilian police for their overall professional competence and dedication under arduous circumstances.[36]

Humanitarian
Before the arrival of UNOMSIL in 1998, humanitarian agencies and NGOs faced perpetual threats, assaults, and kidnappings. Relations between the NGO community and UNOMSIL became tense as a result of the January 1999 RUF/AFRC invasion of Freetown. Humanitarian organizations accused UNOMSIL of failing to share crucial intelligence on the impending invasion in an effort to downplay the strength of the RUF.[37] The Lomé Agreement and the arrival of UNAMSIL failed to open up RUF-controlled territory in the northern and eastern sections of the country to humanitarian relief. RUF resistance to humanitarian aid efforts caused great suffering for hundreds of thousands of Sierra Leone's citizens. Only with the arrival of British troops, the augmentation of UNAMSIL's combat strength, and the

[34] Thirteenth Report of the Secretary-General on the United Nations Mission in Sierra Leone, March 14, 2002, p. 3.

[35] *Ninth Report of the United Nations Mission in Sierra Leone* (March 14, 2001), p. 6.

[36] Malan, Rakate, and McIntyre (2002), Chapter 8.

[37] *A Review of Peace Operations* (2003), p. 80.

successful UK and UN hostage rescue operations did the situation change for the better. Starting with the Abuja I cease-fire agreement of November 2000, and continuing with the capitulation of the RUF in the Abuja II agreement of May 2002, humanitarian agencies became progressively better able to supply aid throughout the country. The appointment of the Secretary-General's Deputy Special Representative for Governance and Stabilization went far to coordinate these efforts and avoid much of the tension that had been associated with UNOMSIL.[38]

The cease-fire negotiated under Abuja II was largely respected. UNAMSIL forces were then able to furnish security and logistical support for the delivery of humanitarian aid, as well as for transporting refugees. All UNAMSIL contingents performed humanitarian work. For example, members of the Pakistani battalion in the contentious Kono District offered medical care, engaged in reconstruction projects, and even shared their rations with the local population when necessary. They also distributed 10,000 soccer balls to children and schools.[39] The Bangladeshi battalion engaged in similar humanitarian projects and also promoted various agricultural projects. Battalion members transported 2,288 internally displaced persons and 2,499 people requiring resettlement, treated 6,686 medical patients in May 2002 alone, and routinely shared their rations with the local population.[40] Units from every contributing nation provided humanitarian assistance.

Civil Administration

The destruction of public facilities, revenue and logistical shortcomings, lack of communication equipment, and shortages of qualified administrators severely constrained the Sierra Leone government's ability to expand its authority into previously held RUF territory. Before the Abuja II agreement, the 37 members of UNAMSIL's Civil Affairs Sector played a central role in facilitating communication between the government of Sierra Leone and the RUF. Thereafter, UNAMSIL facilitated the return of government officials. In addition to basic security and logistical support, the Civil Affairs Sector was instrumental in organizing meetings with government officials, RUF cadres, and important tribal chiefs to resolve a wide range of problems. These included administrative disputes over property rights,

---

[38] *A Review of Peace Operations* (2003), p. 85.

[39] Clifford Bernath and Ayre Nyce, "UNAMSIL—A Peacekeeping Success Lessons Learned: Report on the United Nations Mission in Sierra Leone," Washington, D.C.: Refugees International, 2002, p. 13.

[40] Mark Malan, "UNMASIL After the Elections," in ISS (2003), p. 64.

revenue collection, illicit mining, and regularizing the status of caretaker chiefs appointed by the RUF.[41] Subsequently, the Civil Affairs Sector worked with youth groups to resolve housing disputes, and aided important chiefs in assessing reconstruction priorities. The Civil Affairs Sector assisted in reestablishing branches of Freetown banks in the provinces, monitoring a trust fund project established by UNAMSIL to reintegrate ex-combatants and war victims into civil society, ascertaining the number of small arms remaining in the country, and reestablishing judiciary functions.[42]

Democratization

UNAMSIL furnished essential security and logistical services for the 2002 presidential election and worked to promote the transformation of the RUF into a legitimate political party. The United Nations Development Program established an Election Trust Fund that covered three-fourths of the costs of the election.[43] UNAMSIL closely monitored the election, in which there were a minimal number of voter irregularities. UNAMSIL sent both military and civilian UN personnel to inspect 4,700 out of the total 5,256 polling stations.[44] Radio UNAMSIL played a crucial role in promoting the registration drive, and provided the political parties with air time. UNAMSIL troops furnished transportation and security to distribute and collect the ballot boxes; UNAMSIL civilian police advisers and troops helped the 6,500-man Sierra Leone police force maintain order.

From an operational perspective, the election proved to be a great success. The result was an overwhelming victory for President Kabbah and his ruling SLPP party, which had over 70 percent of the vote. Unfortunately, this renewed democratic mandate only served to reinforce the generally corrupt administration's hold on power.

In response to the hostage crisis of May 2000, the Security Council passed Resolution 1315, which authorized the Secretary-General to work with the government of Sierra Leone to set up a special court for the investigation

---

[41] "Seventh Report of the Secretary-General on the United Nations Mission in Sierra Leone," S/2000/1055, October 31, 2000, p. 4.

[42] UNAMSIL Press Briefing, 21 February 2003.

[43] Twelfth Report of the United Nations Mission in Sierra Leone, S/2001/1195, December 13, 2001, p. 6.

[44] United Nations Department of Public Information, *UN Peace Operations Year in Review 2002*, "Sierra Leone," New York: United Nations, 2002, p. 1.

and prosecution of war crimes and crimes against humanity.[45] UN Secretary-General Annan became personally active in establishing the Truth and Reconciliation Commission and the Special Court for Sierra Leone.[46] The decision to set up a Special Court was taken in part in response to criticism leveled at the Lomé Agreement, which had given a blanket amnesty to war criminals. UNAMSIL provided much of the security, logistical, and technical support for this undertaking. After much planning, negotiation, fund-raising, and organization, the Special Court finally commenced operations. It had a budget of $71.5 million for three years. Although its tasks were eased somewhat when Sankoh died in prison in 2003, forestalling the need for an expensive and contentious trial, the Special Court still requested that Nigeria hand over Charles Taylor. He had been given asylum in Nigeria, but faced 17 counts of crimes against humanity for his role in Sierra Leone's civil war. The Special Court has also indicted Johnny Paul Koroma, the chief of the AFRC, who remained at large following an unsuccessful attack on the Armed Forces Wellington barracks armory on January 13, 2003, which he allegedly masterminded.[47] In an effort to be evenhanded, the Special Court indicted Sam Hinga Norman, the leader of the CDF, provoking considerable protest in the streets of Freetown.

Economic Reconstruction

UNAMSIL coordinated the efforts of bilateral donors, NGOs, and UN agencies to help reconstruct educational and health facilities and to put together a government administration for Sierra Leone. It conducted surveys of government facilities in territory previously held by the RUF to help the government rebuild the local administration. UN-sponsored reconstruction programs used the labor of demobilized RUF and AFRC troops, teaching them basic skills. UNAMSIL military engineering units helped reconstruct roads. Individual tactical units also took their own initiative to participate in local construction projects. Units repaired mosques and churches, rebuilt schools, and reconstructed hospitals and orphanages. Such efforts helped improve the security climate as they generated a substantial amount of goodwill among the local population.

[45] United Nations Security Council Resolution 1315, August 14, 2000, p. 2.

[46] For an in-depth analysis of the Special Court and Truth and Reconciliation Commission, see Mark Malan, "The Challenge of Justice and Reconciliation" in ISS (2003), pp. 142–154.

[47] Seventeenth Report of the Secretary-General on the United Nations Mission in Sierra Leone, S/2003/321, March 17, 2003, pp. 1–2.

UNAMSIL was less successful in assisting the Sierra Leone government to regain control of diamond exports. The government earned $17.34 million in diamond export revenues between October 2000 and May 2001, up from less than $1.5 million the year before.[48] However, it is estimated that Sierra Leone shipped between $200 million and $400 million in diamonds in 2002, in contrast to officially reported exports of $40 million. Many demobilized RUF and AFRC troops flocked to illegal diamond mining sites. UNAMSIL was unable to prevent these movements. The Kimberly Process Certification Scheme, which the Kabbah administration had set up to control underground diamond mining, lacked centralized control, and its audit process was inadequate.[49] International and local efforts have been under way to channel more of Sierra Leone's diamond exports through official channels.

The United Nations and other international organizations have supported the Peace Diamond Alliance. The alliance consists of organizations of miners, tribal chiefs, dealers and exporters, government officials, representatives of NGOs, and donors. With support from USAID and encouragement from UNAMSIL, the alliance pursued such practical tasks as offering training courses in diamond evaluation, providing credit to miners, and establishing more robust tracking mechanisms.[50] However, living conditions in Kono, the heart of the diamond district, remained grim, despite the efforts of UNAMSIL to improve the situation.

LESSONS LEARNED

UNAMSIL went through two distinct phases, the first marked by failure and the second by some success. The first phase illustrated how not to run a nation-building operation; the second demonstrated how even a badly compromised effort can be turned around. In the first phase, the UN operations exhibited weaknesses that almost led to the collapse of the operation. These included

---

[48] Malan, Rakate, and McIntyre (2002), Chapter 10.

[49] Osman Benk Sankoh, "In Diamonds We Trust," *Concord Times* (Freetown), March 23, 2004.

[50] For more information on the Peace Diamond Alliance, see Report of the Second General Meeting of the Peace Diamond Alliance, pp. 27–28, August 2003, Koidu Town, Sierra Leone, Prepared by Management Systems International Under USAID Cooperative Agreement No. 636-A-00-03-00038 (September 2003). Also see http://www.peacediamonds.org/home.asp (accessed November 24, 2004).

- willingness to proceed on best-case assumptions

- reliance on poorly trained, ill-equipped, and unprepared units

- dependence on a hastily assembled and personally incompatible management team

- lack of interest, focus, and support from the major powers.

The second phase of the operation demonstrated how much could be achieved rapidly when these deficiencies were remedied. The original UN-AMSIL mandate and force structure were premised on the assumption that the RUF would comply with the disarmament provisions of the Lomé Agreement. Since the RUF had complied with neither of its two previous undertakings, such an assumption was unjustified.

In the aftermath of the Somalia debacle, the United States and most West European governments had steered clear of engagement in African peace-keeping missions. They were also preoccupied with the war in Kosovo and the challenges of its postwar peace stabilization. Consequently, there was little prospect for a significant American or European engagement in Sierra Leone in mid-1999. However, a regional force under Nigerian command had already failed to stabilize the situation in Sierra Leone. There was no reason to believe that a largely regional force under UN command, no better manned or equipped than its ECOMOG predecessor, would do any better.

Divisions within the international command structure further weakened the United Nations' efficacy in Sierra Leone. Personalities undoubtedly played a role. Several factors contributed to the dysfunctional result: the existence of two separate international peacekeeping forces with similar mandates; the role of Nigeria, which was seeking to withdraw the bulk of its units even as its nationals occupied leadership positions in both forces; and the isolated position of the Indian force commander.

By mid-2000, Kosovo had been occupied and largely stabilized. The United Kingdom and, in a more limited way, the United States were able to shift attention and resources to Sierra Leone. In combination with the personal intervention of UN Secretary-General Annan, the modest application of military force from a major power, money, and influence turned the situation around rather quickly. With UK and U.S. backing, the United Nations adopted a more robust peace enforcement stance, disarmed the dissident forces, and organized democratic elections. However, by insisting that British forces remain separate from the UN command structure, the United Kingdom reinforced the unhappy precedent set by the United States in Mogadishu seven years earlier. The brevity of the British operational engagement in Sierra Leone helped limit the dangers resulting from allowing two separate international forces to operate in the same area of responsibility. In addition, the important positions held by British commanders in UNAMSIL helped to smooth coordination between the two forces.

Table 8.1
UN Operations in Sierra Leone—Key Facts

Population (1998): 4,895,337; Area: 27,698 square miles; Capital: Freetown

Operation	Mandate	Special Representative	Peak Military Size	Peak Police Size	Civilian Components
UNOMSIL (1998–1999)	Resolution 1181 Monitor the military and security situation Monitor disarmament and demobilization of former combatants	Francis G. Okelo (Uganda)	192 military observers, 15 other military personnel	No police component	Advise the government of Sierra Leone and local police officials on policing practices, training, re-equipment, and recruitment Report human rights violations
UNAMSIL (1999–Present)	Resolution 1270: Assist government in implementation of Peace Agreement and disarmament, demobilization, reintegration. Monitor adherence to the cease-fire Facilitate the delivery of humanitarian assistance Provide support to the elections Resolution 1346: Guard weapons collected from ex-combatants Provide security for government buildings, the airport, the free flow of goods, services, and people, and the disarmament program	Daudi Ngelautwa Mwakawago (Tanzania) Oluyemi Adeniji (Nigeria)	15,255 troops, 256 military observers Major Contributors: Bangladesh, Kenya, Nigeria, Pakistan	52 civilian police	Political affairs Civil governance Policy planning Child protection Human rights Public information Disarmament, demobilization, and reintegration

Chapter Nine

EAST TIMOR

The Portuguese colonized the island of Timor in the sixteenth century. Except for a brief period of Japanese rule during World War II, the eastern portion of the island remained a Portuguese colony until 1975, when, following the withdrawal of Portugal, Indonesia invaded and annexed East Timor.[1] Despite the passage of several United Nations Security Council resolutions during the Cold War demanding the withdrawal of Indonesian military forces, the major powers were not prepared to employ effective pressure to compel Indonesia's compliance.[2] The United States, for example, was unwilling to pressure Indonesia to withdraw because Indonesia was perceived as an anti-Communist bulwark in Southeast Asia. Recently declassified documents show that U.S. policymakers were concerned about East Timor's communist and pro-independence movement and worried that an independent Timor would lead to an increase in Chinese influence in the region.[3]

The end of the Cold War, the 1997 Asian economic crisis, and the fall of Indonesian President Suharto created conditions more favorable for a resolution of East Timor's status. In January 1999, newly installed President B.J. Habibie permitted a referendum to be conducted in East Timor on its future status. The original rationale for Indonesia's occupation—concern that the territory might become a haven for communist influence—was of

---

[1] On the history of East Timor, see John G. Taylor, *East Timor: The Price of Freedom*, New York: Zed Books, 1999; Paul Hainsworth and Stephen McCloskey, *The East Timor Question: The Struggle for Independence from Indonesia*, New York: I. B. Tauris, 2000.

[2] UN Security Council Resolution 384, S/RES/384, December 22, 1975; UN Security Council Resolution 389, S/RES/389, April 22, 1976.

[3] Memorandum to President Ford from Henry A. Kissinger, "Your Visit to Indonesia," c. November 21, 1975; "Indonesia and East Timor," State Department Briefing Paper, c. November 21, 1975. Both are in National Archives, Record Group 59, Department of State Records, Executive Secretariat Briefing Books, 1958–1976, Box 227, President Ford's Visit to the Far East.

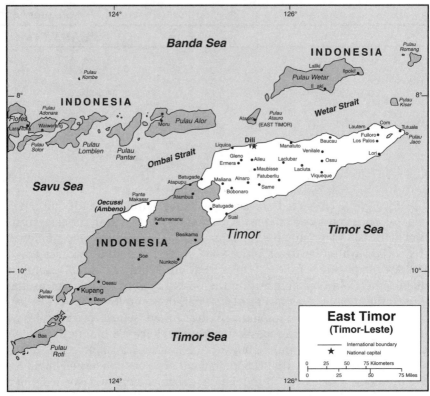

RAND *MG304-9.1*

Figure 9.1—Map of East Timor

less concern in the post–Cold War era.[4] After a series of negotiations among the United Nations, Indonesia, and Portugal, the UN Mission in East Timor (UNAMET) organized and conducted a referendum, which was held on August 30, 1999.[5] When UN Secretary-General Kofi Annan announced on September 4 that 78.5 percent of registered voters rejected the proposal that East Timor remain in Indonesia, fighting broke out. Rampaging mobs of militia backed by the Indonesian military killed over 1,000 people in what

---

[4] Tim Huxley, *Disintegrating Indonesia? Implications for Regional Security*, Adelphi Paper 349, London: International Institute for Strategic Studies, 2002, p. 34.

[5] Voters were asked the following questions: "Do you accept the proposed special autonomy for East Timor within the unitary state of the Republic of Indonesia? Or do you reject the proposed special autonomy for East Timor, leading to East Timor's separation from Indonesia?" On the referendum, see Ian Martin, *Self-Determination in East Timor: The United Nations, the Ballot, and International Intervention*, Boulder, Colo.: Lynne Rienner Publishers, Inc., 2001.

was referred to as "Operation Clean Sweep." The mobs caused considerable damage to East Timor's physical infrastructure.[6]

Under pressure from the United States, the International Monetary Fund, World Bank, and countries in the region such as Australia and New Zealand, the Indonesian government permitted the deployment of an Australian led multinational force, the International Force in East Timor (INTERFET), to quell the violence.[7] INTERFET quickly restored order to most of East Timor, encountering little resistance from pro-Jakarta militia and suffering no casualties. With order largely restored, the UN Security Council authorized the establishment of the United Nations Transitional Administration in East Timor (UNTAET) to provide an interim administration, oversee the process of reconstruction and prepare the territory for independence. UNTAET was followed by a successor mission, the United Nations Mission of Support in East Timor (UNMISET), which is still deployed to East Timor.

CHALLENGES

The United Nations was responsible for governing and preparing for independence the poorest society in Asia, which had no experience in democracy and in which 90 percent of the population had lately been driven from their homes, civil administration had collapsed, and the local infrastructure had been devastated.

Security

The United Nations faced three major security challenges. The first came from the Indonesian-backed militias. During "Operation Clean Sweep" in

---

[6] Australian intelligence and UN documents leaked to the press indicate that the Indonesian army was involved in the violence. Shawn Donnan, "Evidence Grows Over Jakarta Hand in Violence," *Financial Times*, November 25, 1999, p. 6; Desmond Ball, "Silent Witness: Australian Intelligence and East Timor," *Pacific Review*, Vol. 14, No. 1, 2001, pp. 35–62; Craig Skehan, Hamish McDonald, Lindsay Murdoch, and Mark Dodd, "Jakarta's Bloody Hands: Military Backs Violence," *Sydney Morning Herald*, September 6, 1999, p. 1; Report of the Security Council Mission to Jakarta and Dili, S/1999/976, September 14, 1999.

September 1999, locally organized militia and Indonesian armed forces had killed over 1,000 East Timorese and systematically ravaged the territory.[8] Militias harassed displaced persons near both the West Timorese border and Oecusse, an enclave of East Timor located in Indonesian West Timor. They also threatened INTERFET and subsequently UNTAET forces. IN-TERFET skirmished with militias several times near the border with West Timor. However, the pro-Indonesian militia lacked sufficient arms, command and control capabilities, and discipline to pose a significant insurgent threat. Some militia possessed modern semi-automatic assault rifles and hand grenades, but most carried decrepit bolt-action rifles, shotguns, pistols, homemade pipe guns, machetes, and knives.[9]

The military wing of the East Timorese resistance movement, Falintil, also presented a potential security concern. It had been engaged in armed resistance against the Indonesian military since the latter's arrival in the 1970s. UNTAET feared that the prospect of independence might embolden Falintil to respond to pro-Indonesian militia attacks in kind, triggering a spiral of violence. Falintil's leaders agreed to place their forces in four cantonments and to refrain from conducting military operations or carrying weapons outside these areas.[10] However, UNTAET remained concerned that increased attacks by the militias would lead Falintil commanders to break this commitment.[11]

Finally, little was left of the Indonesian police and justice system in East Timor. Indonesian military, police, and judicial personnel left the country en masse following the referendum; few East Timorese had worked in these institutions. When Indonesian civil administrators, judges, and lawyers fled, East Timor was without a justice system. The courts and legal buildings were heavily damaged. Because of the legacy of distorted justice left by the

---

[7] Nicholas J. Wheeler and Tim Dunne, "East Timor and the New Humanitarian Interventionism," *International Affairs*, Vol. 77, No. 4, 2001, pp. 805–827.

[8] Estimates of the number of East Timorese killed have ranged from 1,000 to 2,000. See, for example, Amnesty International, *Indonesia and Timor-Leste: International Responsibility for Justice*, New York, p. 1; Human Rights Watch, *Justice Denied for East Timor*, New York, 2002.

[9] Ian Bostock, "East Timor: An Operational Evaluation," *Jane's Defense Weekly*, Vol. 33, No. 18, May 3, 2000, pp. 23–27.

[10] Letter dated 15 October 1999 from the Secretary-General Addressed to the President of the Security Council, S/1999/1072, October 18, 1999.

[11] Michael G. Smith, *Peacekeeping in East Timor: The Path to Independence*, Boulder, Colo.: Lynne Rienner Publishers, Inc., 2003, pp. 48–49.

Indonesians, the public had no confidence in the judiciary.[12] Remaining police were poorly trained. They lacked community-based policing skills, did not know how to handle weapons or how to manage civil disturbances.[13] The militia had destroyed barracks, police stations, and equipment used by the military, police, and judiciary.[14] The United Nations had to fill the immediate security void while building a police force, military, and justice system from scratch.

Humanitarian

East Timor had been one of the poorest areas of Indonesia and, indeed, of Asia. According to the 1999 United Nations Development Program index, which uses a combination of indicators on life expectancy, levels of education, and standards of living, East Timor had the lowest ranking in Asia and was on par with Rwanda.[15] The violence that followed the September 1999 referendum displaced close to 90 percent of East Timor's total population of 967,000. Approximately 265,000 East Timorese became refugees, and 500,000 East Timorese escaped to the interior of the island. Roughly 265,000 refugees were transported under Indonesian and militia control to West Timor and neighboring islands in ships and trucks.[16] Most UN personnel were temporarily evacuated to Darwin, Australia, although the chief military liaison officer, Brigadier Rezaqul Haider, and a small staff remained in Dili.

Three-quarters of all clinics, hospitals, and doctors' offices in East Timor were damaged, senior medical staff evacuated the island, and most medicines and medical equipment were looted or destroyed. This resulted in a total breakdown of the health system. Only 48 percent of all households had

---

[12] Hansjorg Strohmeyer, "Collapse and Reconstruction of a Judicial System: The United Nations Missions in Kosovo and East Timor," *The American Journal of International Law*, Vol. 95, No. 46, 2001, pp. 50–51.

[13] U.S. Department of Justice, *East Timor Project Overview*, Washington, D.C.: International Criminal Investigative Training Assistance Program, U.S. Department of Justice, 2002.

[14] Letter dated 4 October 1999 from the Secretary-General Addressed to the President of the Security Council, S/1999/1025, October 4, 1999.

[15] United Nations Development Programme (UNDP), *The Way Ahead: East Timor Development Report, 2002*, Dili, East Timor, 2002, pp. 1–2.

[16] *A Review of Peace Operations: A Case for Change*, London: Conflict Security & Development Group, King's College, 2003, p. 228; U.S. Committee for Refugees (USCR), *World Refugee Survey Country Report 2002: East Timor*, Washington: U.S. Committee for Refugees, 2002; *Evaluation of UNHCR's Repatriation and Reintegration Programme in East Timor*, 1999–2003, EPAU/2004/02, New York: United Nations, February 2004, p. 12; Jarat Chopra, "The UN's Kingdom of East Timor," *Survival*, Vol. 42, No. 3, Autumn 2000, p. 27.

access to clean water and only 38 percent to sanitation during the Indonesian occupation. Both the water supply and sanitation systems were heavily damaged during the violence.[17]

Civil Administration

The exodus of Indonesian officials and the post-referendum violence brought about the near total collapse of the civil administration. Roughly 8,000 civil servants fled to Indonesia. This left East Timor with virtually no senior civil servants or senior policemen. Even before the violence, the Indonesian government had not served East Timor well. The adult population was 46 percent illiterate. East Timor had few secondary school teachers and almost no doctors.[18] As a report from the UN Secretary-General's permanent representative in East Timor concluded: "On deployment, INTERFET encountered an environment where civil infrastructure had been seriously degraded and where there was no effective civil administration. The scope of the problem that will be generated by those conditions will quickly outstrip the very limited capacity available."[19]

Democratization

East Timor had no meaningful history of democracy. In 1974, a year before the Portuguese left, the colonial governor of East Timor called for the creation of political parties to prepare for decolonization. Shortly thereafter, two political parties, the Timorese Democratic Union (UDT) and the Timorese Social Democratic Association (ASDT), were created. But the Indonesian government suppressed these parties after it annexed East Timor in 1975. Following annexation, the Indonesian military controlled political and administrative affairs. In the 1990s, the growing independence movement contributed to the emergence of East Timorese political organizations. In addition to the Catholic Church, which is the dominant element in East Timor's civil society, the East Timorese established a number of nongovernmental organizations, youth groups, newspapers, magazines, and radio stations. In 1998, the National Council of Timorese Resistance was

---

[17] Luis M. Valdivieso, *East Timor: Building Blocks for a Nation,* New York: United Nations, November 2000, pp. 10–11.

[18] Jonathan Steele, "Nation Building in East Timor," *World Policy Journal*, Vol. 19, No. 2, Summer 2002, p. 79; UNDP (2000), p. 33.

[19] Letter dated 4 October 1999 from the Secretary-General Addressed to the President of the Security Council, S/1999/1025, October 4, 1999.

formed to coordinate a common strategy for the resistance movement. It included representatives from the UDT, the ASDT successor organization (Fretilin), and most other pro-independence parties. The National Council of Timorese Resistance played a crucial role in the transition to independence and establishment of a democratic political system.

Economic Reconstruction

The Indonesian-backed militias destroyed the already impoverished East Timor economy and much of its infrastructure. Gross domestic product dropped 30 percent in 1999, inflation soared, and both the government's fiscal system and the financial system broke down.[20] The militias destroyed 70 percent of public infrastructure and private housing and razed the Oecusse enclave. Following the breakdown of the banking and payments systems, all transactions in East Timor were conducted in cash. The government ceased collecting tax revenue and the provision of public services stopped. During the violence, telecommunications transmission towers, switchboards, and telephone cables were heavily damaged and about half of all livestock, goats, cattle, and pigs were slaughtered.[21] As one account summarized it:

> The militias wrecked East Timor in a very distinctive way. The country was burned, not bombed. From the street, whether in Dili or the smaller provincial towns, concrete slabs of foundations are still visible, as are the side and often the front and back walls of buildings—but no windows, doors, or roofs. The houses are hollow, scorched clean of paint, wiring, or fixtures of any kind. In some neighborhoods, the dwellings are intact; in others, every house has been gutted.[22]

---

[20] "Birth of a Nation: East Timor Gains Independence, Faces Challenges of Economic Management, Poverty Alleviation," *IMF Survey*, Vol. 31, No. 11, June 10, 2002, p. 179.

[21] *A Review of Peace Operations* (2003), p. 228; Smith (2003), p. 44; Participatory Potential Assessment (PPA): East Timor (Dili, East Timor: UNDP, ADB, ETTA/ETPA, World Bank, 2002), p. 1; Luis M. Valdivieso, Toshihide Endo, Luis V. Mendonca, Shamsuddin Tareq, and Alejandro López-Mejía, *East Timor: Establishing the Foundations of Sound Macroeconomic Management,* Washington, D.C.: International Monetary Fund, 2000.

[22] James Traub, "Inventing East Timor," *Foreign Affairs*, Vol. 79, No. 4, July/August 2000, p. 80.

Even before the violence, economic conditions in East Timor were bleak. East Timor was one of the poorest provinces in Indonesia, with an annual per capita income that ranged from $304 to $424 between 1995 and 1999. Its economy was largely agricultural, with approximately 90 percent of the population based in rural areas and 75 percent engaged in agriculture—primarily on a subsistence level.[23] Under Indonesian rule, tax revenues raised in East Timor were collected by the Indonesian central government and taken to Jakarta. Government expenditures were financed by the central government and determined by the central planning agency, also in Jakarta. Budgets were based on national, not local priorities. During the violence, Indonesian civil servants and managers fled and the civil administration collapsed. Indonesian managers failed to return after independence. East Timor lacked a coterie of indigenous managers.[24] During the first few years of reconstruction, East Timor's economy would be highly dependent not only on external financing but also on foreign managers and administrators.

THE UN AND INTERNATIONAL ROLES

UNTAET took over responsibility for East Timor from the Australian-led multinational force, INTERFET, in February 1999. Much of its staff was originally housed in the Veksa, a floating 133-room hotel moored a few hundred yards from the old Portuguese Governor's House. UNTAET had dual responsibilities. On the one hand, it had the leading role in rebuilding East Timor during the transition to independence. On the other hand, it actually *was* the government through May 20, 2002, when East Timor gained its independence. One member of UNTAET referred to its status as "comparable with that of a pre-constitutional monarch in a sovereign kingdom."[25] Its successor mission, UNMISET, which took over in May 2002, had a much less obtrusive mandate of providing assistance to core administrative structures and helping develop the police and other security institutions.

---

[23] Valdivieso (2000).

[24] Valdivieso et al. (2000); Luis M. Valdivieso and Alejandro López-Mejía, "East Timor: Macroeconomic Management on the Road to Independence," *Finance and Development*, Vol. 38, No. 1, March 2001; Valdivieso (2000).

[25] Chopra (2000) p. 29. As *Time* magazine argued: "The UN is legally the holder of East Timor's sovereignty, the first time in its history the world body has played such a role." Terry McCarthy, "Rising From the Ashes," *Time*, March 20, 2000, p. 14.

A number of governments played decisive roles in support of the UN operation. Australia took the lead role in deploying INTERFET forces under the command of Australia's Major General Peter Cosgrove. It then provided the core element of the UNTAET force headquarters, much of the aviation and logistics support, and roughly 5,000 troops. The United States provided substantial logistical, communications, and intelligence support; U.S. strategic lift was used to transport many of the forces deployed to East Timor. The USS *Bellevue Wood,* with a contingent of Marines from the 31st Marine Expeditionary Unit, was stationed just offshore in case additional support became necessary.[26] U.S. support was critical to convince the Indonesian army not to contest East Timor's independence or lend further support to militias operating in the area. By accepting the August 1999 ballot outcome, Indonesia removed the major political obstacle to East Timor's independence. The Indonesian government withdrew its military forces from East Timor. It also curbed its support of the militias, although they continued to exist in West Timor.

Military and Police

In September 1999, the Indonesian government accepted a UN-authorized International Force in East Timor to quell the violence.[27] Acting under Chapter VII of the UN Charter, this force was led by Australia and was authorized to restore peace and order, protect and support UN activities, and facilitate humanitarian assistance operations throughout East Timor.[28] INTERFET included nearly 12,000 troops composed primarily of combined-arms, light infantry brigades with naval and air supporting elements, and Special Forces. It possessed virtually no heavy equipment, such as main battle tanks or armored fighting vehicles, which would have been difficult to use on the mountain roads.[29]

---

[26] Alan Ryan, "The Strong Lead-Nation Model in an Ad Hoc Coalition of the Willing: Operation Stabilise in East Timor," *International Peacekeeping,* Volume 9, Number 1, Spring 2002, pp. 23–44.

[27] Nicholas J. Wheeler and Tim Dunne, "East Timor and the New Humanitarian Interventionism," *International Affairs,* Vol. 77, No. 4, 2001, pp. 805–827.

[28] United Nations Security Council Resolution 1264, S/RES/1264, September 15, 1999.

[29] On INTERFET see Alan Ryan, *Primary Responsibilities and Primary Risks: Australian Defence Force Participation in the International Force East Timor,* Duntroon, Australia: Land Warfare Studies Centre, 2000; Ryan, "The Strong Lead-Nation Model in an Ad Hoc Coalition of the Willing: Operation Stabilise in East Timor," *International Peacekeeping,* Vol. 9, No. 1, Spring 2002, pp. 23–44; Joan Blaxland, *Information-Era Maneuver: The Australian-Led Mission to East Timor,* Duntroon, Australia: Land Warfare Studies Centre, June 2002.

UNTAET took over responsibility for security in East Timor from INTER-FET in February 2000, deploying both military and armed police forces. Its mandate included the following:

- Provide security and maintain law and order throughout East Timor

- Disarm, demobilize, and reintegrate ex-combatants

- Assist in the construction of an East Timor Defense Force

- Help in the development of the East Timor Police Service.

The military force included roughly 8,000 troops and 200 military observers organized into four geographical sectors: East, Central, West, and Oecusse. Over 30 countries contributed forces, of which nearly two-thirds came from six countries in the region: Australia, New Zealand, Pakistan, Philippines, Thailand, and Bangladesh.[30] The civilian police component consisted of 1,250 individual officers and two rapid reaction units with 120 officers each.[31] Following disturbances involving gangs of youth in April 2000, all police were required to carry sidearms. The police were placed within the governance element of UNTAET, and the police commissioner reported to the deputy administrator. Approximately 40 countries contributed police officers.

Civil and Economic

All legislative and executive powers were concentrated in the hands of Sergio Vieira de Mello, the transitional administrator. UNTAET had the authority to do everything from sign treaties to stamp passports at the Dili airport. It was treated as a de facto government by countries and international organizations, with the power to negotiate projects, disburse funds, and make reporting arrangements. UN Security Council Resolution 1272 gave UNTAET a broad mandate to

- create an effective administration

- help develop civil and social services

---

[30] Smith (2003), pp. 68–74, 173–178.

[31] *A Review of Peace Operations* (2003), p. 235.

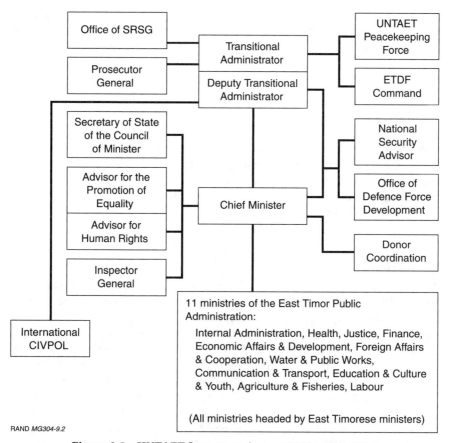

Figure 9.2—UNTAET Structure: August 2001 to May 2002

- facilitate the coordination and delivery of humanitarian, rehabilitation, and development assistance

- support capacity-building for self-government

- assist in the establishment of conditions for sustainable development.[32]

UNHCR and the International Organization for Migration assisted in the return of refugees and internally displaced persons. The International Committee of the Red Cross, the UN Office for the Coordination of Humanitar-

---

[32] United Nations Security Council Resolution 1272, S/RES/1272, October 25, 1999.

ian Affairs, and the Commission for Reception, Truth, and Reconciliation in East Timor assisted UNTAET in providing humanitarian relief. The World Bank, IMF, and Asian Development Bank played prominent roles in economic reconstruction.

WHAT HAPPENED

Thanks to a favorable international climate, comparatively abundant resources, and high-quality leadership, the United Nations was able to maintain security, restore governance, begin reconstruction, hold democratic elections, and turn power over to the representative government of an independent East Timor.

Security

The Australian-led multinational force INTERFET went ashore on September 20, 1999. It encountered little resistance from the pro-Jakarta militias and was able to quickly restore order to most of East Timor, suffering no casualties. By the end of the month, INTERFET had set up an operational force headquarters in Dili's charred public library. INTERFET deployed in three stages: first to Dili, then to regional centers, and finally throughout East Timor. In its early phase of deployment, INTERFET's combat power came primarily from Australia's 3rd Brigade and Special Air Services Regiment. The eastern districts were quickly freed of militia activity, but the western districts took somewhat longer. Militia groups harassed displaced people near the West Timorese border and Oecusse, the East Timor enclave located in Indonesian West Timor. On October 16, 1999, for example, an INTERFET patrol was ambushed by nearly two dozen armed militiamen near the town of Bobonaro. The INTERFET patrol sustained no casualties, but three militiamen were killed and three more were wounded.[33]

Military command shifted from INTERFET to UNTAET in February 2000. Initially relying on UN military and civil police for security, UNTAET sought to disarm, demobilize, and reintegrate the militias and Falintil fighters and to build an East Timorese army and police force.

---

[33] Letter dated 15 October 1999 from the Secretary-General Addressed to the President of the Security Council, S/1999/1072, October 18, 1999; Letter dated 29 October 1999 from the Secretary-General Addressed to the President of the Security Council, S/1999/1106, October 29, 1999.

The disarmament, demobilization, and reintegration program encountered numerous hurdles.[34] The UN peacekeeping force attempted to implement a search-and-seize campaign to disarm militia and checked returning refugees for weapons at border crossings. These efforts were undermined by the Indonesian government's refusal to disarm militias based in West Timor. Consequently, the militias were never disarmed.[35] In January 2001, the Falintil High Command and UNTAET agreed on a disarmament plan for Falintil fighters. However, many never gave up their weapons. Those weapons that were surrendered were made available to the East Timor Defense Force. The Falintil Reinsertion Assistance Program, funded by USAID, the World Bank, and Japan, assisted in the reintegration of Falintil fighters.[36] A number of dissatisfied ex-Falintil members nevertheless turned to robbery, extortion, and other crimes.[37]

UNTAET military forces focused their efforts on preventing militias in West Timor from infiltrating into East Timor, primarily by patrolling the border in cooperation with the Indonesian army. They also assisted UN civilian police by providing internal security when necessary. Although UNTAET was not as large, mobile, or militarily robust as INTERFET had been, it was large in proportion to the population and had little difficulty maintaining a secure environment. Its most difficult task was rooting out militia activity in the West and Central sectors. Vieira de Mello's decision to adopt a proactive policy targeting militia groups helped stabilize the security situation.[38] In January 2000, the UN Secretary-General concluded: "For most people, there is now no threat of violence and they can circulate freely."[39]

The next step was the UN construction of the East Timor Defense Force.[40] Although the United Nations had often supported the development of new

---

[34] Report of the Secretary-General on the Situation in East Timor, S/1999/1024.

[35] Centre for Defence Studies, *Independent Study on Security Force Options and Security Sector Reform for East Timor*, London: King's College, August 8, 2000, pp. 231-233.

[36] The Falintil Reinsertion Assistance Program was implemented by the International Organization for Migration. See, for example, Cara Chester, Eben Forbes, Tasha Gill, Heather Kelly, Heather Kulp, Jeff Merritt, Sharon Otterman, *Bridging the Gap: An Assessment of IOM's Community Assistance Programs in East Timor*, New York: Columbia University School of International and Public Affairs, 2000.

[37] Elsina Wainwright, *New Neighbour, New Challenge: Australia and the Security of East Timor*, Barton, Australia: Australian Strategic Policy Institute, 2002, pp. 12-13.

[38] Interview with former UNTAET officials, April 29, 2004.

[39] Report of the Secretary-General on the United Nations Transitional Administration in East Timor, S/2000/53, January 26, 2000, p. 1.

[40] *A Review of Peace Operations* (2003), pp. 233-235; Smith (2003), pp. 79-82.

or reformed police forces, this was its first foray into building a military. The purpose of the East Timor Defense Force was to defend East Timor against militia incursions, deter foreign aggressors, and provide assistance during natural disasters and other emergencies. Australia and Portugal took the lead in funding and training the force. Donor conferences were held in November 2000 and June 2001 to seek international assistance.

Officially established in January 2001, the East Timor Defense Force consisted of two light infantry battalions, comprising 1,500 regular soldiers and 1,500 volunteer reservists. A small navy of fifty sailors and two patrol craft was added later. There were some initial problems, such as UNTAET's failure to publicly articulate the criteria for including some Falintil fighters in the force but not others. However, the construction of the East Timor Defense Force proceeded relatively smoothly.[41] Nevertheless, in 2002, Secretary-General Annan concluded that the East Timor military forces were still not capable of handling growing militia threats on their own: "The military component lacks the necessary capacity and mobility to respond effectively or take a sufficiently proactive role to address the threats, and has inadequate ability to obtain and process information."[42]

UNTAET experienced more difficulties with its civil police component than its military. Recruitment of international police officers proceeded slowly. Officers were of uneven quality. Language barriers were a major problem. Virtually none of the international police spoke the local language.[43] The slow pace at which the justice sector was rebuilt led to delays in prosecuting pretrial detainees.

Beginning in December 1999, UN civilian police developed a curriculum for basic police training and compiled and reviewed names of potential police officers. The UN civil police tested and selected candidates for training at the newly rehabilitated Police College in Dili. The United Nations recruited some officers who had served in the Indonesian police force. After completing a three-month basic training course, East Timorese officers were given an additional six months of field training alongside international police counterparts. By the time of East Timor's independence in 2002, over 1,700

---

[41] *A Review of Peace Operations* (2003), pp. 234–235.

[42] Special Report of the Secretary-General on the United Nations Mission of Support in East Timor, S/2003/243, March 2, 2003, p. 4.

[43] Interview with Peter Galbraith, Director for Political, Constitutional, and Electoral Affairs for UNTAET, January 9, 2004; United Nations Security Council Resolution 1272, S/RES/1272, October 25, 1999; *A Review of Peace Operations* (2003), pp. 235–237.

officers had gone through the Police College and field training.[44] Although UN efforts to establish a viable East Timor police force were largely successful, the force suffered from a lack of funds. As UN Secretary-General Kofi Annan noted, the paucity of funds led to significant shortages of police communications and transport equipment and made it difficult to meet recurring costs for the maintenance of vehicles, weapons, and other equipment.[45]

UNTAET developed a fairly close relationship with the Indonesian government over several issues: the withdrawal of Indonesian forces from East Timor, Indonesia's support of the militias, and refugee returns. UNTAET and the Indonesian government also established a Joint Border Committee to improve coordination on such sensitive issues as border security, cross-border trade, movement of returnees, demarcation of borders, and police cooperation.[46]

Following independence, the UN Security Council authorized the creation of the United Nations Mission of Support in East Timor as a follow-on peace-keeping mission. It provided interim law enforcement and helped build the East Timor Police Service.[47] The United Nations retained executive control of the police, but had transferred command of all 13 districts to the East Timor Police Service by the end of 2003. The mission was authorized to deploy 1,250 civilian police, 5,000 military troops, and 120 military observers. The United States contributed over 40 police officers to help rebuild the police force.

Riots erupted in Dili in December 2002 and several armed attacks occurred throughout East Timor in 2003 that the police were unable to control without UNMISET assistance. There was also growing evidence that former militia and other armed groups had established bases within the country following the departure of UNTAET.[48] Inadequate training, the absence of a legal and procedural framework, and lack of judicial oversight hampered the East Timor Police Service's development. So did the lack of clarity regarding the security structure, as illustrated by the January 2004 confron-

---

[44] *A Review of Peace Operations* (2003), pp. 237–240.

[45] Report of the Secretary-General on the United Nations Transitional Administration in East Timor, S/2002/80, January 17, 2002, p. 4.

[46] *A Review of Peace Operations* (2003), p. 230; Smith (2003), pp. 60–62.

[47] UN Security Council Resolution 1410, S/Res/1410, May 17, 2002.

[48] Report of Secretary-General on the United Nations Mission of Support in East Timor, S/2003/449, April 21, 2003; Special Report of the Secretary-General on the United Nations Mission of Support in East Timor, S/2003/243, March 3, 2003.

tation between East Timor's armed forces and police in Los Palos.[49] In May 2004, the UN Security Council extended UNMISET for at least one more year through May 2005.[50]

Humanitarian

UNTAET established a Humanitarian Assistance and Emergency Rehabilitation component, with support from UNHCR and the International Organization for Migration.[51] The humanitarian operation was effective, despite some setbacks. Militia members killed three UNHCR staff in September 2000. Emergency humanitarian relief proved initially difficult due to inclement weather, faulty communications, misdirected airdrops, and insufficient quantities of essential commodities. Nevertheless, UNTAET was able to avert a potentially severe humanitarian crisis. Rice and non-food assistance were distributed to returning refugees and other at-risk individuals. All hospitals in East Timor were reopened and mobile health clinics were established shortly after UNTAET received its mandate. Piped and well-water systems and sanitation systems were repaired, so most of East Timor now has adequate, affordable, water supplies and sanitation services.[52]

The vast majority of internally displaced persons came out of hiding in 2000. Initially, most of them had nowhere to go. The widespread destruction of homes and buildings following the September 1999 violence forced many East Timorese to live in either makeshift housing or with family and friends. UNTAET was able to encourage refugees to return to East Timor by steadily improving security and economic conditions, offering transportation and other assistance from UNHCR, and granting repatriation bonuses. Nearly 150,000 refugees were repatriated from West Timor in the last quarter of

[49] Report of Secretary-General on the United Nations Mission of Support in East Timor, S/2004/333, April 29, 2004.

[50] United Nations Security Council Resolution 1543, S/RES/1543, May 14, 2004.

[51] Armando Duque González, Francesco Mezzalama, and Khalil Issa Othman, *Evaluation of United Nations System Response in East Timor: Coordination and Effectiveness*, JIU/REP/2002/10, Geneva: United Nations Joint Inspection Unit, 2002.

[52] World Bank, *Report of the Joint Assessment Mission to East Timor, Annex 1*, Washington: World Bank, 1999b; Asian Development Bank, *Sixth Progress Report on Timor-Leste*, Dili: Asian Development Bank, 2003, pp. 39–47.

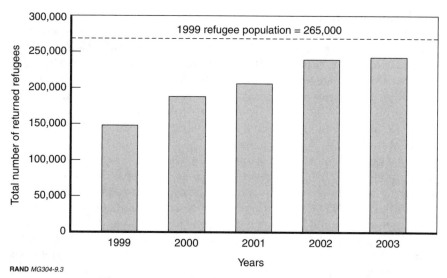

RAND *MG304-9.3*

Figure 9.3—Total Refugee Returns, 1999–2003

1999, 40,000 in 2000, 18,000 in 2001, 32,000 in 2002, and a few thousand in 2003 (Figure 9.3). An estimated 25,000 refugees remained in West Timor in 2004.[53]

Staff from UNTAET, the UN peacekeeping force, UNHCR, and the International Organization for Migration met the returnees at the East Timor border. These organizations ensured that the refugees were indeed civilians, verified that they were returning voluntarily, and provided transportation to their villages of origin. They offered each returning civilian family up to $165. Returning members of the military or civil service received a payment of between $550 and $1,650, depending on their length of service.[54] Most of these programs were discontinued at the end of 2002. UNMISET, UNHCR, and the International Organization for Migration continued to address the problem of refugees in West Timor camps in 2003 and 2004. These refugees decided to remain in Indonesian West Timor, despite attempts by NGOs to encourage them to return. Finally, there are still numerous unresolved cases to reunify families whose children were separated in 1999.

---

[53] USCR (2003, 2002, 2001); González, Mezzalama, and Othman (2002), p. 20; Author's estimates.

[54] USCR (2003).

Civil Administration

UNTAET had to fill the administrative vacuum resulting from the departure of 8,000 civil servants to Indonesia in 1999, the termination of all civil administration activities, and the destruction of 70 percent of public infrastructure and private housing.[55] The UN Security Council gave UNTAET extraordinary executive and legislative powers to deal with this situation.

UNTAET initially filled most civil administration positions with UN international staff. Not all were competent.[56] UNTAET formed the National Consultative Council, in which most political parties were represented, as was the Catholic Church and various special interest groups. The National Consultative Council was a strictly advisory body with no legislative or executive authority. UNTAET staff frequently presented regulations on complex matters to the council but gave it little time for study—and then warned of dire consequences if the council failed to express its support.[57] A somewhat more representative and influential National Council later replaced the National Consultative Council.[58] UNTAET also had little flexibility on how it could spend its assessed budget, including for such basic costs as paying East Timor teachers.[59]

UNTAET initially envisioned building capacity from the bottom up, ceding senior positions to local control only in the latter phases. Responding to growing local pressure, however, UNTAET began to accelerate the hand-off of civil administration to the East Timorese. This process of "Timorization" proceeded in three phases. The first step was made in August 2000, when UNTAET established the East Timor Transitional Administration, which was to become the nucleus of the new government. The Transitional Administration consisted of a cabinet with nine de facto ministries. Five were headed by East Timorese and four by international staff.[60] East Timorese complaints that UNTAET was a neocolonial administration began to decline. The second step took place in September 2001, when UNTAET created the East Timor

---

[55] United Nations Development Programme (2002), pp. 32–39.

[56] Interview with former UNTAET officials, April 29, 2004.

[57] Interview with Peter Galbraith; Joel C. Beauvais, "Benevolent Despotism: A Critique of UN State-Building in East Timor," *New York University Journal of International Law and Politics*, Vol. 33, 2001, pp. 1101–1178.

[58] *A Review of Peace Operations* (2003), pp. 247–257.

[59] Interview with former UNTAET officials, April 29, 2004.

[60] East Timorese were assigned five cabinet posts: Infrastructure, Economy, Social Affairs, Internal Administration, and Foreign Affairs. International staff were assigned the remaining four posts: Police and Emergency Services, Justice, Finance, and Political Affairs. See, for example, Smith (2003), pp. 64–66; Beauvais (2001), pp. 1127–1130.

Public Administration following the election of a Constituent Assembly. Still under the control of Vieira de Mello, the East Timor Public Administration consisted of ten ministries and four secretariats, all headed by East Timorese. A cabinet was selected through consultation with Vieira de Mello and the newly elected Constituent Assembly. By the end of UNTAET's tenure in 2002, it had recruited nearly 11,000 East Timorese civil servants. The education and health sectors were the largest employers, representing almost two-thirds of civil service staffing. Appointments were primarily at lower levels; less than half of all management positions remained unfilled because of a paucity of qualified candidates.[61] The third step came on May 2002, when East Timor gained independence and UNTAET was dissolved.

Reflecting on the pace of Timorization, Vieira de Mello later noted, "While consultation and partnership were established early on, it became clear by April of this year that it was not sufficient. . . . Faced as we were with our own difficulties in the establishment of this mission, we did not, we could not involve the Timorese at large as much as they were entitled to."[62]

The lack of experienced East Timorese had a particularly negative effect on justice sector reform.[63] UNTAET found that only about 70 East Timorese who had graduated from law school were actually living in East Timor. None had been practicing law when East Timor was under Indonesian control.[64] Severe shortages of prosecutors, investigative police, bailiffs, and judges resulted in delays in the administration of justice. So did the absence of courtrooms, holding facilities, and prisons. The accused were subject to prolonged pre-trial detentions; convicts were consigned to overcrowded prisons.[65] Vieira de Mello vested exclusive judicial authority in East Timor's courts and considered their judicial decision making to be entirely outside his sphere of power.[66] In light of the severe shortages of qualified indigenous personnel,

---

[61] Report of the Secretary-General on the United Nations Transitional Administration in East Timor, S/2002/80, January 17, 2002; Report of the Secretary-General on the United Nations Transitional Administration in East Timor, S/2002/432, April 17, 2002.

[62] Sergio Vieira de Mello, Address at the First CNRT Congress, Dili, August 21, 2000.

[63] Report of the Secretary-General on the United Nations Transitional Administration in East Timor, S/2002/432, April 17, 2002, pp. 3-4. Also see Smith (2003), pp. 82-83.

[64] Traub (2000), p. 83; Beauvais (2001), p. 1154.

[65] Report of the Secretary-General on the United Nations Mission of Support in East Timor, S/2003/449, April 21, 2003, p. 5.

[66] Jonathan Morrow and Rachel White, "The United Nations in Transitional East Timor: International Standards and the Reality of Governance," *The Australian Year Book of International Law*, Vol. 22, Canberra, Australia: Centre for International and Public Law, Australian National University, 2002, p. 18.

this trust was ill placed. In hindsight, UNTAET might have retained control of this sector and drawn in foreign judges for the transitional period, just as it used foreign police to support the embryonic East Timorese police force.

UNTAET initially declared that Indonesian laws were to remain applicable and began a review of existing legislation to determine which were inconsistent with international human rights standards or the objectives of UNTAET's mission. Several Indonesian laws, such as the Law on Anti-Subversion and the Law on Social Organizations, were immediately abrogated, as was capital punishment.[67] The Office of the Principal Legal Adviser drafted new legislation, including regulations for a provisional tax and customs regime, licensing of banks and currency exchange, appropriations, environmental protection, judicial institutions, and establishment of a defense force. UNTAET regulations and laws were published in the *Official Gazette* and were endorsed by East Timorese transitional structures such as the National Consultative Council and its successor, the National Council.

More than 1,000 people died in the violence in East Timor. This total is significantly smaller than in Rwanda or Bosnia, but East Timor is a smaller country.[68] UNTAET established the Special Panels for Serious Crimes, located in the Dili District Court, to deal with cases arising from the 1999 post-referendum violence. These panels had jurisdiction over genocide, war crimes, crimes against humanity, and other serious offenses committed in East Timor between January 1 and October 25, 1999. The initial Special Panel included judges from Italy, Burundi, and Brazil, along with provisionally appointed East Timorese judges. The Special Panel's efforts have been hamstrung by the Indonesian government's unwillingness to cooperate. Most of those indicted—including members of the Indonesian military forces and Jakarta-backed militia leaders—remain at large. In 2004, the Special Panels issued an arrest warrant for Indonesian General Wiranto, former commander of the Indonesian Armed Forces and Minister of Defense and Security. According to Indonesian Foreign Minister Hassan Wirajuda, the Special Panels are "not at all an international tribunal. Yes, they are assisted by the UN mission in East Timor, but they don't have international jurisdiction and, for that matter, legally they don't have the capacity to reach non–East Timorese."[69] As a result of Indonesian noncooperation, few of those responsible for atrocities in 1999 have been prosecuted.

---

[67] Regulation No. 1999/1 on the Authority of the Transitional Administration in East Timor, UNTAET/REG/1991/1, November 27, 1999, Section 3.

[68] See, for example, Samantha Power, "A Problem From Hell" in Power (2002).

[69] "East Timor: UN Indicts General Wiranto for Crimes Against Humanity," ABC Radio, February 25, 2003.

Indonesia set up its own forum to deal with these abuses. The Ad Hoc Human Rights Court on East Timor was established by the Indonesian government in August 2001. A preliminary national commission of inquiry had found that gross human rights violations were committed in East Timor between January and October 1999, concluded that they were planned and conducted systematically, and that the Indonesian military, police, and civil administration appeared to have close ties with the militia groups who committed the violence.[70] In January 2002 President Megawati Sukarnoputri appointed 18 non-career judges to sit on this court, and 24 prosecutors were appointed a month later. While the Ad Hoc Court has convicted some individuals of crimes against humanity, it has been widely criticized by human rights groups as unfair, politically biased, and unwilling to prosecute senior Indonesian civil and military officials.[71]

UNMISET continued to provide support to East Timor's civil administration after the country's independence. UN civilian advisers have tried to improve East Timor's ability to run an efficient government by developing standard operating procedures and manuals, training Timorese counterparts, and assisting with other crucial tasks where necessary. This has been particularly urgent in those areas that are critical to short-term stability, such as the ministries of Finance, Interior, and Defense. Grave problems also exist within the administration of justice; most courts outside Dili are still inoperative.[72]

Democratization

East Timor's democratic institutions were constituted in three steps: the election of a Constituent Assembly; the elaboration of a constitution; and the holding of presidential elections. The World Bank's Community Empowerment Program, in which democratically elected village councils were established to make decisions concerning local development projects, contributed to the germination of a democratic culture.[73]

---

[70] Amnesty International (2003), pp. 3–4.

[71] Human Rights Watch (2002); ICG, *Indonesia: Implications of the Timor Trials*, Jakarta and Brussels: International Crisis Group, 2002; Amnesty International (2003).

[72] S/2004/333.

[73] World Bank, *Trust Fund for East Timor*, Update No. 2 (Dili: World Bank, September 6, 2000), pp. 1–2; Richard Caplan, *A New Trusteeship? The International Administration of War-Torn Territories*, Adelphi Paper 341, London: International Institute for Strategic Studies, 2002, p. 42.

In August 2001, elections were held for the 88-member Constituent Assembly. Over 90 percent of eligible voters participated. Fretilin won 57 per cent of the vote and 55 representatives, giving it a majority and the dominant role in shaping the new constitution. The Democrat Party took second place with seven seats. The Assembly established a committee to make recommendations on the constitution and to oversee its drafting. In March 2002, after six months of intensive discussions, input from the United Nations and NGOs, and public consultations held in the 13 districts, the Constituent Assembly approved a constitution providing for a unitary democratic state. It was based on the rule of law and the principle of separation of powers among four "organs of sovereignty": the presidency, national parliament, the government (including the prime minister and other ministers), and the courts.[74] The president and parliament were to be elected through universal direct suffrage.

Approval of a constitution prepared the way for presidential elections. Two candidates, Francisco Xavier do Amaral and Kay Rala Xanana Gusmão, competed during a four-week campaign period leading up to the elections on April 14, 2002. Gusmão received 82.3 percent and Xavier do Amaral 17.3 percent of the vote.[75] After gaining independence and holding elections, East Timor now faces the difficult task of building viable democratic institutions from scratch. There is a burgeoning civil society: a number of nongovernmental organizations now provide social services and promote human rights. Most are dependent on foreign aid. The constitution provides for freedom of speech and the press, and the East Timor government has generally respected these rights. However, government officials have attempted to interfere with the press on several occasions.[76]

Economic Reconstruction

In September 1999, the United Nations agreed to send a Joint Assessment Mission under World Bank leadership to assess East Timor's reconstruction needs. The Bank was a logical choice because it had created a Post-Conflict and Reconstruction Unit and a separate Post-Conflict Fund two years earlier, and it had identified East Timor as a potential target. The Joint Assessment Mission prioritized critical short-term

[74] Constitution of the Democratic Republic of East Timor, Section 67.

[75] Report of the Secretary-General on the United Nations Transitional Administration in East Timor, S/2002/432/Add.1, April 24, 2002.

[76] U.S. Department of State, *2003 Human Rights Reports,* Washington, D.C.: United States Department of State, 2004.

reconstruction initiatives and provided estimates of external financing requirements.[77] It incorporated international technical expertise from an amalgam of donor countries, UN agencies, the European Commission, the Asian Development Bank, and the World Bank. In the economic sector, it identified several urgent priorities:

- Restart commerce: the sale and production of goods and services.

- Create a payments system.

- Agree on a currency and create currency conversion facilities.

- Reestablish branch units of Indonesian banks.

- Develop a budget.

- Establish key economic institutions such as a department of finance and planning, procurement and audit agencies, revenue agency, and statistical agency.

One of the next steps was to raise funds. The December 1999 Tokyo Donors' Meeting led to $366 million in reconstruction pledges and $157 million in humanitarian aid pledges. This amount was surpassed during the implementation phase—at least $518 million was disbursed by June 2002.[78] Donors' meetings were then held every six months to discuss implementation of the core program for reconstruction and restitution of government services. Efforts to raise tax revenues were largely successful. These included a 5 percent import duty, an assortment of excise taxes, a 5 percent sales tax on commercial imports, a 10 percent tax on services, and royalties from—as well as taxes on—the production of oil and gas.[79] The negotiation with Australia on the "Timor Gap"—a coffin-shaped area in the Timor Sea between Darwin and the Timor Trench with proven oil fields—provided East Timor with a future source of revenue on which to make budgetary plans and against which to borrow.

Reconstruction aid was channeled through several modalities: (1) the assessed contribution budget of UNTAET, (2) a UN-administered

[77] World Bank, *Report of the Joint Assessment Mission to East Timor,* Washington, D.C.: World Bank, 1999b.

[78] Klaas Rohland and Sarah Cliffe, *The East Timor Reconstruction Program: Successes, Problems and Tradeoffs,* CPR Working Paper No. 2, Washington, D.C.: World Bank, 2002, pp. 6–9.

[79] Valdivieso and López-Mejía (2001).

Consolidated Fund for East Timor, (3) a Trust Fund for East Timor, (4) projects financed by several UN agencies, and (5) bilateral development assistance, most of which was channeled through NGOs and contractors.[80] The division of funds was somewhat complicated. The Consolidated Fund for East Timor, which was administered by UNTAET, mobilized funds for the recurrent expenses of government, rehabilitation of administrative buildings, civil service capacity-building, and rebuilding of the justice sector. The Trust Fund for East Timor, which provided grants for economic reconstruction and development in East Timor, was supervised by the World Bank and Asian Development Bank. Activities included employment schemes in the capital city of Dili, loans and training for East Timorese small enterprises, and emergency repairs on roads and ports.[81] Bilateral projects and those implemented by other UN agencies covered all sectors.

Unfortunately, coordination among the various aid vehicles was poor. Planning and implementation procedures varied greatly across the agencies. The separation of recurrent cost financing (provided through the Consolidated Fund for East Timor) and reconstruction financing (provided from the Trust Fund) posed the most difficult problem. This arrangement made it difficult to incorporate funding from multiple sources into East Timor's budget because the funds could only be used for specific purposes. These arrangements also made it challenging to synchronize reconstruction efforts. East Timorese civil servants needed to be recruited to manage the various projects, but project funds could not be used to pay their salaries, creating the difficult problem of finding funding for steps that needed to be taken before major reconstruction projects could begin. As a World Bank assessment concluded:

> East Timor also demonstrates the inappropriate complexity of aid financing for post-conflict countries with low capacity.... These differing and complex modes of aid provision created barriers to national ownership of the reconstruction planning process in the initial period, and prevented the integration of all funding sources into the national budget.[82]

---

[80] Salvatore Schiavo-Campo, *Financing and Aid Management Arrangements in Post-Conflict Situations*, Washington, D.C.: World Bank, 2003, pp. 22–23; Rohland and Cliffe (2002), pp. ii–iii.

[81] Asian Development Bank, *Trust Fund for East Timor*, Lisbon, Portugal: Asian Development Bank, 2000; World Bank, World Bank-Administered Trust Fund for East Timor: Fact Sheet, Washington, D.C.: World Bank, April 11, 2000.

[82] Rohland and Cliffe (2002), p. ii. Also see Schiavo-Campo (2003), pp. 22–23.

The International Monetary Fund played a critical role in helping UNTAET stabilize the economy. The IMF advised the East Timorese government to adopt the U.S. dollar as the only legal tender.[83] It also helped the East Timorese set up the Central Payments Office. The Office clears payments and transfers funds. It also performs many of the functions of a central bank: It acts as a repository for foreign governments and banks, ensures an adequate supply of bank notes and coins, and issues licenses to banks and dealers.[84] The IMF also helped the East Timorese create a fiscal framework. It helped design and set up a tax system and budgeted expenditures. A Central Fiscal Authority, which later became East Timor's Ministry of Finance, was set up to formulate tax policy, collect tax revenues, and plan and implement the budget. East Timor also received technical assistance from the IMF and other financial institutions to design a macroeconomic policy framework and establish and run the Central Fiscal Authority and Central Payments Office.[85]

Economic activity in East Timor recovered quickly from the September 1999 destruction. GDP has returned to precrisis levels. The large inflows of foreign aid, expenditures by international staff located in East Timor, and a revival in agricultural production drove the recovery. The new monetary and fiscal framework and appropriate policies resulted in a fall in inflation from 140 percent at the end of 1999 to 7 percent in early 2003. The monetary authority is functioning, and three foreign-owned commercial banks and one micro-credit institution are operating. Despite this progress, problems remain. The financial system is still rudimentary. Lending is restricted and few financial instruments are available.[86] Growth moderated sharply after independence, partly because of the drawdown of UN and other staff involved in the reconstruction effort and the expenditures that they made in the local economy. Investment is partially restricted because property rights are ill-defined. The World Bank failed to set up a titling and property registration system, leading to confusion about laws, regulations, and property in urban areas.

---

[83] The East Timorese leadership wanted to introduce a national currency, but the IMF strongly urged that this step not be taken until a financial market became functional and well-developed institutional and legal frameworks were in place.

[84] Regulation No. 2000/6 on the Establishment of a Central Payments Office of East Timor, UNTAET/REG/2000/6, January 22, 2000.

[85] Valdivieso and López-Mejía (2001); "Birth of a Nation," pp. 177–181; José Ramos Horta and Emilia Pires, "How Will the Macroeconomy Be Managed in an Independent East Timor? An East Timorese View," *Finance & Development*, Vol. 38, No. 1, March 2001.

[86] IMF, Public Information Notice, No. 03/90, July 28, 2003; *Democratic Republic of Timor Leste: Selected Issues and Statistical Appendix*, No. 03/228, Washington, D.C.: International Monetary Fund, July 2003.

LESSONS LEARNED

The UN mission in East Timor was similar to the earlier effort in Eastern Slavonia in several respects. First, the United Nations had plenary powers to secure and govern both territories. Second, the territories were comparatively small. Third, the resources provided were comparatively large. On a per capita basis, these two operations are the best resourced of any UN- or U.S.-led nation-building effort to date. Fourth, both efforts had strong international backing, which in turn helped ensure a favorable regional environment. Because of these factors, operations were correspondingly successful.

Coming at the end of a decade of UN nation-building, the East Timor operation was able to build on a number of earlier models:

- The employment of a two-stage process for establishing control: a UN mandated nationally commanded multinational force to establish initial security and a UN peacekeeping force to maintain it

- The establishment of an interim administration employing international personnel under UN authority

- The deployment of international police armed with weapons and arrest authority

- The early implementation of plans for disarmament, demobilization, and reintegration and the establishment of new security institutions

- The establishment of cooperative arrangements with neighboring states, in this case Indonesia.

Nevertheless, there were also familiar shortcomings in the United Nations' performance:

- Failure to prepare for the outbreak of violence following the August 30, 1999 referendum

- Slowness in recruiting civil administrators and police, and the variable quality of those deployed

- Reluctance to cede authority, once acquired, to local actors

- Inability to effectively coordinate assistance from bilateral and international financial institution donors.

The absence of a UN plan or capability to deal with the violence precipitated by the May 1999 referendum, which the United Nations organized, is characteristic of the UN tendency to proceed on the basis of best-case assumptions. The United Nations assumed that Indonesia would peacefully accept and effectively implement any outcome, including independence. Unfortunately, although the UN Secretariat may be proactive in making contingency plans, it is usually more difficult to persuade the Security Council to make contingent decisions.

In East Timor, Australia effectively played the same military role that the United States had played in Somalia and Haiti. As the United States had done in Haiti in 1995, the Australians then proceeded to provide the core of the UN peacekeeping force and its commander. Coincident with its unexpected responsibility for governing East Timor, the United Nations was handed the equally unanticipated task of administering Kosovo. The United Nations' earlier role in Eastern Slavonia was its only recent preparation for these responsibilities. Not surprisingly, the Secretariat had some difficulty meeting the personnel requirements of these two substantial and unanticipated charges, including the need to recruit 5,000 civil police for Kosovo and 1,250 for East Timor. The demand for international civil administrators and police may not always reach such a high level. But the consistency of the need, and the usually late and often indifferent quality of the delivered product, suggest the need for improvements in the United Nations' capacity to generate these resources.

Nation-building operations almost invariably require the phase-out of old security structures and the creation of new ones. Nation-building modules have accordingly emerged for this task, including programs for police training and the disarmament, demobilization, and reintegration of former combatants. There is growing understanding, however, that police are not enough. In most instances the entire security sector needs to be reformed, including the judiciary, the corrections system, and the military. East Timor was the first instance in which the United Nations had to assume responsibility for the latter. And despite bitter experience going back at least to Somalia, the United Nations was slow to fill the judicial vacuum. Experience in East Timor, as in Kosovo, suggests the need to mobilize international judges alongside international police in many nation-building missions, particularly those under some sort of interim international administration.

The complaint voiced most often about UNTAET was its slowness in devolving administrative power to local officials. In fact, Vieira de Mello seems to have altered course on this matter comparatively quickly once local objections had been registered.

In most developing countries, the recipient government is supposed to be responsible for coordinating donor assistance. Failed states and wards of the international system are obviously unable to perform this function. Thus far, the international community has not worked out a satisfactory alternative. Bilateral donors are reluctant to accept from a UN representative the kind of direction they would accept as normal from a recipient government. International financial institutions, such as the World Bank and the regional development banks, often have the most money to offer. But they are generally unwilling to let the United Nations coordinate it because they regard the UN as a less expert competitor. The United Nations' standing to perform this role assisting or substituting for nonexistent or incompetent recipient governments could usefully be strengthened by including language to this effect in the relevant Security Council resolutions establishing nation-building missions.

Table 9.1
UN Operations in East Timor—Key Facts

Population (1999): 967,000; Area: 5,794 square miles; Capital: Dili

Operation	Mandate	Special Representative	Peak Military Size	Peak Police Size	Civilian Components
UNAMET (1999)	Resolution 1246: Organize and conduct a referendum on East Timor's status	Ian Martin (UK)	50 military liaisons	280 civilian police	Electoral component Information component
UNTAET (1999–2002)	Resolution 1272: Provide security and order Establish an effective civil administration Assist in the development of civil and social services Ensure coordination and delivery of humanitarian assistance, rehabilitation, development assistance Support capacity-building for self-government	Sergio Vieira de Mello (Brazil)	8,000 troops and personnel Major Contributors: Australia, New Zealand, Pakistan, Philippines, Thailand	1,500 civilian police	Political component Governance and public administration component Humanitarian assistance and emergency rehabilitation component Electoral component Human rights component Gender component Political component Donor coordination component

Table 9.1—Continued

Operation	Mandate	Special Representative	Peak Military Size	Peak Police Size	Civilian Components
UNMISET (2002–Present)	Resolution 1410: Provide assistance to core administrative structures Provide interim law enforcement and public security and assist in the development of a new law enforcement agency in East Timor Contribute to the maintenance of the external and internal security of East Timor	Kamalesh Sharma (India) Sukehiro Hasegawa (Japan)	5,000 troops and personnel Major Contributors: Australia, New Zealand, Pakistan, Bangladesh	1,250 civilian police	Civilian component to oversee gender and HIV/AIDS issues Serious Crimes Unit Human Rights Unit

Chapter Ten

IRAQ

The United States argued on several grounds for an invasion of Iraq designed to topple the regime of Saddam Hussein. Principal among these were Iraqi development and possession of weapons of mass destruction. Iraq's failure to comply with multiple UN Security Council resolutions, its links with terrorist organizations and its gross abuses of the human rights of its own citizens were others.

The United States and the United Kingdom sought, but ultimately failed, to secure a mandate from the United Nations Security Council for the intervention. The two countries proceeded nonetheless. U.S. and UK troops, assisted by smaller contingents from several other countries, invaded Iraq on March 21, 2003, took Baghdad on April 9, and suppressed the last organized, open resistance on April 15.

American officials expected most Iraqis to welcome their liberators. They believed that Iraqi police and military forces would remain available to provide for public security and that the Iraqi administration would continue to provide basic public services during the post-conflict transition period while a new Iraqi government was being formed. The American objective was to establish Iraq as a peaceful democratic state, a source of stability, and a model of political reform for its region.

CHALLENGES

The post–World War I British-installed Hashemite monarchy had failed to forge a united Iraqi nation before its eventual overthrow in 1958. Thereafter a succession of military rulers, leading eventually to Saddam Hussein's Baathist regime, gave Iraq 45 years of ever-worsening dictatorship. The effects of Baathist mismanagement were compounded by a trade embargo

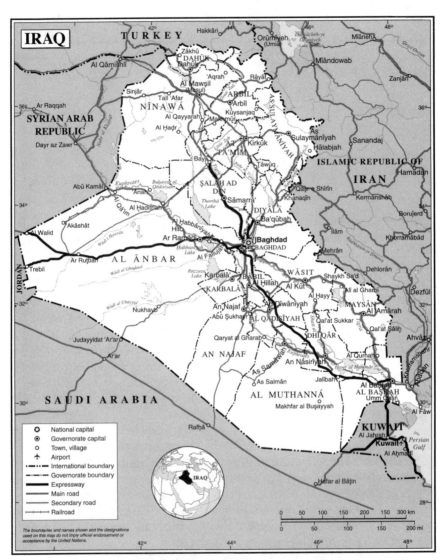

SOURCE: United Nations Cartographic Section, Iraq, no. 3835 Rev. 4, January 2004.
Available online at http://www.un.org/Depts/Cartographic/english/htmain.htm.

RAND MG304-10.1

Figure 10.1—Map of Iraq

the United Nations imposed on Iraq after its invasion of Kuwait in 1990. By 2003, two major wars, more than a decade of economic sanctions, and several waves of massive internal violence had reduced Iraq's population to penury and destroyed most societal institutions.

The U.S.-led coalition's rapid military victory demonstrated the fragility of Saddam Hussein's regime. The Iraqi army was unable to put up an effective conventional defense against coalition forces: Most Iraqi soldiers showed little loyalty to the regime. Because of the collapse of resistance and the effectiveness of coalition operations, the conventional war ended quickly. Prewar concerns that combat would precipitate a humanitarian disaster proved unwarranted. The population was well supplied with food; most Iraqis continued to have access to potable water, although the water systems functioned poorly, in part because of the disruption in electric power. Clinics and hospitals remained open at the conclusion of the conventional battle, although some subsequently suffered extensive damage from looting, especially in Baghdad.[1] However, the United States was confronted with a wholesale collapse of government. The U.S.-led coalition was compelled to take over all government functions while simultaneously seeking to transform the Iraqi polity into a democracy and create a market economy. Shortly after U.S. President George W. Bush announced the end of major combat operations on May 1, 2003, a growing insurgent and terrorist campaign, spearheaded by members of the former regime, began to pose an increasing security threat to the U.S.-led coalition and Iraqis alike.

Security

During the course of the campaign, Iraqi military units were quickly destroyed or dispersed. In many instances, individual soldiers took their weapons and went home. In other cases, regular units whose equipment and bases had been pulverized by coalition airpower and artillery gave themselves up and then disbanded. Although "elite" military units such as the Republican Guard and Special Republican Guard sometimes fought hard, they were quickly destroyed; once this occurred, soldiers blended back into the population.[2] Irregular groups that supported the former regime, such as the Saddam *fedayeen*, emerged as serious irritants. They operated out of towns and cities from which they attacked coalition lines of communica-

---

[1] Katie Razzall, "Looting Rife," Channel Four News-United Kingdom, April 11, 2003, http://www.channel4.com/news/2003/04/week_2/11_war.html.

[2] Williamson Murray and Major General Robert H. Scales, Jr., *The Iraq War: A Military History*, Cambridge, Mass.: The Belknap Press of Harvard University Press, 2003.

tion. Although poorly trained, equipped, and led, these irregulars proved to be precursors for the organization of more extensive insurgent networks that former regime elements mobilized to fight the occupation. Those forces, which became increasingly better organized over the course of the summer and into the fall, were often led by men from Saddam's many internal security and intelligence agencies and from the Baath Party who had gone underground. Although immediately after the conflict some of these individuals had been tracked down and killed by opposition party militias or vigilantes, others fell back on networks of supporters, taking with them cash, weapons, and documents that they used to set up underground networks.

All of Iraq's security organs melted away in the dying days of the regime. Conscripts assigned to the border security forces packed up and went home. The regular police, who had always been treated as a second-class organization by the security services and were reviled by Iraqis for being corrupt and brutal, largely deserted their posts. Security guards responsible for protecting industrial facilities or government buildings either abandoned their posts or refused to perform their duties when looters began to attack.

Some ethnic groups and nascent opposition groups had created militias before the collapse of the Saddam regime. Once the regime was toppled, these groups rapidly expanded. They ranged from the well-organized, disciplined *peshmerga* guerrillas created by the Kurdish parties under the protection of American airpower in the north of the country to ragtag private armies of the smaller, exile opposition groups such as the Iraqi National Congress (INC). The Supreme Council for the Islamic Revolution in Iraq (SCIRI) controlled a large Iranian-trained paramilitary force, the *Badr* Brigade. Underground movements, such as *al-Daawa,* had fighters and agents operating in cells across the country. These various militias moved quickly during and after the war to stake out territory.

The most immediate security challenge in the aftermath of the fall of Baghdad was the complete breakdown of order on the streets. Iraqis engaged in widespread looting of stores, warehouses, and public facilities, from ministries to hospitals. These looters caused more damage to Iraqi infrastructure than had the campaign. Armed gangs instituted a reign of terror: robbing, kidnapping, raping, and murdering. Much of the looting was the result of spontaneous anger against the former regime and the desire to make good on years of deprivation. Some of it was more organized. Criminal gangs, many composed of convicts released by Saddam shortly before the war and the smugglers and racketeers who had flourished in symbiosis with the former regime, carried out a number of the more-directed attacks. Regime loyalists and foreign intelligence agencies were undoubtedly behind some of the destruction of government records and buildings. This extensive destruction did much to set reconstruction back, especially the resumption of water and electricity service.

Humanitarian

The humanitarian problems caused by the conflict were much less severe than expected. The Office for Reconstruction and Humanitarian Assistance (ORHA), which had been set up to handle the civil administration of the country, had expected that upward of 2 million people would flee their homes, in addition to the 800,000 internally displaced people and 740,000 refugees, primarily in Turkey and Iran, who were estimated to be dispersed before the war.[3] ORHA also feared widespread hunger. Roughly three-fifths of the population was dependent on food rations provided through the Oil for Food (OFF) program. ORHA assumed that there would be a six-week interval between the time of the invasion and when food could once again be distributed across the country. The swiftness of the coalition military victory quickly relieved these fears. ORHA also was also concerned about the effects of chemical and biological weapons attacks on the civilian population and the provision of potable water.

Civil Administration

Before the war, civil administration in Iraq was split between the three Kurdish-controlled provinces (Arbil, Dohuk, and Sulaimaniyah) and the remainder of the country. Above the "Green Line," the Kurdistan Democratic Party (KDP) and the Patriotic Union of Kurdistan (PUK) had consolidated control over what was effectively a quasi-autonomous Kurdish state with its own, semi-democratic governing institutions. After the cessation of internecine warfare between the KDP and PUK in the mid-1990s, elections were held. The Kurdish governments that emerged (there were two, one for the region controlled by the KDP and one for the region controlled by the PUK) successfully provided such services as education, health, policing, and border control. To pay for these services, the governments levied taxes. Even in the Kurdish governorates, which were by far the most democratic area in Iraq, clan leaders dictated government decisions from behind the

---

[3] Robert Woodward, *Plan of Attack,* New York: Simon and Schuster, 2004, p. 276.

scenes. The decades of autonomy made reintegrating the Kurdish region into the Iraqi state a major challenge for the occupation authorities.

In the remainder of Iraq, civil administration was nominally provided by ministries that reported to the prime minister, who in turn was appointed by Saddam. These ministries executed the typical functions of a developing Middle Eastern state, from providing education, health care, and transportation services to the management of the oil and agricultural sectors. Saddam's regime was highly centralized; it discouraged civil servants from taking the initiative. A number of capable civil servants emigrated in the 1980s and 1990s because of the oppression of the Baath Party and the sharp declines in incomes caused by government mismanagement and the UN sanctions. The loss of skilled administrators and technicians and the decline in morale resulted in a reduced ability of the government to deliver basic services, from potable water to child health care.

The administrative structure of the Iraqi government displayed many of the worst characteristics of central planning combined with a "divide and rule" approach to government. The finance and planning ministries exercised minute control over the plans and spending of individual ministries. Coordination between departments was discouraged; all decisionmaking powers were pushed upward, ultimately to the president himself. The Baath Party, the secret police agencies, and the clan networks surrounding Saddam Hussein were the real sources of power. They came to control virtually all areas of government activity. Informal networks of influence were much more important than formal administrative procedures.

At the local level, administration was provided by provincial governors and city managers, who were tightly controlled by the Ministry of Interior. They worked with local representatives of the central ministries to implement plans devised in Baghdad. Although local notables, especially tribal leaders in rural areas, were involved in advisory councils, their role was more to assist in the maintenance of order than to provide societal input into decisionmaking. Civil administrative structures at the local level were supplemented by the Baath Party, which maintained order, gathered information, and spread propaganda at the block and street level in the cities.

Because ministerial, gubernatorial, and senior official appointments had been gifts of the Baath Party and, more narrowly, Saddam Hussein's clan, most holders of these posts either left their positions, were removed by coalition forces or, in some instances, were deposed by local citizens in the immediate aftermath of the war. The parallel Baath Party structures were also swept away. In a highly centralized, hierarchical system, the removal of these individuals left an already dysfunctional system rudderless. Because the remaining officials were generally unable or unwilling to take initiative without written orders from Baghdad, the operations of the creaky Iraqi government slowed even further and in many instances stopped. Further confusion arose as prominent individuals, tribal leaders, or representatives of political parties and militias grabbed for power, undermining what little authority remained to civil servants. These power grabs occurred in several cities, most notably Baghdad.

Democratization

Throughout its entire history, Iraq enjoyed no more than a façade of democracy. Under the Hashemite monarchy, elections for the national legislature had been held, and elected politicians had coexisted with ministers appointed by the king in accordance with thinly disguised British behind-the-scenes influence. Although mass movements—such as the Communist Party, Arab nationalists, and the Muslim Brotherhood—had arisen, democratic values had never penetrated deeply into Iraqi society, which was dominated by tribal ties and an unelected monarchy. The series of military and party coups that began with the 1958 revolution and ended with the second Baath coup in 1968 eliminated most political opposition. By the time Saddam Hussein formally took over the presidency in 1979, Iraq was becoming a totalitarian, one-party state, consciously modeled on Stalin's Soviet Union. By 2003, even the Baath Party had become a hollow shell. The state had come to be dominated by a small network of families loyal to Saddam Hussein, who exercised authority through a web of secret police agencies.

At the time of the invasion, the majority of the Iraqi population was too young to remember a time before Baath Party rule. Many of the educated middle classes had gone into exile. For most Iraqis who remained in the country, the concept of civil society had no meaning. The totalitarian system had succeeded in atomizing the population and replacing bonds of social trust and community with the fear of informers and reversion to the more easily manipulated primordial loyalties of clan and tribe. This "retribalization" of Iraqi society was to have a significantly negative impact on the coalition's attempt to promote democratization.

Another, unnoticed, trend in Iraq paralleled that in many other Arab nations oppressed since the 1960s by dictatorship and limited economic opportunities—the recourse to the mosque. Although religious leaders had played an important role in Iraqi politics as far back as the 1920s, many of the parties that were active in the 1950s, including the Baath Party, had been determinedly secular. In Saddam's Iraq, however, the mosque provided a social network and a space outside the tight control of the regime for Sunni and Shia alike. Despite brutal state repression during the 1990s, it became rapidly evident in 2003 that clerics retained considerable authority in the eyes of the Iraqi public. Their views on democracy proved to be as varied as any in the Islamic world. However, the Shiite clerics were attracted to elections because they believed that a democratic majority would, for the first time, give their community the upper hand in determining Iraq's political future.

Reconstruction

When organized and overt resistance ended on April 15, 2003, the Iraqi economy had come to a standstill. Oil exports had been halted because pipelines were closed. As a consequence, oil production had to be severely cut back. Iraq's rickety telecommunications system shut down because the major switches had been destroyed in the war or damaged during looting. Although the electric power system had not been attacked, looters destroyed important controls. To compound the problems posed by looting, organized gangs knocked down power line pylons to steal the metal in the cables, further reducing the availability of electricity. In early May, electric power generation was at one-third the output level of the previous year. Without electricity, pumps needed to operate the water systems failed, resulting in sharp reductions in the availability of potable water. Sewage treatment plants were also unable to operate properly.

These immediate problems pummeled a system that had seen very little investment since before the Gulf War. Western engineers were both amazed and horrified at the stopgap measures devised by the Iraqis to keep the electric power system up and running, from ingenious substitutes for important components to running power lines around circuit breakers, endangering the entire system. Needs assessments conducted by U.S. contractors and the United Nations and World Bank found multibillion-dollar backlogs of maintenance, refurbishment, and new investment needed to restore power supplies, increase supplies of potable water, and treat sewage.[4]

---

[4] United Nations Development Programme and World Bank, *Joint Iraq Needs Assessment,* Washington, D.C., October 2003, pp. 21, 28.

THE U.S., UN, AND OTHER INTERNATIONAL ROLES

Since the U.S. and British governments had been unable to secure a UN Security Council resolution explicitly authorizing the military overthrow of the Iraqi regime, their authority in Iraq was derived from the Geneva Conventions on the Laws of Armed Conflict. Initially, the legal status of the coalition forces was kept in limbo, but when the U.S. government announced on May 11, 2003, that a new Coalition Provisional Authority (CPA) was to supersede ORHA,[5] the coalition members officially recognized that they were occupying powers. As such, they were responsible for ensuring the security and well-being of the Iraqi population and for the interim government of the country. Although subsequent UN Security Council resolutions, such as UN Security Council Resolution (UNSCR) 1483 passed on May 22, 2003, recognized CPA's role, this mission differed from most other cases of post-conflict nation-building in that it was explicitly an occupation rather than a UN-mandated peacekeeping or peace enforcement operation.

The occupying authorities in Iraq, formally the United States and the United Kingdom, theoretically had unity of command. All coalition military forces reported to the American Secretary of Defense via the U.S. Central Command. The civilian authority, first ORHA and then CPA, also reported to the Secretary of Defense. ORHA and CPA were U.S. Department of Defense (DoD) operations, supported and staffed by DoD or detailees from other agencies. In practice, however, full unity of command was never achieved. American civil and military operations in Iraq reported to Washington through separate channels. The British operated with considerable autonomy in the southern region, centered in Basra, which they had occupied. Political and reconstruction activities were meant to be CPA's domain. Development of Iraqi security institutions was a shared mission; combat operations were the domain of the military. Although there were often amicable working relationships at all levels between CPA and the military, the two were never able to achieve true unity of effort because of the dispersion of authority, the difficulties in communicating among the different groups, and different institutional goals.

Military
Once conflict operations had ended, the U.S.-led ground forces that had fought the war were transformed into a stabilization force: Combined Joint

---

[5] L. Elaine Halchin, "The Coalition Provisional Authority: Origin, Characteristics, and Institutional Authorities," CRS Report for Congress, RL32370, Washington, D.C.: Congressional Research Service, April 29, 2004, p. 1.

Task Force 7 (CJTF-7). Prewar planning had envisaged drawing down this force substantially within months of the occupation of Baghdad, and some withdrawals had already begun before the security situation began to deteriorate. U.S. troop levels remained at about 105,000 until May 2004, when DoD announced they would be increased to 138,000 to counter escalating violence. Coalition forces from some 31 countries provided an additional 22,700 troops as of June 28, 2004;[6] contributions ranged from the United Kingdom's 8,000 troops to fewer than a dozen from Norway. The deteriorating security situation and domestic discontent among some coalition partners led to the withdrawal of some contingents, most notably the Spanish in the spring of 2004.

At the heart of CJTF-7 was the U.S. Army's V Corps. The forces deployed as part of CJTF-7 consisted of division-strength armored, cavalry, and light infantry/airborne units, along with supporting units, such as special forces, artillery, logistics and communications, medical, intelligence, civil affairs, and military police.

Command arrangements for CJTF-7 mirrored those for the combat phase. Although it had a coalition structure, CJTF-7 answered to the U.S. Central Command, which in turn answered to the U.S. Department of Defense and the president of the United States. Major coalition partners, such as the United Kingdom and Australia, had senior officers in key positions—for example, the CJTF-7 deputy commanding general was British. These slots, combined with close consultations between national capitals, allowed coalition partners to influence military strategy and operations. Coalition members determined their own rules of engagement in areas under their control. Nonetheless, CJTF-7 was very much a U.S.-led force answering to the U.S. national chain of command.

Civil and Economic

Iraq was the first American-led nation-building operation without an accompanying American diplomatic mission since the occupations of German and Japan nearly 60 years earlier. DoD had assembled ORHA shortly before the war and assigned it the task of working with U.S. forces to undertake immediate reconstruction and humanitarian tasks.

It rapidly became clear that a more wide-ranging program of civil governance was required. On May 6, 2003, President Bush appointed a former

---

[6] CPA, Working Papers: Iraq Status, Unclassified Briefing, June 29, 2004, Slide 33.

ambassador, L. Paul Bremer III, as his envoy to Iraq, and on May 11, 2004, the Coalition Provisional Authority succeeded ORHA.[7] CPA was explicitly a U.S.-UK construct, albeit with other states participating. CPA's authority to administer Iraq was recognized by UN Security Council Resolution 1483, which called on CPA to restore security, to promote the welfare of the Iraqi people, and to create conditions in which the Iraqi people "can freely determine their own future."[8]

The precise legal basis for CPA was always a little unclear, with U.S. and British government lawyers often interpreting CPA's powers rather differently. UNSCR 1483 clearly placed CPA under an obligation to act according to international law, and in particular, to act as an occupying power under the Geneva Conventions. This gave CPA freedom to undertake measures to ensure security and promote the welfare of the Iraqi people. However, the resolution did restrict CPA from undertaking fundamental changes in the Iraqi state, for instance by disposing of state property.

Supported by CJTF-7, CPA ended up with many tasks and roles that it had to pursue concurrently, including

- the day-to-day governance of Iraq at all levels from local to national

- the day-to-day operation of Iraqi security forces and essential services

- reconstruction and rehabilitation of infrastructure and improvement in the delivery of essential services such as electricity and water

- building the capacity of Iraqi civil administration and security forces

- implementing a process of political transition to a fully sovereign government

- implementing a wide-ranging program of democratization and economic transformation

- laying the basis for a process of "truth and reconciliation"

- conducting a counterinsurgency and counterterrorist campaign.

---

[7] Halchin (2004), p. 3.

[8] UNSCR 1483, S/RES/1483, May 22, 2003.

The UN Role

Before the war, UN agencies had made extensive preparations to alleviate humanitarian suffering. At the urging of the United Kingdom, the U.S. administration had agreed that the United Nations should play a "vital" role in post–Saddam Iraq, but U.S. officials initially interpreted this mandate rather narrowly, essentially seeking to limit it to humanitarian activities. UNSCR 1483 authorized the Secretary-General to appoint a Special Representative to Iraq and reaffirmed the "vital" role to be played by the United Nations in humanitarian relief, reconstruction, and the establishment of governance institutions. On August 14, 2003, UNSCR 1500 established the UN Assistance Mission for Iraq (UNAMI).[9]

Under this mandate, UN agencies played an important role in Iraq until the fall of 2003. The World Food Program (WFP), a UN agency, carried on with its support for the Iraqi government's Public Distribution System, the food-rationing network, in the center and south of the country. The WFP continued to operate the program in the north through contractors under its own auspices. Before the onset of the conflict, in the first part of 2003, the WFP launched the largest emergency operation in its history, delivering 2.1 million tons of food through the Iraqi Ministry of Trade in the central and southern areas and its own contractors in the Kurdish areas.[10] Because of these efforts, households had sufficient food to survive the disruption in supplies caused by combat operations. Extra deliveries of medical supplies before the onset of the conflict also helped tide clinics and medical services over until regular supplies were once again available. The International Organization of Migration (IOM) began registering demobilized military personnel. Other agencies worked on humanitarian and health issues. The Secretary-General's Special Representative, Sergio Vieira de Mello, worked effectively to advance political dialogue among Iraqi leaders and with CPA, playing an important behind-the-scenes role in the selection of the Iraqi Governing Council and a very public role in the announcement of the Governing Council's members.

UN operations were severely cut back after the August 19, 2003, bombing of the UN Headquarters in Baghdad that killed de Mello and 21 others. After the bombing, UN personnel were directed to withdraw from the country.[11] The bombing was followed by escalating violence in the winter and spring

---

[9] UNSCR 1500, S/RES/1500, August 14, 2003.

[10] World Food Program, "World Hunger—Iraq," May 2004, http://www.wfp.org/country_brief/index.asp?region=6, accessed on November 20, 2004.

[11] United Nations, *Report of the Independent Panel on the Safety and Security of UN Personnel in Iraq,* 20 October 2003.

against foreign aid agencies, NGOs, and contractors, all of which made UN-related activities in Iraq very difficult and forestalled a larger role.

In January 2004, at the request of the U.S. and British governments, the United Nations once again became meaningfully engaged in Iraq. On November 15, 2003, the U.S. administration had greatly accelerated plans transfer sovereignty to an Iraqi government. Facing difficulties in achieving Iraqi buy-in to the process of selecting this government, Washington and London asked the United Nations to play an expanded role in negotiating a more broadly acceptable agreement and in facilitating the process of political transition. The Secretary-General's representative, Lakhdar Brahimi, was asked to take the lead in negotiating the formation of an interim government to take power after CPA was dissolved. (Brahimi had earlier been the United States' principal UN partner in Haiti and Afghanistan and was Washington's first choice to head the Kosovo administration). The United Nations was also asked to take over supervision of the plans for local and national elections. Further UN involvement in the process of constitutional development and aid coordination was also envisaged. However, the UN leadership in New York remained reluctant to overextend itself in Iraq, recognizing that UN personnel would remain prime targets for attacks.

WHAT HAPPENED

The initial civil authority was the Office of Reconstruction and Humanitarian Assistance (ORHA), under Lieutenant General (ret.) Jay M. Garner. ORHA's goals and mandate were not well defined. In May 2003, ORHA (along with Garner) was replaced by the Coalition Provisional Authority under Ambassador L. Paul Bremer III. CPA, representing the occupying powers, was responsible for governing Iraq. CPA interpreted its mandate broadly: It decided not merely to restore order and basic services but also to initiate a wide-ranging transformation of Iraq. CPA's goal was to create a pluralist democracy governed along "modern," technocratic lines. This transformation was to be achieved by CPA, a civilian-led authority—albeit one responding to the U.S. Department of Defense—rather than through a military-led occupation. In that respect, it differed from the U.S. experience in Japan after World War II.

Four features of CPA detracted seriously from its effectiveness. First, CPA was put together on an ad hoc basis: DoD had no permanent staff with experience and responsibility for representing the United States abroad and assisting foreign governments on political and economic development issues. Consequently, the CPA leadership had to build an organization from scratch while simultaneously learning to govern Iraq and build Iraqi institutions. In part because of its ad hoc nature, which necessitated recruiting from across the government, and in part because of the dangers of serving in Iraq, CPA had difficulty recruiting and retaining a full complement of staff. From its inception to its end on June 28, 2004, CPA was always woefully understaffed. According to a report of the CPA Inspector General, of 2,117 authorized positions, CPA had only 1,196 personnel on staff as of March 8, 2004—56 percent of total authorized slots.[12] Most of those people stayed no longer than three to six months. Thus, only a small fraction of CPA-authorized personnel had been at their desks long enough to know what they were doing and were not due to depart. An even smaller proportion had relevant experience and were qualified to fill the positions to which they were assigned. Even its full proposed complement of personnel would have been inadequate to the task of both managing and transforming the Iraqi government.

The "hollowness" of CPA led to the second feature of the operation: CPA's reliance on CJTF-7 to implement many policies. In Baghdad, almost 30 percent of CPA billets were filled by military detailees, many of them reserve officers. In the regions where CPA presence on the ground was extraordinarily thin, virtually all functions were handled by CJTF-7. Consequently, CPA was largely dependent on the military for the execution of policy. This dependence extended to areas as diverse as protection of contractors, police training, and the establishment and mentoring of local councils.

Third, there was relatively poor coordination between the British and CPA in Baghdad. During the war, the British operated in the south around Basra. They had fought fairly independently of the wider U.S.-led campaign. The UK government and UK military put considerable effort into building Iraqi capacity and giving aid in the south. They did so in a fairly structured and organized fashion. This "British autonomy" persisted, exacerbated by CPA's failure to establish effective, secure communications between its regional offices and Baghdad.

Fourth, CPA's relationship with Iraqi institutions was never quite clear. In July 2003, CPA appointed the 25-member Iraqi Governing Council (IGC) to serve as the interim representative body for Iraq. The IGC was not accepted by the United Nations as the representative government of Iraq. Many CPA

---

[12] Inspector General of the Coalition Provisional Authority, "Audit Report: Management of Personnel Assigned to the Coalition Provisional Authority in Baghdad," Report Number 04–002, June 25, 2004, p. 1.

employees were deeply distrustful of the competence and probity of much of Iraqi officialdom, including the members of the IGC. Nonetheless, CPA had promised to consult and coordinate with the IGC on major issues. At least until late 2003, CPA's general approach was to treat the IGC only as an advisory group. CPA made policy and undertook implementation unilaterally. Although CPA adopted more of a partnership approach as the deadline for transfer of authority approached, it was never quite able to resolve the dilemma of whether CPA was meant to work in support of Iraqi institutions, however imperfect, or to impose unilateral reform from above.[13] These features dogged the CPA mission throughout its 13-month life.

Security

The first security challenge to face coalition forces was an unanticipated breakdown of law and order across much of the country during and after the war. The disappearance of the organs of state repression and law enforcement opened the way for an explosion of street crime and organized criminality. Fueled by an abundance of military-grade weapons (especially AK-47s and rocket-propelled grenades) and the presence on the streets of former convicts, this crime wave overwhelmed ordinary Iraqis and disrupted reconstruction efforts. Looters destroyed ministerial offices, control centers, and other key facilities, setting back reconstruction efforts greatly. Truck hijackings and kidnappings were prevalent. The disappearance of Iraq's border security forces permitted organized criminals to engage in massive smuggling of gasoline and diesel fuel, further straining Iraq's economy.

By the summer of 2003, politically motivated violence in the form of insurgent and terrorist campaigns had begun to threaten the coalition. A disparate set of groups orchestrated an increasingly deadly and disruptive campaign of sabotage and terror against coalition forces, CPA, civilian contractors, the infrastructure, and Iraqi ministries. The core of the insurgency consisted of former regime loyalists, notably personnel from the security and intelligence services, who had been excluded from power after the war. Sunni Islamist extremists, both home-grown and linked to networks such as al-Qaida, Ansar al-Sunna, and Abu Musa al-Zarqawi's group, constituted another source of violence. These groups sought to humiliate the U.S. gov-

---

[13] A good example was CPA's relationship with the Iraqi court system. CPA was clearly in a supporting role vis-à-vis the judiciary. Judicial reform was driven by the Chief Justice and Minister of Justice. However, the Commission on Public Integrity was established outside the Iraqi court system to ensure that it reported only to the future U.S. embassy rather than to Iraqi politicians.

ernment, to make Iraq ungovernable, and to lay the political groundwork for the eventual imposition of a radical Islamist state. These groups sometimes cooperated tactically. They were able to exploit discontent among Iraqis, largely in the "Sunni triangle" area, where a lack of employment opportunities and anger at coalition occupation tactics had generated widespread disaffection. In addition to these groups, Moqtada al-Sadr, scion of a prominent Shiite clerical family, mobilized unemployed, discontented Shiite youth into an armed militia to support his struggle for power within the Shiite community. He perceived himself as being excluded from the political process and believed that U.S. forces were determined to "capture or kill" him.[14] In April 2004, in reaction to CPA's closure of his movement's newspaper and the arrest of a senior lieutenant, he launched a widespread uprising against U.S. forces.

The overall level of violence ebbed and flowed, peaking in November 2003, April–May 2004, and again in the weeks following the June 28 transfer of sovereignty. During the April–May escalation, CJTF-7 and CPA lines of communication were frequently cut, CPA locations had to be evacuated, and the coalition lost control over a number of cities, notably Najaf, Karbala, Kut, and Fallujah. In addition to attacks on coalition forces and CPA, spectacular terrorist strikes against the United Nations and NGOs and regular ambushes and kidnappings of foreign contractors significantly slowed the pace of reconstruction. The lack of security slowed and at times halted the nascent economic recovery. As the new Iraqi government institutions, from the IGC and government ministers to the police, judiciary, and army, began to take an increasingly prominent role in running the government and setting policy, they also came under fire. Insurgents targeted local council-members and Iraqi nationals working with NGOs and reconstruction contractors and Iraqis standing in line in front of recruiting centers for the police and the army. These attacks spread a climate of fear and hampered CPA's attempts to build a democracy and civil society in Iraq. Insurgents also attempted to spark communal violence, including suicide bombings of Shiite religious festivals and against the Kurdish leadership.

Faced with escalating violence, coalition forces initially believed they were dealing primarily with regime "bitter-enders" and a small number of foreign *jihadist* fighters. Coalition tactics included cordon and search and strike operations. However, coalition forces were always hampered by poor intelligence. Heavy-handed operations, including indiscriminate arrests and heavy use of firepower, including fixed-wing attack aircraft, often acted

---

[14] An Iraqi judge had issued an arrest warrant for him in connection with the murder of Abdul Majid al-Khoei, which took place in April 2003.

as a recruiter for the insurgents. By fall 2003, CJTF-7 recognized that it faced a combination of terrorist and insurgent threats. Coalition intelligence predicted that these threats would escalate in severity over the coming months. Coalition forces, which had expected to leave Iraq, found themselves engaged in a vicious guerrilla war for which they were not trained, postured, or resourced. U.S. armored forces had to learn on the job how to control an urban environment by patrolling on foot and developing human intelligence networks.

The initial deployment had been criticized for insufficient numbers of troops by no less a figure than Army Chief of Staff General Eric Shinseki.[15] Shinseki was proven right: There were never enough troops in the country to undertake such key tasks as border security and guarding arms depots or to surge troops to hotspots of unrest like Ramadi and Fallujah to preempt insurgent consolidation.

As the violence surged in April–May 2004, shortly before the promised handover to a sovereign Iraqi government, the major political-military setbacks experienced by the coalition forced a serious reevaluation of strategies and tactics. It became evident to the CJTF-7 leadership and to CENTCOM that the political-military campaign was faltering. This reevaluation led coalition forces to reposture for extended combat operations, to increase U.S. and UK troop levels in part to replace coalition partners, such as Spain, that had withdrawn their forces, and to develop a more-integrated counterinsurgency strategy in partnership with Iraq's embryonic security forces.

One of CPA's first acts had been to abolish the Iraqi armed forces, the Ministry of Defense (MoD), and the intelligence and security services. This decision was controversial. Critics argued that the army should have been kept intact until a disarmament, demobilization, and reintegration program could be implemented under which soldiers would relinquish their weapons in exchange for financial assistance and help in finding employment. CPA responded that its decision merely recognized facts on the ground: These organizations had disintegrated during the course of the conflict. The decision was also driven in part by a desire to start afresh and build democratically accountable and modern institutions for the new Iraqi state. CPA and CJTF-7 also were skeptical that these institutions, the bedrock of Saddam's regime, could be reformed. The Ministry of Interior was not abolished, but it was radically pruned, losing its control over prisons and its special security

---

[15] Seymour M. Hersh, "Offense and Defense: The Battle Between Donald Rumsfeld and the Pentagon," *The New Yorker,* April 7, 2003.

and emergency units. The police force was not disbanded; the breakdown in law and order after the fall of Baghdad led ORHA to recall Iraqi police officers to work in an effort to provide security on the streets.

From the outset, CJTF-7 and CPA had stressed the importance of building indigenous security forces. Because of the worsening security environment, Washington and London applied constant pressure to accelerate the stand-up of these forces. The coalition was especially anxious to pull back its forces from the front lines. Yet CPA did not begin with a coherent strategy for the reform and development of the Iraqi security sector; an integrated strategy only emerged beginning in December 2003. The long-term vision that had been developed in the summer of 2003 was frequently revised in light of the urgent need to deploy Iraqi security forces to meet the growing insurgent threat. The original program for the gradual and deliberate development of a new Iraqi army was replaced by an accelerated program. The push to deploy Iraqi security forces had counterproductive results. Many who enlisted in the army did so because they were informed that its mission was external defense; they believed they would not be called on to fight their fellow Iraqis. Not surprisingly, therefore, when the 2nd Battalion of the Iraqi Armed Forces (IAF) was deployed to fight the insurgency in April 2004, the unit mutinied on its first contact with the insurgents. In addition to the problems of morale, the development of the security sector was consistently hampered by delays in the delivery of funds for personnel and equipment.

The program for development of the security sector that belatedly emerged was ambitious in scope and scale. CPA intended to create a small but effective Iraqi military force under civilian management, focused on external defense. The program called for the creation—from the ground up—of a new army, a coastal defense force, an air component, and a defense ministry. It was to be operated according to the standards of a first-world force. This program was managed by a Coalition Military Assistance Training Team and civilian MoD advisors. On the internal security front, the program called for the redesign of the Ministry of Interior. The ministry was to be transformed from a corrupt, authoritarian instrument of repression to a protector of public safety and national security. The police force was to be rebuilt by purging and retraining existing personnel and gradually increasing the number of new recruits, who would be trained and mentored by international police advisors. The border security forces were also to be reconstituted. Although some personnel were reemployed, a large-scale recruitment, training, and infrastructure development program was to be set up to recruit new officers.

At the same time, the judiciary and prison system were to be transformed from politicized servants of the dictatorship to upholders of the rule of law. The judiciary was purged and made independent of the Ministry of Justice. The Iraqi Correctional Service was purged and an ambitious program of training and monitoring by expatriate civilian prison experts instituted. On the intelligence front, the previous plethora of competing secret police agencies was to be replaced by a democratically accountable Iraqi National Intelligence Service working in partnership with police and military intelligence agencies.

In addition to these forces, coalition military regional commands sought to fill the immediate security gap by raising auxiliary troops, known as the Iraqi Civil Defense Corps (ICDC). Locally recruited and quickly trained for basic paramilitary tasks, the ICDC became a mainstay of coalition security policy simply because it could be rapidly generated and, operating under the wing of coalition forces, put an Iraqi face on coalition operations. The ICDC was enthusiastically taken up by the Interim Iraqi Government in July 2004 and was rebadged as a "National Guard."

In the spring of 2004, with the transfer of authority fast approaching, CPA also turned its attention to building national security management and decisionmaking institutions and policies that would ensure civilian control over the security forces and institutionalize effective decisionmaking on national security issues. CPA worked intensively with the IGC and ministers to develop mechanisms (e.g., a Ministerial Committee on National Security) and legislation that would shape the practices of the Interim Iraqi Government.

UNSCR 1483 had called on the United Nations to encourage international efforts to assist the Iraqi civil police force, but, by the time the United Nations withdrew its staff in the wake of the August 19, 2003, bombing of its headquarters, it had made no significant progress in this regard. The police program remained under the direction of the U.S. government, shared uneasily among the State Department, Department of Justice, and CENTCOM.

When the United Nations began to envisage deploying back into the country to support the political and reconstruction process after CPA dissolved, its primary concern was its own security. UNSCR 1546, passed on June 8, 2004, called for the creation of a special UN security force reporting to the Multi-National Force–Iraq, which replaced CJTF-7, to protect UN personnel and facilities inside Iraq. .

With the inauguration of a new Iraqi government under Prime Minister Ayad Alawi, U.S. and coalition forces have sought where possible to step back and allow Iraqi authorities to assume more visible responsibility for security. Alawi's government has adopted an approach emphasizing both toughness, in the form of provisions for martial law, and reconciliation, in the form of an amnesty—while at the same time seeking to further accelerate the training and equipping of new Iraqi security forces. These forces and their recruiting efforts have in turn been heavily targeted by insurgent attacks, as have national and local government leaders.

Humanitarian

The WFP, U.S. forces, and the Ministry of Trade quickly started delivering food after combat operations ended. International staff of the WFP reentered Iraq in May 2003. In the north, WFP continued its operations through subcontractors. In the rest of the country, it worked with the Ministry of Trade to facilitate transportation of food and other materials, and assisted with the renegotiation of contracts that had been signed under the Oil for Food Program. Under UNSCR 1472 and 1476, the WFP helped ensure the delivery of five months worth of food rations. Although WFP's mandate to provide food for Iraq was to expire on November 21, 2003, CPA decided that it lacked the administrative capacity to take over contracting for food operations. In January 2004, CPA, WFP, and the Iraqi Ministry of Trade signed a Memorandum of Understanding requesting WFP to provide continued support for contracting and assistance in capacity-building for the Iraqi Ministry of Trade.[16]

Although it played a less-prominent role than WFP, the World Health Organization was also active in Iraq, providing emergency medical supplies and help in staffing major hospitals.[17]

Civil Administration

In the immediate aftermath of the war, an early priority for coalition forces was to restart the functions of government. The centralized nature of the Iraqi state and the fact that most senior positions had been filled by Baath Party loyalists meant that local government and basic public services ceased functioning with the fall of the regime. Initially, many military re-

---

[16] World Food Program (2004).

[17] United Nations, "Iraq Situation Report," July 18–24, 2004, at www.who.int/disasters/repo/14032.pdf, accessed November 22, 2004.

gional commands took over the management of such basic services as sanitation. As soon as possible, however, the coalition installed Iraqi officials at the municipal and provincial levels and provided logistical and financial support to enable the resumption of local services, such as education. Lacking local knowledge, mistakes were often made. At times, appointed officials were removed for corruption or past human rights abuses. Moreover, because local administration decisions were so decentralized and communications so poor, there was frequently no consistent policy throughout the country. Nonetheless, the regional commands got the local civil administrations functioning fairly quickly. The slow deployment of CPA teams to the provinces hampered the transfer of authority from the military to the civilian authority. However, the military handed over the job of working with the local civil administrations as soon as the CPA teams were established. Because of the fairly small numbers of CPA employees and the continued need for security and logistic support, CJTF-7 actively worked with the local civil administration throughout CPA's existence.

At the national level, CPA, heavily supported by military Civil Affairs officers, found itself responsible for the day-to-day management of the whole of the Iraqi government machinery. As noted above, de-Baathification had stripped the senior management layer from most ministries. Not until September 2003, when the IGC and CPA appointed interim ministers, did Iraqis begin to once again take a lead role in running day-to-day operations of the government. Until that time and often after, CPA "advisors" found themselves handling the operations of ministries, from refurbishing ministry buildings through making salary payments to setting policy, and instigating long-term reform programs.

The quality and depth of the Iraqi ministries with which the advisors worked varied considerably. The Health and Education Ministries were relatively functional and reform-minded. Interior and Industry and Minerals were either in disarray or had vested interests in resisting reform. Human Rights and Defense had to be constructed from scratch. Government operations were severely hampered by the catastrophic state of Iraq's physical and social infrastructure. Damage to the telephone network during the war and CPA's failure to rapidly restore phone service made coordination difficult. The state of Iraq's banking system and the archaic practices of the Finance Ministry meant that inordinate efforts had to be expended to move cash securely around the country simply to pay salaries. Corruption was endemic and most ministry payrolls featured large numbers of "ghost workers."

By late 2003, CPA had begun to move beyond "firefighting" to develop a broader program of civil service reform. Building on the good practices that were emerging in some ministries, CPA envisaged a multiyear program of institutional reform and capacity-building, as well as a wide-ranging anticorruption program. By late spring of 2004, work had also begun on the development of a central government coordinating mechanism to provide professional policy staff to support the prime minister and presidency. However, by the time these programs had begun to come together, CPA's focus was on "graduating" the ministries, i.e., turning them over to full Iraqi control. In some cases, this process reinforced the reformist trend as empowered ministers became able to work with their advisors to plan long-term programs; in others, the transition negated much of CPA's work as Iraqi ministries reverted to traditional practices of centralization, patronage, and corruption.

UNSCR 1483 had pledged the United Nations to assist with civil administration. This was an area of comparative advantage for the United Nations, especially in light of the familiarity of a number of UN agencies with the country. However, the withdrawal of the UN mission in August 2003 stopped any such programs. Although the UN strategic plan for Iraq stressed the United Nations' desire to assist in this area,[18] in the absence of a UN presence civil administration was undertaken by CPA and military personnel, along with coalition aid agencies (notably the U.S. Agency for International Development [USAID] and the UK Department for International Development [DfID]) and their contractors. The UN and other international bodies, such as the World Bank and International Monetary Fund, limited themselves to programs such as offering out-of-country training for Iraqi officials.

Democratization

U.S. planning for Iraq's post–Saddam governance veered back and forth several times between a prolonged American administered transition to democracy on the post–World War II German and Japanese models and a rapid hand-off of power to an unelected interim Iraqi government on the Afghan model. Two months before the war, U.S. planners were focusing on the former approach. As hostilities approached, the latter, more rapid transition came into favor and was the approach the United States first attempted to implement.

---

[18] United Nations, *A Strategy for Assistance to Iraq*, draft for stakeholder consultation, February 7, 2004.

On April 15, 2003, ORHA and CENTCOM hosted a meeting in Nasiriyah of Iraqi notables from both inside and outside Iraq. Serious tensions were evident between returning exiles who envisaged a leading role for themselves in the new Iraq and Iraqis who had remained in the country under Saddam's rule. However, at the end of the meeting, the United States announced a series of consultative meetings that would lead to the formation of a transitional government by the end of May 2003. This government was to be followed by the formation of a provisional government, which would draft a constitution and prepare for national elections.

At the end of May, however, CPA Administrator Bremer announced that he would delay the selection of the transitional government because of the worsening security situation. It was not until July 13, 2003, that CPA formed the IGC—a body with largely advisory powers. The IGC was dominated by six largely émigré opposition parties (the INC, the INA, the KDP, the PUK, SCIRI, and the Daawa Party), but it also included a number of respected individuals from across the country. In addition to a widespread perception among Iraqis that the IGC was an American puppet, the legitimacy of the IGC was called into question from the outset by the absence of weighty figures representing the Sunni community.

Under the plan for political transition drawn up by CPA, the IGC's role was to draft a constitution and to appoint ministers to run the interim government. Ministers were eventually appointed by September 2003, but disagreements between the IGC and CPA over the appointment of deputy ministers continued into the spring of 2004, leaving most ministries with a leadership vacuum on the level immediately below the top. The IGC's constitutional committee meanwhile made little progress. Although the committee agreed on a process, it failed to resolve the many controversial issues that needed to be tackled in the constitution. In any case, CPA's plan for transition was coming under attack on two fronts. A broad-based popular movement, whose views were generally captured in statements by Shiite cleric Ayatollah Sistani, called for full elections as a precursor to drawing up a constitution. At the same time, insurgent violence was growing—destabilizing all aspects of Iraqi reconstruction, increasing frustration of the Iraqi populace with the coalition, and generating domestic political reverberations in the United States and the United Kingdom.

In response to these setbacks, the U.S. administration switched once again back to its second alternative, a more rapid transfer of authority to an unelected Iraqi government. This move was codified in a November 15, 2003, agreement between CPA and IGC calling for the drafting of a "Basic Law"—

an interim constitution—by February 28, 2004, the appointment of a larger Iraqi governing council through a national caucus by May 2004, and the election of an interim government by the transitional council and the dissolution of CPA by July 1, 2004. This was to be followed by the adoption of a constitution and full elections by the end of 2005.[19]

Under this revised and accelerated program, the IGC made considerable progress on the Basic Law, known as the Transitional Administrative Law (TAL). The TAL was signed on March 8, 2003. Although it was a progressive document in terms of its attitude to individual rights and it resolved issues such as the role of Islam in public life, it left for the future such controversial issues as the status of the Kurdish governorates and the geographic extent of Kurdish areas.[20] Portions of the TAL, which were perceived as giving the Kurds veto power over further constitutional amendments, became the target of sustained opposition by Sistani's camp on behalf of the Shiite community.

Sistani and a Shiite bloc on the IGC further disrupted CPA's plans by continuing to demand that the interim government be selected through national elections rather than caucuses. CPA argued that free and fair elections could not be held in the time available. However, by the end of 2003, CPA had been unable to win the public argument. To resolve the issue, in January 2004, the IGC, encouraged by the U.S. government, asked the United Nations to rule on the issue of elections. A UN election team visited Baghdad and determined that it would, indeed, be infeasible to hold elections in the time available but that it would be worth exploring other options rather than caucuses for the selection of the interim government.[21] By this stage, the United States was eager to share the process of selecting the interim government with veteran U.N. troubleshooter Lakhdar Brahimi.

Between February and May 2003, Brahimi made several visits to Iraq and floated a number of formulas. Members of the IGC fought hard to preserve their positions within the post-transition power structure. After a complex, multisided process of consultations, Brahimi, the IGC, and CPA agreed on an Interim Iraqi Government consisting of a president, two vice-presidents, a prime minister, and a Council of Ministers. The mandate of the Interim

---

[19] "Transfer Does Not Affect Troops," BBC News Online, November 16, 2003, www.news.bbc.co.uk, accessed November 16, 2003; "Bremer: U.S. in Tough Fight in Iraq," BBC News Online, November 16, 2003, www.news.bbc.co.uk, accessed November 16, 2003.

[20] For instance, Kirkuk was a major bone of contention.

[21] Betsy Pisik, "UN Sides with U.S. on Voting in Iraq," *Washington Times,* January 16, 2004; Betsy Pisik, "UN Iraq Advisor Issues Vote Warning," *Washington Times,* January 28, 2004.

Iraqi Government (IIG) was to manage Iraq through elections for a transitional assembly, scheduled for January 2005. The elections, in turn, would pave the way for drawing up a full constitution. The IIG would be supplemented by a 100-member Interim National Council, chosen from a 1,000-member National Conference, held in August of 2004.[22]

Although the process of national political transition attracted most of the limelight, CPA's program of grassroots democratization and local governance reform also went forward. The pace of democratization was slowed by a failure to deploy CPA personnel rapidly into Iraq's regions, by funding delays, and by the worsening security situation. The Sadr uprising in April–May 2004, for instance, targeted many of the local offices for CPA, RTI International (working under contract for USAID), and their Iraqi partners.

CPA's democratization and local governance reform program had several aims. First, it sought to build the fabric of a civil society that would support democratic values and a pluralist party system. This involved education programs, support for women's groups, and support for an independent, professional media. Second, it sought to build the capacity of accountable local government institutions. Despite the lack of a democratic tradition and the ever-present threat of insurgent violence, this program made significant strides. In Baghdad, neighborhood and district councils elected a City Council that displayed surprising signs of political maturity. Aside from the aid programs, CPA sought to encode its reforms in a Local Governmental Powers Order, issued in April 2004, in the face of opposition from members of the IGC, who opposed the decentralizing tone of the legislation.

The third main plank of CPA's democratization program was the protection of human rights and the administration of transitional justice. CPA created a new human rights ministry and worked with the IGC to create an Iraqi Special Tribunal to try officials of the former regime for crimes against humanity. CPA also sought to instill in government officials, notably members of the security forces, notions of the rule of law and respect for human rights; these values were encoded in the TAL and relevant government orders. CPA also began the process of investigating the crimes of the previous regime, but efforts to investigate mass gravesites and to collate documents were slowed by logistical and security concerns. On the pressing issue of internally displaced people, CPA founded an Iraqi Property Claims Commission to resolve property claims, primarily of Kurds who had been expelled from their homes under Saddam's policy of Arabization of Kurdish areas, especially around Kirkuk.

---

[22] CPA, *Interim Iraqi Government Press Packet,* June 24, 2004.

Although the United States did not initially envisage a leading UN role in the process of political transition and democratization, Sergio de Mello exercised significant behind-the-scenes influence in bridging the gap between CPA and Iraqi politicians, even engaging in dialog with Ayatollah Sistani, who consistently refused to meet with CPA officials. De Mello's death at a critical phase in the political process contributed to the problems CPA faced in fall 2003.

Starting in January 2004, CPA and the U.S. government ceded more and more authority to the United Nations as they sought early end to an increasingly unpopular occupation. Although closely shadowed by U.S. officials, Brahimi was given quite a free hand in the selection of the interim government that took power on June 28, 2004. The UN election team under Carina Perelli was given full CPA support in its efforts to prepare Iraq for the January 2005 elections. Although CPA and the coalition military were to underpin preparations for elections, policy direction was largely left to the United Nations.[23]

Reconstruction

CPA and CJTF-7 made the restoration of essential services, especially electric power, water, sewage, and garbage pickup, a top priority. Unless the population could be supplied with potable water, epidemics threatened. Unless the water authority had access to electricity, pumps could not be operated. Electricity and fuel were key to returning economic activity to normal. During the summer of 2003, shortages of gasoline and diesel fuel were blamed for triggering riots and disturbances, including a major riot in Basra that led to a number of deaths.[24] The resumption of oil production and export was given very high priority because oil exports were the sole source of revenue for the Iraqi government.

Funding for reconstruction came from three sources: Iraqi assets deposited in a special account, the Development Fund for Iraq (DFI), in the Federal Reserve Bank of New York; oil export revenues, also deposited in this account; and U.S. grant aid. The grant aid pledged to the reconstruction of infrastructure in Iraq has been extraordinary. The U.S. Congress has provided over $20 billion in assistance, $18.4 billion of which was granted through the Emergency Supplemental Appropriations Act on November 6, 2003. This

[23] United Nations, The Political Transition in Iraq: Report of the Fact-Finding Mission, S/2004/140, February 23, 2004.

[24] Charles Recknagel, "Iraq: Al-Basrah Riot Underlines Frustration With Energy Shortages," Radio Free Europe, Washington, D.C., August 11, 2003.

figure was 2.5 times the entire budget request for USAID in 2002. Of this amount, two-thirds, or $12.4 billion, was earmarked for the construction of infrastructure projects. Other donors have promised an additional $3.7 billion in grant aid and much larger sums in the form of subsidized loans.

The use of grant aid to finance infrastructure projects is a highly unusual. Grant aid is generally considered best spent on projects that are difficult to finance through borrowing, such as education, improving government operations, and developing health care systems. Long-term investments in electric power, water systems, and the oil sector are almost always financed through equity or loans. These projects are very expensive. The financing requirement forces the borrower to evaluate the project more carefully by stipulating that it will bring positive return on the investment. This exercise contributes to better project design and more efficient use of funds.

Despite the extraordinarily large sums committed to the reconstruction of Iraq, the coalition has had mixed success in restoring Iraqi services. After rising sharply from May 2003 to October 2003, electric power generation stagnated; production fell in April 2004. Output still runs about the same level as before the war. Oil production had failed to reach the pre-conflict levels by mid-year 2004. At the end of June 2004, sabotage, an ongoing problem, had reduced output to just 1.1 million barrels per day (mbd), a level last seen just after the war, compared to an immediate prewar peak of 2.5 mbd.[25]

The slower-than-planned pace at which essential services have been restored is due to a variety of reasons. First, the coalition underestimated the magnitude of the task. Not only did the coalition have to repair war damage, but years of poor maintenance and underinvestment had caught up with Iraq. In many instances, electric power generating equipment was not worth repairing and had to be replaced. This slowed the process of reconstruction. Second, looting immediately after the war and sabotage since have knocked out refurbished installations, resulting in frequent setbacks in restoring service levels. Third, the continued use of subsidies and price controls has exacerbated problems. Iraqis have used their rising incomes to purchase refrigerators and air conditioners that have increased demand for electric power, power for which they do not pay. Because diesel fuel is free for state-owned enterprises, the Ministry of Electricity has used it for power generation rather than natural gas. Not surprisingly, diesel fuel is in

---

[25] U.S. Department of Defense, Iraq Status Report, June 29, 2004.

short supply. The Ministry of Electricity has not been able to operate newly installed generating capacity because of fuel shortages.

CPA has been criticized for not spending funds more quickly. The slower-than-promised pace of disbursal is due to a variety of reasons. U.S. congressional concerns about properly monitoring contract expenditures have necessitated a reasonable period of time for issuing requests for proposals, evaluating bids, and choosing winners. Only after the winning bidders have been selected does the process of developing specific projects, contracting for equipment, and installing the equipment begin. The time needed to manage this process correctly has stretched out the reconstruction process. In addition, the high degree of violence has raised contractor costs, slowed reconstruction, and generally retarded the effort.

The United Nations, through UNDP and in conjunction with the World Bank, has played a subsidiary role to CPA and CJTF-7 in the reconstruction of Iraq. In the summer of 2003, UNDP and the World Bank prepared a joint assessment of Iraq's needs. They examined education, health, water and sanitation, transport, telecommunications, electricity, and housing, among other key areas. As part of this evaluation, they set targeted levels of service and estimated the cost of meeting these targets. This study was completed before a donors' conference for Iraq held in Madrid on October 23 and 24, 2003, to raise funds for reconstruction.[26]

At the conference, donors authorized the creation of two trust funds, one to be run by the World Bank and the other by UNDP, through which donors could channel funds for assistance. The trust funds have received very little in the way of donations. Of over $21 billion in grants to be given Iraq, donors have committed to channeling only $1 billion through the funds.[27]

Although the needs assessments were used as a basis for requesting funds at the Madrid conference, UNDP and the World Bank have played a relatively small role in setting priorities or plans for reconstruction in Iraq. Separate needs assessments for the oil sector by Halliburton and for the electricity, water, and sewage sectors by Bechtel (funded by the U.S. government) became the basis for setting priorities and planning reconstruction in these areas.[28] These assessments were used to put together the detailed project plans that are guiding current reconstruction activity.

---

[26] UNDP and World Bank (2003).

[27] Mona Megalli and Heba Kandil, "Iraq Donors Commit About $1 Billion to Iraq Funds," Reuters, February 29, 2004.

WFP has also played a role in reconstruction, a legacy of its role in running the OFF program. Under this program, Iraq was permitted to buy equipment and components needed to provide essential services such as electricity and potable water. At the time of the war, a multibillion-dollar backlog of contracts for this equipment existed. WFP continued to monitor and oversee these contracts through the handover to CPA on November 21, 2003, and assisted CPA and the Ministry of Trade with contract oversight after that date.

To date, neither the World Bank nor UNDP has been taking a lead role in reconstruction. The security situation has remained so precarious that almost all personnel employed by these organizations who are assigned to Iraq remain outside the country, usually in Amman, Jordan.

LESSONS LEARNED

U.S. nation-building efforts in Iraq have exhibited many of the characteristic weaknesses for which the United Nations has been so often and so justly criticized:

- Planning for stabilization and reconstruction was based on unrealistic, best-case assumptions.

- The original stabilization force was too small.

- The United States was slow to deploy civil administrators and police in adequate numbers.

- When deployed, those individuals proved of variable quality.

The United States failed to anticipate that

---

[28] Because Halliburton had already been engaged to evaluate the needs of the oil sector, UNDP and the World Bank deliberately chose not to undertake their own needs assessment (UNDP and World Bank, 2003, p. v.).

- the fall of Saddam would be accompanied by the collapse of the Iraqi state

- a power vacuum would open

- this vacuum would be immediately filled by a combination of criminal and extremist elements

- the Iraqi security apparatus would be unavailable to challenge these elements

- criminals and extremists would become extremely difficult to displace if they were allowed to move into the power vacuum, organize and consolidate, intimidate the populace, and cow what was left of the police.

Similar developments had attended the collapse of regimes in Somalia, Haiti, Bosnia, Kosovo, and Afghanistan. It seems clear, therefore, that America's planning for Iraq gave inadequate attention to its own recent experiences in the field of nation-building.

The U.S. decision to model the Iraqi operation on its post–World War II occupations of Germany and Japan, rather than post–Cold War Bosnia or Kosovo, and to actually term its presence an "occupation" rather than a "peace enforcement action" heightened resistance among the Iraqi and neighboring populations. For Americans, the term *occupation* conjures up relatively benign images of the very successful U.S. role in European reconstruction. For the rest of the world, in particular for the rest of the Arab world, the word evokes the Israeli occupation of the West Bank and Gaza.

Given the manner in which the war unfolded, the United States may not have had the option of treating "post-conflict" Iraq as a fully international operation. Nevertheless, there was probably a window of opportunity in the early weeks following the end of conventional combat in which a greater role for the UN, NATO, the World Bank, and other international institutions might have been forged. The rapid and relatively bloodless U.S. victory had created favorable global opinion. Most Iraqis were apparently grateful for their liberation, little significant resistance had developed, and weapons of mass destruction were still generally expected to be found. It was precisely at this moment of apparent victory, however, that American opinion seemed inclined to regard Iraq as a prize won rather than a burden acquired. That is when decisions were made to exclude noncoalition countries from reconstruction contracts and to limit the UN role. The UN was not particularly popular in Iraq, and greater international involvement might have added only marginally to the actual military manpower and economic assistance available to stabilize the country. Nevertheless, a more balanced partnership between the United Nations and the United States, on the model of Afghanistan, could well have accelerated the eventual return of power to representative Iraqis. It could also have assuaged opinion in neighboring countries if not in Iraq itself, and helped secure greater cooperation from regional governments in stemming the flow of men, money, arms, and moral support to an Iraqi resistance.

In executing its ambitious plans for Iraqi reconstruction, the United States failed to employ in a timely fashion the many techniques of nation-building that had been developed over the previous fifteen years in the course of several dozen U.S. and UN operations. U.S. officials disbanded the Iraqi army without having put in place a program for disarmament, demobilization, and reintegration. They banned former Baathists from government office without having established a process to adjudicate individual cases and rehabilitate those unassociated with major crimes. They failed to move expeditiously to recruit and train a new police force. They did not deploy international civilian police to monitor and mentor that new force as it emerged from training.

The decision to transfer responsibility for overseeing the civil aspects of nation-building—for developing the police, courts, administration, parties, press, civil society, elections, and the like—from the Department of State to the Department of Defense complicated the U.S. task. In Korea, Vietnam, the Dominican Republic, Grenada, Panama, Somalia, Haiti, Bosnia, Kosovo, and Afghanistan, U.S. diplomatic missions had operated alongside U.S. military forces to oversee such functions. Throughout the 1990s, as the frequency of such missions increased, the Department of State, USAID, and the Department of Justice had gradually strengthened their capabilities to perform such functions, although never to an entirely adequate degree. Shifting oversight of these civil programs to the Department of Defense, and doing so only weeks before the war commenced, imposed massive additional start-up costs on an already dauntingly difficult operation.

Perhaps the primary lesson be drawn from the early U.S. experience in Iraq is that the United States has not adequately absorbed the lessons of its abundant nation-building experience over the previous decade. Had the United States planned for the collapse of governance and the power vacuum that developed with the fall of Saddam, had it deployed forces adequate in number and quality to provide minimal public security during those early weeks, had it put in place a well-conceived program for disarmament, demobilization, and reintegration, had it conducted de-Baathification in a more discriminate manner, and had it involved the UN more centrally from the beginning in the selection of an interim Iraqi leadership, Iraq would still have been a stunningly difficult exercise in nation-building. Having failed to take those steps in a timely fashion, the United States now faces challenges of a very different order, in which a counterinsurgency struggle must be won before even the most competent nation-building efforts can have much effect.

Chapter Eleven

LESSONS LEARNED

As the 1980s ended and the Cold War wound down, the pace and scope of UN peacekeeping missions began to increase. Throughout the preceding four decades, East-West confrontation had foreclosed most opportunities for concerted international military action. The few UN military operations that were agreed on were limited in scale and scope. UN peacekeepers monitored cease-fires and patrolled disengagement zones on contested ground in places such as Cyprus, Palestine, and Kashmir. Their purpose was not to enforce resolution of these longstanding disputes but rather to discourage their escalation.

There were two notable exceptions to this limited model of United Nations military activity. One was the Korean War, in which the defense of South Korea was undertaken by a UN-mandated, U.S.-led multinational coalition. The second was the Congo, where the United Nations organized and led a robust peace enforcement and nation-building mission. These Cold War anomalies reemerged in the post–Cold War era as the two principal prototypes for international military action. The first was facilitated by an ill-conceived Soviet boycott of the UN Security Council, the second by an unusual conjunction of U.S., Soviet, and nonaligned interest in keeping Africa's decolonization on track.[1]

The first volume of this series dealt with the American experience with nation-building, defined therein as the use of armed force in the aftermath of a crisis to promote a transition to democracy. It examined eight instances in which the United States took the lead in such endeavors: Germany and

---

[1]The United Nations assisted in at least one other decolonization case during this period. In 1962, it deployed a small peacekeeping force to West New Guinea to facilitate the transfer of territory from Dutch to Indonesian control. The territory had been a Dutch colony since 1828. The United Nations established a temporary executive authority to administer the territory, maintain law and order, protect the rights of the population, and supervise the buildup of a local police force. In May 1963, the UN transferred full administrative control to Indonesia.

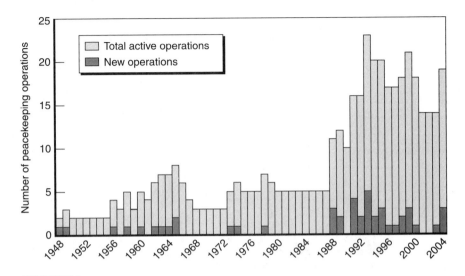

RAND *MG304-11.1*

Figure 11.1—Number of Peacekeeping Operations, 1948–2004

Japan after World War II; Somalia, Haiti, Bosnia, and Kosovo after the Cold War; and Afghanistan after 9/11. This volume deals with the United Nations' experience with comparable operations. It looks at eight instances in which the United Nations led multinational forces toward generally similar ends: the former Belgian Congo, Namibia, Cambodia, El Salvador, Mozambique, Eastern Slavonia, East Timor, and Sierra Leone. This volume, like the last, concludes with a review of ongoing nation-building efforts in Iraq, examining both the UN and the much more substantial U.S. roles there.

In both volumes, our intent has been to draw from these individual experiences lessons that are applicable to future operations and to look across all the cases for conclusions about the nation-building process as a whole. In comparing and contrasting the various cases, this volume draws on data assembled for the last, thereby allowing consideration of both the U.S. and the UN experiences and illuminating some important differences between the two.

INTO THE CAULDRON: THE UN IN THE FORMER BELGIAN CONGO

The Republic of the Congo failed almost from the moment of its birth. Belgium, among the most rapacious of colonial regimes, opposed the very notion of independence until, in an abrupt reversal at the last moment, it suddenly granted independence to the Congo on June 30, 1960. As a result, almost nothing had been done to prepare the Congolese for self-government. Within days of the Congo's independence, its army mutinied, the remaining white administrators fled, the administration and the economy collapsed, Belgian paratroops invaded, and the mineral-rich province of Katanga seceded. These developments cast a serious shadow over the prospects for the successful and peaceful completion of Africa's decolonization, at that point just gathering momentum. Responding to this threat, the United States, the Soviet Union, and the nonaligned states of the Third World made rare common cause. On July 14, 1960, acting with unusual speed, the Security Council passed the first of a series of resolutions authorizing the deployment of UN-led military forces to assist the Republic of the Congo in restoring order, and, eventually, in suppressing the Katangese rebellion.

Among UN-led military operations, the Congo mission was long unmatched in size, scope, and ferocity of combat. In the following four decades, only one operation was larger, and none was as lethal. The Congo remains the only operation in which UN-led forces engaged in sustained combat, mounted a series of set-piece offensives, or employed fixed-wing attack aircraft. UN-led units sustained more combat deaths in the Congo (135) than in all subsequent UN operations combined. To that number must be added the loss of Secretary-General Dag Hammarskjöld, whose plane went down flying to a rendezvous with the Katangan President Moise Tshombe in 1961.

Given the unprecedented nature of its mission and the consequent lack of prior experience, existing doctrine, designated staff, or administrative structure to underpin the operation, the United Nations performed remarkably well in the Congo. Significant forces began to arrive within days of the Security Council's authorization, a performance matched in few subsequent UN peacekeeping missions. The United Nations was quickly able to secure the removal of Belgian forces. Over the next three years, UN troops forced the removal of foreign mercenaries and suppressed the Katangan succession, while civil elements of the mission provided a wide range of humanitarian, economic, and civil assistance to the new Congolese regime. Measured against the bottom-line requirements of the international community—that decolonization proceed, colonial and mercenary troops depart, and the Congo remain intact—the United Nations was largely successful. Democracy did not feature heavily in the various Congo resolutions passed by the UN Security Council; there was, in any case, no agreement during the Cold War on the definition of that term. The Congo never became a functioning democracy, but large-scale civil conflict was averted for more than a decade following the United Nations' departure, and the country more or less held together for another three decades, albeit under a corrupt and incompetent dictatorship. Of at least equal importance to the Security Council sponsors of the Congo intervention, the principle of territorial integrity was preserved, and decolonization was able to proceed throughout the rest of Africa on that basis.

UN achievements in the Congo came at considerable cost in men lost, money spent, and controversy raised. For some people, the United Nations' apparent complicity in the apprehension and later execution of Prime Minister Patrice Lumumba overshadowed its considerable accomplishments. As a result of these costs and controversies, neither the United Nations' leadership nor its member nations were eager to repeat the experience. For the next 25 years, the United Nations restricted its military interventions to interpositional peacekeeping, policing cease-fires, and patrolling disengagement zones in circumstances where all parties invited its presence and armed force was to be used by UN troops only in self-defense.

HEALING COLD WAR WOUNDS

The end of the Cold War presented the United Nations with new opportunities and new challenges. For 40 years, regional disputes and proxy wars had been the currency of East-West competition. Alert to the danger of uncontrolled escalation, the two superpowers were occasionally able to agree on tactical cease-fires, which they were content to have the United Nations observe. They remained ever wary, however, of allowing any problem to be definitively solved to the other's advantage. In consequence, few major international disputes were definitively resolved, and many conflicts ground on for decades. By the end of the 1980s, however, the United States and the Soviet Union had begun to disengage from proxy wars in Latin America, Africa, and Asia and were finally prepared to work together in pressing former clients to resolve their outstanding differences. Again, the United Nations was asked to oversee implementation of the resultant, but now much more definitive, accords.

The early post–Cold War UN-led operations in Namibia, Cambodia, El Salvador, and Mozambique followed similar patterns. The international community, with U.S. and Soviet backing, first brokered a peace accord. The Security Council then dispatched a UN peacekeeping force to oversee its implementation. In each case, the responsibilities of the UN mission included initiating an expeditious process of disarmament, demobilization and reintegration; encouraging political reconciliation; holding democratic elections; and overseeing the inauguration of a new national government. Operations in each of these countries were greatly facilitated by war-weary populations, Great Power support, and neighboring-country cooperation. The United Nations became adept at overseeing the disarmament and demobilization of willing parties. The reintegration of former combatants was everywhere more problematic, for nowhere did the international community provide the necessary resources. Economic growth accelerated in most cases, largely as a result of the cessation of fighting. Peace, growth, and democracy were often accompanied by an increase in common crime, as old repressive security services were dismantled, and demobilized former combatants were left without a livelihood.

All four of these operations culminated in reasonably free and fair elections. All four resulted in a sustained periods of civil peace which endured after the UN withdrawal. Cambodia had the least successful democratic transformation and experienced the greatest renewal of civil strife, although at nothing like the level that preceded the UN intervention. The United Nations' lesser success in Cambodia can be attributed to the deeper trauma that society had experienced during the decades of genocidal conflict; the unwillingness of the Khmer Rouge and the ruling party, the Cambodian People's Party, to live up to their commitments; the absence of nearby democratic role models; the more limited international inputs in the form of troops, money and time; and the briefness of the UN intervention, less than two years.

Cambodia was also the first instance in which the United Nations became responsible for actually governing a state in transition from conflict to peace and democracy. The United Nations was ill-prepared to assume such a role. In addition, although the government of Cambodia had agreed to UN administrative oversight as part of the peace accord, it was unwilling to cede effective authority. As a result, UN control over Cambodia's civil administration was largely nominal.

Despite the substantial success of these early post-Cold War operations, a number of weaknesses in the United Nation's performance emerged that would cripple later missions launched in more difficult circumstances. Deficiencies included the slow arrival of military units, the even slower deployment of police and civil administrators, the uneven quality of military components, the even greater unevenness of police and civil administrators, the United Nations' dependence on voluntary funding to pay for mission-essential functions such as the reintegration of combatants and capacity building in local administrations, the frequent mismatches between ambitious mandates and modest means, and the premature withdrawal of missions, often following immediately on the successful conclusion of a first democratic election. The latter was a particular problem in Cambodia, where UN troops left less than two years after their arrival, well before democratic processes had time to take root.

COPING WITH FAILED STATES

In the early 1990s, the United Nations enjoyed a series of successes. This winning streak and a consequent optimism about the task of nation-building came to an abrupt end in Somalia and were further diminished by events in the former Yugoslavia. In both those instances, UN-led peacekeeping forces were inserted into societies where there was no peace to keep. In both cases, UN forces eventually had to be replaced by larger, more robust U.S.-led peace enforcement missions.

Although the Cold War divided some societies, it was the glue that held others together. Former East-West battlegrounds—Namibia, Cambodia, El Salvador, and Mozambique—were able, with UN assistance, to emerge as viable nation-states. But other divided societies, such as Somalia, Yugoslavia, and Afghanistan—which had been held together by one superpower or the other, and sometimes by both—began to disintegrate as external supports and pressures were removed. Not surprising, the United Nations had a harder time holding together collapsing states than brokering reconciliation in coalescing ones.

The original UN mission in Somalia was undermanned and overmatched by warring Somali clan militias. The U.S.-led multinational force that replaced it was built on a core of 20,000 American soldiers and marines. This force was quickly able to overawe local resistance and secure the delivery of famine relief supplies, its principal mission. Washington then chose to withdraw all but 2,000 U.S. troops. The United States passed overall responsibility back to the United Nations while also supporting a radical expansion of that organization's mandate. The previous UN and U.S. forces had confined their mission to securing humanitarian relief activities. Even as the United States withdrew 90 percent of its combat forces and saw them replaced by a smaller number of less-well-equipped UN troops, it joined in extending the mission of those remaining forces to the introduction of grass-roots democracy, a process which would put the United Nations at cross-purposes with every warlord in the country. The result was a resurgence of violence to levels that residual U.S. and UN troops proved unable to handle.

As the first volume of this series makes clear, it was largely American errors of judgment that led to the collapse of the Somalia operation. The UN leadership certainly shares responsibility for the gross disparity between its mission and its means. But it was the United States that refused to put its remaining troops under UN command, it was the United States that took up the hunt for General Mohamed Farah Aideed, it was the United States that failed to arrange backup or rescue for its lightly armed Rangers, and it was the United States that abandoned the Somali mission after losing 18 men. By contrast, it was a UN-led unit that helped rescue the surviving American Rangers, and it was UN-led troops who remained in Somalia for more than a year after the U.S. departure, providing both military and political cover for America's graceless exit.

Insuperable difficulties also arose in the former Yugoslavia, where UN peacekeepers were again deployed into an ongoing civil war without the mandate, the influence, or the firepower needed to end the fighting. UN deficiencies contributed to the failure of its efforts in Bosnia as they had in Somalia. But at least equal responsibility lies with its principal member governments: with Russia, for its stubborn partisanship on behalf of Serbia; with the United States, for its refusal to commit American forces or to support the peacemaking initiatives of those governments that had; and with Britain and France, the principal troop contributors, for failing to enforce the mandate they had accepted to protect the innocent civilians entrusted to their care.

Nevertheless, UN forces, not NATO forces, remained in Bosnia at war's end to oversee initial implementation of the Dayton peace accords and presided over the final cease-fire, the demarcation of boundaries, the withdrawal of troops, and the establishment of liaison among former combatants. The last shot of the war was fired on October 11, 1995. Only ten weeks later, on December 21, the lead elements of a 60,000-man NATO force took over from a departing UN force one-third its size.

The failure of UN missions in both Somalia and Bosnia, when contrasted with the more robust U.S.-led multinational efforts that succeeded them, led to a general conclusion that, although the United Nations might be up to peacekeeping, peace enforcement was beyond the organization's capacity. This conclusion, not uncongenial to the UN's own leadership, is belied by that organization's performance in the Congo. Its subsequent conduct of a small, but highly successful, peace enforcement mission in Eastern Slavonia in 1996–1998 and another in East Timor beginning in 1999 suggests that the UN is perfectly capable of executing a robust peace enforcement mandate in circumstances where the scale is modest, the force includes a core of capable First World troops, and the venture has strong international backing.

Eastern Slavonia was the last Serb-held area of Croatia at the end of the conflict between these two former Yugoslav Republics. Here, the United Nations once again became responsible for governing a territory in transition, in this case from Serb to Croat control. The operation was generously manned, well led, abundantly resourced, and strongly supported by the major powers, whose influence assured the cooperation of neighboring states. Not surprisingly, given these advantages, the UN peace enforcement mission in Eastern Slavonia was highly successful.

At decade's end, new nation-building responsibilities in Kosovo were divided between NATO, which took the lead on security, and the United Nations, which provided the interim administration. The process of disarmament, demobilization, and reintegration in Kosovo was smoothly handled by the two organizations in concert, aided by a joint decision to enlist many of the former combatants into a civil reconstruction corps. Successful local and then general elections were held. Unfortunately, East-West divisions and differences among NATO allies over Kosovo's final status have made reconciliation between ethnic Serb and Albanian communities more difficult, and the UN administration was excessively prolonged.

U.S.-led multinational missions in Somalia and Bosnia contrasted positively with the UN missions that preceded them, primarily because they were better resourced and employed those larger capabilities in a more determined way. Had the United States been willing to provide a military commander and 20,000 American troops to the UN-led operations in Somalia or Bosnia, UN efforts would likely have fared better, thereby obviating the need for subsequent multinational interventions.

All multinational coalitions are coalitions of the willing. In the case of UN-led operations, such coalitions include both the troop contributors and the members of the UN Security Council that authorize the mission and provide for its funding. When the Security Council is deeply divided, as it was on the Balkans throughout the 1990s, UN coalitions are correspondingly weak and often ineffective. Since 1989, serious divisions within the UN Security Council, particularly among its permanent members, have been the exception rather than the rule. Kosovo and Iraq are the only cases where the United States felt compelled to proceed with an operation without explicit UN support. In the latter case, West-West disagreements made NATO equally unavailable and forced the United States to rely on an even more limited and much less satisfactory coalition, one too small to adequately enhance either the power or the legitimacy of the effort. In sum, NATO has proved to be an effective alternative to the UN in the relatively narrow range of post–Cold War circumstances where there was strong East-West disagreement and strong West-West agreement.

Even as most of the Cold War's legacies were being cleared away, newly failed or failing states continued to emerge and to require international attention. In 1995, the United Nations took over a U.S.-led peace enforcement operation in Haiti and ran it for an additional three years. As in Cambodia, the United Nations withdrew from Haiti before the democratic reforms it was trying to introduce could take root. Despite the ultimate failure of this effort and the consequent need for a second intervention a decade later, the 1995–1998 UN operation in Haiti was well managed, adequately resourced, and deemed quite successful at the time. Disarmament and demobilization were handled expeditiously, reintegration went as well as might be expected in a society with very high rates of unemployment, and a new, initially uncorrupted police force was created. The apparent success of the Haiti operation gave both the United States and the United Nations a welcome boost to their rather tarnished reputations for competent nation-building.

NATION-BUILDING IN THE NEW DECADE

In the closing months of 1999, the United Nations found itself charged with governing both Kosovo and East Timor. The latter operation proved an ideal showcase for UN capabilities. Like Eastern Slavonia, East Timor was small in both territory and population; international resources, in terms of military manpower and economic assistance, were unusually abundant. Major-power influence secured neighboring-state cooperation. A multinational coalition, in this case led by Australia, initially secured the territory and then quickly turned the operation over to UN management. Remaining combatants were disarmed, new security forces established, a local administration recreated, elections held, and a democratically elected government inaugurated within the first two years.

Even this showcase operation exhibited certain chronic UN deficiencies. International police and civil administrators were slow to arrive and of variable quality. Once ensconced, UN administrators were somewhat slow to turn power back to local authorities. These were minor blemishes, however, on a generally successful operation.

In less-benign circumstances, such weaknesses continued to threaten the success of UN operations. In Sierra Leone, inadequate UN forces were inserted under unduly optimistic assumptions, encountered early reverses, and eventually suffered the ultimate humiliation of being captured and held hostage in large numbers. Poised on the verge of collapse, the Sierra Leone operation was rescued by the United Kingdom and turned around—thanks in large measure to extraordinary personal efforts by the UN Secretary-General. British forces arrived, extricated UN hostages, intimidated insurgent forces, and began to train a more competent local military. The United States threw its logistic and diplomatic weight behind the operation. The regime in neighboring Liberia, highly complicit in Sierra Leone's civil war, was displaced. Additional manpower and economic resources were secured. So bolstered, the United Nations was able to oversee a process of disarmament and demobilization and hold reasonably free elections.

In recent years, even as the United Nations' reputation for competent nation-building has begun to recover from earlier setbacks in Somalia and Bosnia, the United States has failed to sustain the positive record set in its own Balkan operations. Whereas the United Nations has learned from its failures, the United States has failed to learn from its successes. The U.S. administration that took office in January 2001 initially regarded nation-building as an unsuitable activity for American forces. But by year's end, the United States had overthrown the Taliban regime in Afghanistan and was faced with the need to install and support its successor. Washington reluctantly agreed to support the deployment of an international peacekeeping mission to help secure the capital, Kabul, but rejected pleas from the new Afghan government and urgings from the United Nations that peacekeepers also be deployed to other major cities. Additionally, Washington initially took the position that the mission of U.S. forces was exclusively one of counterterrorism, and that they were not to engage in peacekeeping or public security activities.

In Iraq 18 months later, U.S. planners failed to anticipate the collapse of public order that accompanied the fall of the Saddam regime. U.S. forces were consequently unprepared to fill the security vacuum that emerged and have since proved unable to displace the criminal and extremist elements that filled it instead. In neither Afghanistan nor Iraq did the United States deploy forces in numbers adequate to establish a secure environment, long considered an essential prerequisite for successful nation-building.

Over time, the U.S. administration has acted to remedy these early omissions, substantially reinforcing the U.S. and international troop presence in both Afghanistan and Iraq and expanding the missions of those forces to encompass more of the public security mission.

Afghanistan and Iraq are larger countries with more challenging environments than most other recent cases of UN and U.S. nation-building. Nevertheless, the techniques developed in the earlier operations—to establish a secure environment; disarm, demobilize and reintegrate former combatants; reform and build new security services; vet members of the former regime; set up interim administrations; and launch political and economic reforms—had direct application to Afghanistan and Iraq and, if applied in a timely fashion, could have helped the United States deal more effectively with the challenges that emerged.

The United Nations has not been given a security role in either Afghanistan or Iraq. That organization certainly would not be in a position to conduct military operations in the violent Iraqi environment, but it would have offered a viable and perhaps even superior alternative to NATO in organizing the international peacekeeping force in Afghanistan. In both countries, the United Nations has been charged with overseeing the transition to representative government, and in both countries the UN accomplishments in this regard have been among the few bright spots in otherwise still very problematic operations.

Chapter Twelve

INPUTS AND OUTCOMES

Although each nation-building mission takes place in a unique environment, the objectives, instruments and techniques remain largely the same from one operation to the next. Thus it is possible to compare, across the various cases, the level of international inputs (as measured in men, money, and time) and of outcomes (as measured in security, economic growth, and democratization). While the analysis inevitably suffers from the deficiencies of the data, and while the measures available provide at best crude approximations of the level of effort and results, this methodology does permit more than merely impressionistic or anecdotal comparisons among case studies.

Nation-building outcomes naturally result from much more than the quantity of inputs. Success depends on the wisdom with which such resources are employed and on the susceptibility of the society in question to the changes being fostered. Some strategies work better than others, and some societies are more ready to change. Nevertheless, success also depends in some measure on the quantity of international military and police manpower and economic assistance committed and on the time over which those commitments continue.

The first volume of this study compared inputs and outputs for seven U.S.-led nation-building missions—Germany, Japan, Somalia, Haiti, Bosnia, Kosovo, and Afghanistan. This volume looks at data from eight UN missions and the seven U.S. missions from the previous volume, in addition to Iraq. This permits an evaluation of data from sixteen case studies.

The measures of input are

- military presence

- international police presence

- duration of mission

- timing of elections

- economic assistance.

The measures of outcome are

- military casualties (a negative measure)

- refugee returns

- growth in per capita GDP

- a qualitative measure of sustained peace

- a qualitative assessment of whether or not a country's government became and has remained democratic.

SECURITY

Military Presence

Military force levels for UN missions have ranged from nearly 20,000 UN troops deployed in the Congo and 16,000 in Cambodia, to just over 4,000 in Namibia. Figures 12.1 and 12.2 shows total peak force levels and force levels per thousand local inhabitants. Force-to-population ratios varied widely. Large numbers of UN military forces relative to population were deployed to Eastern Slavonia and East Timor. Force levels in Congo, Namibia, El Salvador, Mozambique, Cambodia, and Sierra Leone were proportionally much smaller. In half the cases, UN peak force levels were at two or fewer soldiers per thousand inhabitants. This was significantly less than the level the United Nations deployed in Eastern Slavonia, which was 34 soldiers per thousand inhabitants. UN missions have nor-

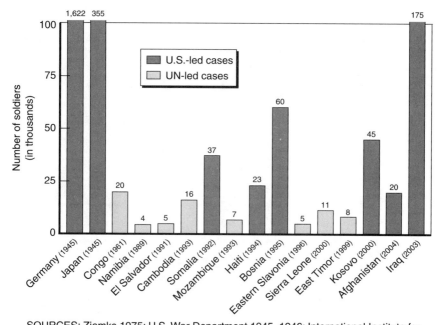

SOURCES: Ziemke 1975; U.S. War Department 1945, 1946; International Institute for Strategic Studies, var.; United Nations Department of Peacekeeping Operations 2004; Jane's Information Group 2004; Ramsbotham et al. 1999; United Nations Department of Public Information, var.

RAND *MG304-12.1*

Figure 12.1—Peak Military Presence

mally fielded much smaller contingents than U.S.-led operations, both in absolute numbers and in relation to the local population. The largest UN mission studied, the Congo, had fewer troops (20,000) than the smallest U.S. mission studied, Haiti (which had 23,000). Of the five smallest operations in proportion to population, four were UN missions: Mozambique, Cambodia, El Salvador, and Congo. Of the five largest operations in proportion to population, only two were UN missions: Eastern Slavonia and East Timor, both very small societies where a few UN troops went a long way.

Duration

UN forces have tended to remain in post-conflict countries for shorter periods of time than have U.S. forces, as illustrated in Figure 12.3. In the early 1990s, both U.S.- and UN-led operations were usually terminated rather quickly, often immediately following the completion of an initial democratic election and the inauguration of a new government. In this period,

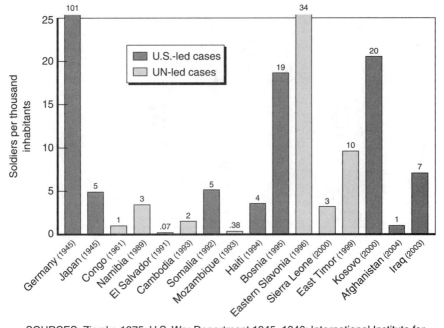

SOURCES: Ziemke 1975; U.S. War Department 1945, 1946; International Institute for Strategic Studies, var.; United Nations Department of Peacekeeping Operations 2004; Jane's Information Group 2004; Ramsbotham et al. 1999; United Nations Department of Public Information, var.; U.S. Census Bureau 2004.

RAND MG304-12.2

Figure 12.2—Peak Military Presence Per Capita

the United States and the United Nations tended to define their objectives rather narrowly, focusing on exit strategies and departure deadlines. As experience with nation-building grew, however, both the United Nations and the United States came to recognize that reconciliation and democratization could require more than a single election. By the end of the decade, both UN and U.S.-led operations became more extended, and peacekeeping forces were drawn down more slowly rather than exiting en masse following the first national election.

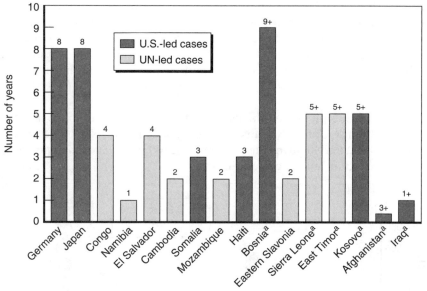

^aOngoing operation

SOURCES: Ziemke 1975; U.S. War Department 1945, 1946; Institute for Strategic Studies, var.; United Nations Department of Peacekeeping Operations 2004; Jane's Information Group 2004; Ramsbotham et al. 1999; United Nations Department of Public Information, var.; U.S. Census Bureau 2004.

RAND *MG304-12.3*

Figure 12.3—Duration of Operations

Civilian Police

International civilian police are an increasingly important component of most UN nation-building operations, in some cases representing 10 percent or more of the overall force. The United Nations has deployed international police to help UN military forces restore security, build and train local police forces, and provide security for local inhabitants. In El Salvador, 315 UN civilian police observers were deployed at the peak of UN activities. These police lacked arrest authority, were unarmed, and depended on the Salvadoran police to make arrests. In contrast, the United Nations deployed over 1,000 civilian police to East Timor and nearly 5,000 to Kosovo; all possessed arrest authority and were required to carry sidearms. As for military presence, the UN operations in the smaller societies of Eastern Slavonia, East Timor, and Namibia had the largest civilian police contingents in proportion to the local populations. Although UN civilian police forces usually left with the troops, in El Salvador, Haiti, and Eastern Slavonia they stayed a year or more after the military component withdrew.

The United States pioneered the use of armed international police in Haiti but looked to the United Nations to supply police for the NATO-led operations in Bosnia and Kosovo. The United States did not include civil police in its last two nation-building operations.

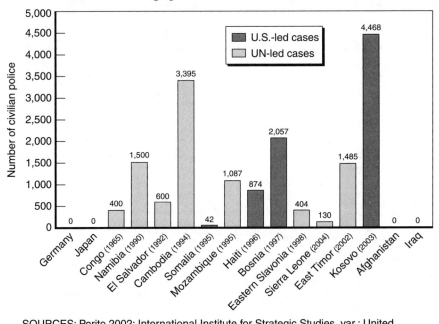

SOURCES: Perito 2002; International Institute for Strategic Studies, var.; United Nations Department of Peacekeeping Operations 2004; Jane's Information Group 2004; Ramsbotham 1999; United Nations Department of Public Information, var.; Oakley et al. 1998.

RAND MG304-12.4

Figure 12.4—Peak Civilian Police Presence

Figures 12.4 and 12.5 illustrate total peak civilian police levels and civilian police levels per capita, and Figure 12.6 shows the military-to-police ratio. UN-led operations have possessed much higher ratios of police to military soldiers. The absence of any international civil police in Afghanistan and Iraq has increased the burden on U.S. and coalition military forces to handle public security and police training functions there.

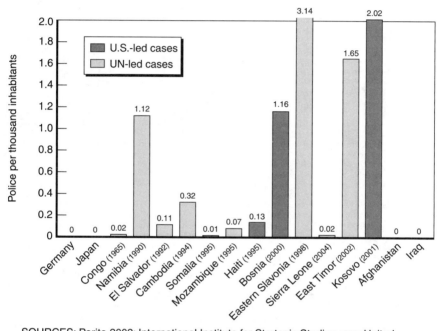

SOURCES: Perito 2002; International Institute for Strategic Studies, var.; United Nations Department of Peacekeeping Operations 2004; Jane's Information Group 2004; Ramsbotham 1999; United Nations Department of Public Information, var.; Oakley et al. 1998; U.S. Census Bureau 2004.

RAND *MG304-12.5*

Figure 12.5—Peak Civilian Police Presence Per Capita

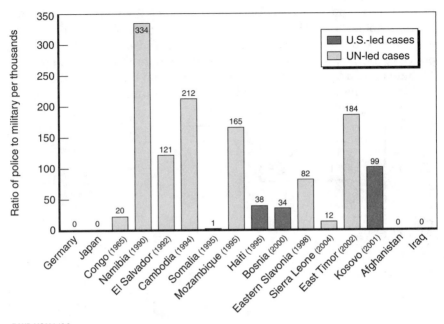

RAND *MG304-12.6*

Figure 12.6—Police-to-Military Ratio

Combat-Related Deaths

Casualties suffered are a good measure of difficulties being encountered. Missions with high casualty levels have been among the least successful. Among UN cases, the Congo had the highest number of casualties, reflecting the peace enforcement nature of the operation. After the Congo, the Cambodian operation, lightly manned as a proportion of the population, had the highest casualty level, followed by Sierra Leone. There were fewer than five combatant deaths in any of the remaining operations. In East Timor, Eastern Slavonia, and Namibia, the United Nations possessed relatively large military forces and experienced few combat deaths.

In Mozambique and El Salvador, the United Nations possessed relatively small military forces but experienced few combat deaths. In both cases, opposing sides had been involved in long, bloody, exhausting civil wars, were committed to peace, and were supported in this commitment by active major and regional power involvement during and after the peace settlement.

Following the loss of 18 U.S. soldiers in Somalia in 1993, the United States took great precautions throughout the rest of the decade to avoid casual-

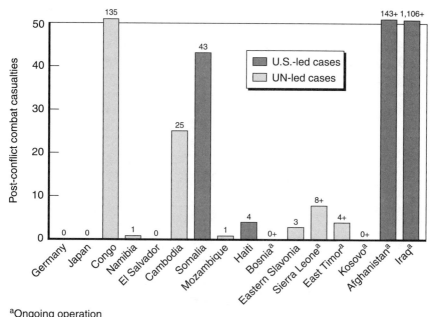

^aOngoing operation

SOURCES: U.S. Department of Defense 2004; United Nations Department of Peacekeeping Operations 2004.

NOTE: Since we could find no information on hostile casualties for U.S. forces in Japan, the U.S. sector of Germany, Kosovo, or Bosnia, we assume there were no casualties. The Iraq data are from May 1, 2003, to November 27, 2004. The Afghanistan data are from December 1, 2001, to November 27, 2004. Iraq and Afghanistan data include both hostile and nonhostile casualties.

RAND MG304-12.7

Figure 12.7—"Post-Conflict" Combat Deaths

ties. The United Nations was slightly less risk averse: Through the end of the 1990s, UN casualty rates were consequently a little higher than U.S. rates. In the aftermath of the September 11 terrorist attacks, American sensitivity to casualties diminished. At the same time, the United States abandoned its strategy of deploying overwhelming force at the outset of nation-building operations. Significantly lower force-to-population ratios in Afghanistan and Iraq than in Bosnia or Kosovo have been accompanied by much higher casualty levels. There have been more combat deaths among U.S. forces in Afghanistan than in all American nation-building operations studied going back to 1945, and the casualty levels in Iraq as of September, 2004 are almost ten times higher than the number for Afghanistan.

Enduring Peace

Peace is the most essential product of nation building. Without peace, neither economic growth nor democratization is possible. With peace, some level of economic growth becomes almost inevitable and democratization at least possible. As Table 12.1 illustrates, among the sixteen cases studied in this and the preceding volume, eleven remain at peace today, five do not. Of the eight UN-led cases, seven are at peace. Of the eight U.S.-led cases, four are at peace, four are not—or not yet. These categorizations are necessarily provisional, particularly for the ongoing operations in Afghanistan and Iraq. Peace in Bosnia, Kosovo, East Timor, and Sierra Leone has been sustained, but so far only with the ongoing presence of international peacekeepers.[1]

Table 12.1
Sustained Peace

Country	At Peace in 2004
Germany	Yes
Japan	Yes
Congo	No
Namibia	Yes
El Salvador	Yes
Cambodia	Yes
Somalia	No
Mozambique	Yes
Haiti	No
Bosnia	Yes
Eastern Slavonia	Yes
Sierra Leone	Yes
East Timor	Yes
Kosovo	Yes
Afghanistan	No
Iraq	No

HUMANITARIAN

Return of Refugees and Internally Displaced Persons

All conflicts generate refugees and displace people within the country. A primary goal of every nation-building operation has been the return of those refugees and internally displaced persons. The number of refugees has varied widely. Among UN cases, the largest numbers of refugees per thou-

---

[1] To code the cases, we used information from the Center for International Development and Conflict Management (CIDCM), *State Failure: Internal Wars and Failures of Governance, 1955–2002*, data set, University of Maryland, CIDCM, www.cidcm.umd, accessed November 22, 2004.

sand inhabitants were in East Timor and Eastern Slavonia. In East Timor, the violence that followed the September 1999 referendum displaced close to 80 percent of the territory's population. Approximately 265,000 East Timorese became refugees; 500,000 escaped to the interior of the island. Most UN personnel were temporarily evacuated to Darwin, Australia. In Eastern Slavonia, most of the Croatian population fled after hostilities broke out in 1991. A reverse flow of roughly 42,000 Serbs from Bosnia and other parts of Croatia had taken refuge in Eastern Slavonia by January 1996 when the UN mission began. Many of them arrived in the summer and fall of 1995, fleeing from Croatian and Bosnian troops, shortly before the UN operation commenced. Mozambique and Sierra Leone also reported high numbers of refugees relative to their total populations.

In most cases, the United Nations High Commissioner for Refugees (UN-HCR) and NGOs were successful in overseeing the timely return of refugees. In Namibia, Mozambique, and East Timor, most refugees had returned home four years after the operation began. In Eastern Slavonia, domestic conflicts stranded a number of refugees. In Sierra Leone, the uncertain se-

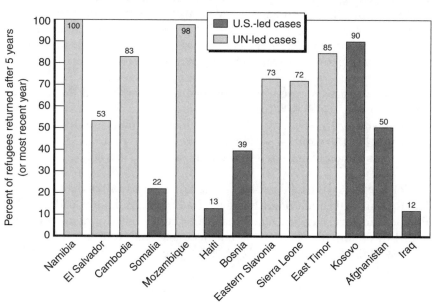

SOURCES: U.S. State Department 1947; United Nations High Commissioner for Refugees, var.; *Statistical Yearbook of Yugoslavia* 1997; U. S. Committee for Refugees, var.

RAND *MG304-12.8*

Figure 12.8—Percentage of Refugee Returns After Five Years

curity situation resulted in an increase in refugees during the first, largely unsuccessful year of the UN operation. Only in the third and fourth years of the operation did a sizable number of refugees feel comfortable returning home.

A low level of refugee return is often a sign of continued conflict in the society in question (e.g., Somalia, Iraq, and Afghanistan) but sometimes is a result of the significantly better living conditions in the places of refuge (e.g., for Salvadoran and Haitian refugees in the United States).

DEMOCRATIZATION

Timing of Elections

The establishment of a democratic political system is a core objective of most nation-building operations. Central to this process has been the planning and conduct of democratic elections, illustrated in Figure 12.9. Although logic might suggest that local elections should precede national ones, this seldom occurs. In Cambodia, the first local elections were held ten years after the intervention; in Eastern Slavonia they were held just 15 months after the operation began. National elections preceded or were held at the same time as local elections in every UN-led operation except Eastern Slavonia.

The U.S.-led cases showed more divergence. In Japan and Bosnia, local elections were held well after national elections. In Haiti, they were held simultaneously. In Germany and Kosovo, local elections preceded national polls by at least 18 months. National elections occurred in the fall of 2004 in Afghanistan and are expected to occur in early 2005 in Iraq.

Initial elections were held to be free and fair in nearly all of the cases studied. In Cambodia and Congo, however, free elections did not lead to stable, democratic governments. Elections are a prerequisite for democracy, but speed in organizing elections is not necessarily an indicator of ultimate success. Haiti, for instance, had one of the quickest of elections but the least enduring success.

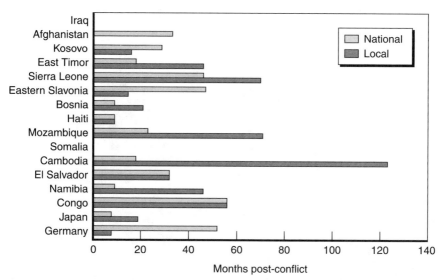

Figure 12.9—Timing of Local and National Elections

Level of Democratization

In Table 12.2, we categorize each of the countries studied as democratic or not democratic. To determine which category to apply, we used the codings from Freedom House and the Polity Project at the University of Maryland. Among the U.S.-led cases, Germany and Japan are clearly democratic; Bosnia and Kosovo are democratic but still under varying degrees of international administration; Somalia and Haiti are not democratic; Afghanistan has held a presidential election but not parlimentary elections; and Iraq's first free election is expected in 2005 under exceptionally difficult conditions. Among the UN-led cases all but the Congo and Cambodia remain democratic—some, of course, more than others.

Table 12.2
Democratic Development

Country	Democracy in 2004	Polity IV (0 low, 10 high)	Freedom House (0 low, 10 high)[a]
Germany	Yes	10.0	10.0
Japan	Yes	10.0	10.0
Congo	No	0.0	2.9
Namibia	Yes	6.0	8.6
El Salvador	Yes	7.0	8.6
Cambodia	No	3.0	2.9
Somalia	No	–	2.9
Mozambique	Yes	6.0	7.1
Haiti	No	1.0	2.9
Bosnia	Yes	–	5.7
Eastern Slavonia[b]	Yes	7.0	8.6
Sierra Leone	Yes	5.0	5.7
East Timor	Yes	6.0	7.1
Kosovo	Yes	–	–
Afghanistan	No	–	2.9
Iraq	No	0.0	1.4

SOURCES: Monty G. Marshall and Keith Jaggers, *Polity IV Project: Political Regime Characteristics and Transitions, 1800–2002,* Dataset Users' Manual, College Park, MD: Center for International Development and Conflict Management, September 2002; Freedom House, *Freedom in the World Country Ratings, 1972 Through 2003,* New York: Freedom House, 2003.
[a] The Freedom House ratings have been converted from a seven-point to a ten-point scale.
[b] Since neither Polity IV nor Freedom House had data for Eastern Slavonia, we used Croatia as a proxy.

ECONOMIC RECONSTRUCTION

Per Capita External Assistance

Figure 12.10 employs per capita external assistance in 2000 dollars in the first two years of the operation to make comparisons across operations. UN-led operations tended to be less well supported with international economic assistance than American operations in both absolute and in proportional terms. This reflects the greater access of the United States to donor assistance funds, both its own and those of the international financial institutions to which it belongs. External assistance on a per capita basis varied greatly among UN cases. Eastern Slavonia received the most money on a per capita basis—more than 10 times that given to Cambodia, Sierra Leone, and Congo. Because of its proximity to Europe and the desire to get the operation "right" after the previous five years of failure in the Balkans, donors, especially the European states, were generous. Since the region

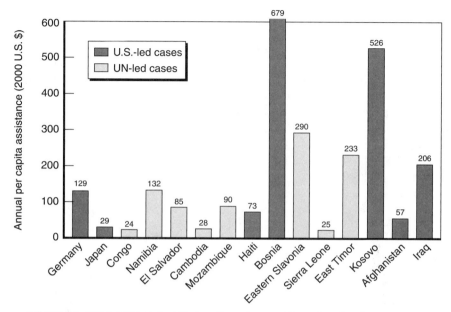

SOURCES: Killick 1997; United Nations Department of Peacekeeping Operations, var.; World Bank 1999a, 2004b; U.S. Government Accountability Office 2004a, 2004b; U.S. Census Bureau 2004.

RAND *MG304-12.10*

Figure 12.10—Average Annual Per Capita Assistance over First Two Years

also has a small population (an estimated 105,000 people in 1998), funds went much further on a per capita basis than in those countries with larger populations. East Timor also received relatively high levels of per capita assistance for its comparatively small population (an estimated 967,000 in 1999).

In general, small societies tended to receive more assistance on a per capita basis than larger ones, with Bosnia, Eastern Slavonia, East Timor, and Kosovo leading this group. On the other hand, Iraq, the largest of the modern nation-building missions, has also been particularly well funded.

As noted, the United States, which has control over its own resources, a powerful voice in the World Bank and regional development banks, and considerable influence with other bilateral donors, has much more control over the level of assistance funding than does the United Nations. In effect, the United States can always ensure that it has the level of funding it deems necessary. The United Nations seldom can. Many UN operations are consequently poorly supported with economic assistance.

Economic Growth

War severely disrupts the economies not just of states in conflict but also of their neighbors. In all the cases studied, conflict resulted in a fall in output and living standards in the societies concerned. As Figure 12.11 shows, peace brought economic growth in all but two.[2] In Bosnia, East Timor, and Kosovo, high levels of external economic assistance resulted in rapid economic recovery. Persistent violence and limited domestic capacity for good governance resulted in slower rates of growth in Sierra Leone. In Mozambique and Congo, these same factors resulted in continued falls in per capita GDP. El Salvador and Cambodia enjoyed strong growth despite less generous inflows of aid.

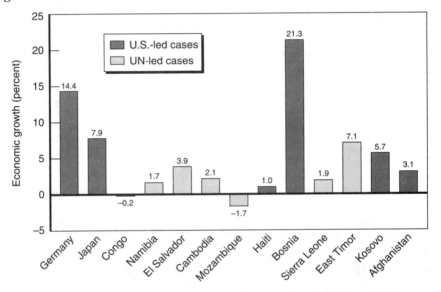

SOURCES: Mitchell 1992, 1998; International Monetary Fund 2002; World Bank 1996b, 1999a, 2004b; *Asian Development Bank Outlook* 2003.

RAND *MG304-12.11*

Figure 12.11—Average Annual Growth in Per Capita GDP over First Five Years

---

[2] We did not include data for Iraq because there were no reliable statistics for economic growth at the time of publication.

The presence of international peacekeepers and their success in suppressing renewed conflict, rather than the levels of economic assistance, seems to be the key determinant of economic growth. As the case of Iraq illustrates anew, security is a prerequisite for growth, and money is no substitute for adequate manpower in providing it. Indeed security without economic assistance is much more likely to spur economic growth than is economic assistance without security. This suggests that initial international investment should be preferentially directed to filling security needs, to include reorganizing and strengthening the local security sector, such as police, military, courts, and prisons.

Chapter Thirteen

THE U.S. AND UN WAYS OF NATION-BUILDING

Over the years, the United States and the United Nations have developed distinctive styles of nation-building derived from their very different natures and capabilities. The United Nations is an international organization entirely dependent on its members for the wherewithal to conduct nation-building. The United States is the world's only superpower, commanding abundant resources of its own and access to those of many other nations and institutions.

UN operations have almost always been undermanned and under resourced, as Figure 13.1 illustrates. This is not because UN managers believe smaller is better, although some do, but because member states are rarely willing to commit the manpower or the money any prudent military commander would desire. As a result, small, weak UN forces are routinely deployed into what they hope, on the basis of best-case assumptions, will prove to be post-conflict situations. Where such assumptions prove ill founded, UN forces have had to be reinforced, withdrawn, or, in extreme cases, rescued.

Throughout the 1990s, the United States adopted the opposite approach to sizing its nation-building deployments, basing its plans on worst-case assumptions and relying on overwhelming force to quickly establish a stable environment and deter resistance from forming. In Somalia, Haiti, Bosnia, and Kosovo, U.S.-led coalitions intervened in numbers and with capabilities that discouraged even the thought of resistance. In Somalia, this American force was drawn down too quickly. The resultant casualties reinforced the American determination to establish and retain a substantial overmatch in any future nation-building operation.

In the aftermath of the September 2001 terrorist attacks, American tolerance of military casualties significantly increased. In sizing its stabilization

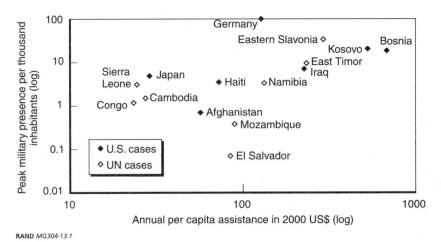

RAND *MG304-13.1*

Figure 13.1—Military Presence and Financial Assistance

operations in Afghanistan and Iraq, the new American leadership abandoned the strategy of overwhelming preponderance (sometimes labeled the Powell doctrine after former Chairman of the Joint Chiefs of Staff General Colin Powell) in favor of the "small footprint" or "low profile" force posture that had previously characterized UN operations. In 2001, the United States led a force into war-torn Afghanistan that was one-sixth the size of the force NATO had led five years earlier into Bosnia, a country with one-eighth the population of Afghanistan. In Bosnia, all parties had agreed to a peace settlement, disengaged their forces, demarcated their respective zones, and established an enduring cease-fire before the first NATO troops arrived. The troop-to-population ratio in Afghanistan is thus one-fortieth what it was in Bosnia. In 2002, the United States led roughly three times as many troops into Iraq as NATO had led into Kosovo four years earlier. But Iraq is twelve times more populous than Kosovo. In consequence, the troop-to-population ratio in Iraq is less than one-third of that in Kosovo. Finally in 2004, the United States deployed one-tenth the number of troops into Haiti than it had sent there a decade earlier for the same purposes.

In all three cases, these smaller American-led forces proved unable to establish a secure environment. In all three cases—Afghanistan, Iraq, and Haiti—the original U.S. force levels have had to be significantly increased (in Haiti, U.S. forces were replaced by a larger number of UN-led troops). In none of these three cases has public security been established at the levels achieved in Bosnia or Kosovo or, in the case in Haiti, at the level achieved in the same country a decade earlier.

It would appear that the low profile, small footprint approach to nation-building is much better suited to UN-style peacekeeping than to U.S.-style peace enforcement. The United Nations has an ability to compensate, to some degree at least, for its hard power deficit with soft power attributes of international legitimacy and local impartiality. The United States does not have such advantages in situations where America itself is a party to the conflict being terminated, or where the United States has acted without an international mandate. Military reversals also have greater consequences for the United States than the United Nations. To the extent that the United Nations' influence depends more on the moral than the physical, more on its legitimacy than its combat prowess, military rebuffs do not fatally undermine its credibility. To the extent that America leans more on hard, rather than soft, power to achieve its objectives, military reverses strike at the very heart of its potential influence. For all of these reasons, the United States would be well advised to leave the small footprint, low profile approach to the United Nations, and resume supersizing its nation-building missions.

The United Nations and the United States tend to enunciate their nation-building objectives very differently. UN mandates are highly negotiated, densely bureaucratic documents. UN spokespersons tend toward understatement in expressing their goals. Restraint of this sort is more difficult for American officials, who must build congressional and public support for costly and sometimes dangerous missions in distant and unfamiliar places. As a result, American nation-building rhetoric tends toward the grandiloquent. American officials tend to emphasize democratization as their chief goal, whereas the UN leadership stresses the more measurable and somewhat more achievable goals of conflict resolution and sustained peace. The United States often becomes the victim of its own rhetoric, when its higher standards are not met.

UN-led nation-building missions tend to be smaller than American, to take place in less demanding circumstances, to be more frequent and therefore more numerous, to have more circumspectly defined objectives, and, at least among the missions studied, to enjoy a higher success rate than U.S.-led efforts. By contrast, U.S.-led nation-building has taken place in more demanding circumstances, has required larger forces and more robust mandates, has received more economic support, has espoused more ambitious objectives, and, at least among the missions studied, has fallen short of those objectives more often than have UN missions.

This does not mean that the United States would be better off emulating the UN style of nation-building. Forced entry and regime change are sometimes essential prerequisites for resolving threats to international security. The United Nations is poorly equipped for such tasks, even when its members can agree on the necessity for them. But if the United States and the United Nations are better at different things, there is still much each can learn from the other's experience.

There are three explanations for the better UN success rate cited above. First, a different selection of cases might produce a different result. Second, the U.S. cases were intrinsically more difficult. Third, the United Nations has done a better job of learning from its mistakes than has the United States over the past 15 years.

Throughout the 1990s, the United States became steadily better at nation-building. The Haitian operation was better managed than Somalia, Bosnia better than Haiti, and Kosovo better than Bosnia. But the U.S. learning curve was not sustained into the current decade. The administration that took office in 2001 initially disdained nation-building as an unsuitable activity for U.S. forces. When compelled to engage in such missions, first in Afghanistan and then in Iraq, the administration sought to break with the strategies and institutional responses that had been honed throughout the 1990s to deal with such challenges.

In contrast, the United Nations has largely avoided the institutional discontinuities that have marred U.S. performance. At present, the United Nations has approximately 60,000 troops deployed in 17 countries. This is a modest expeditionary commitment in comparison with that of the United States, but it exceeds that of any other nation or combination of nations. The current UN Secretary-General, Kofi Annan, was Undersecretary-General for Peacekeeping and head of the UN peacekeeping operation in Bosnia through the first half of the 1990s, when UN nation-building began to burgeon. He was chosen for his current post by the United States and other member governments largely on the basis of demonstrated skills in managing the UN's peacekeeping portfolio. Some of his closest associates from that period moved up with him to the UN front office; others remain in the Department of Peacekeeping Operations. As a result, UN nation-building missions have been run over the past 15 years by an increasingly experienced cadre of international civil servants. Similarly, many peacekeeping operations are headed and staffed in the field by veterans of earlier operations.

The United States, in contrast, tends to staff each new operation as if it were its first and destined to be its last. Service in such missions has never been regarded as career enhancing for American military or foreign service officers. Whereas the United Nations, despite a generally dysfunctional personnel system, has gradually built up a cadre of experienced nation-builders, including several retired senior U.S. officials, the United States starts each mission more or less from scratch. Whereas the United Nations established a Best Practices unit in its Peacekeeping Department to study and adopt lessons learned in prior operations in 1995, the U.S. Department of State created a similar unit only in 2004.

IS NATION-BUILDING COST-EFFECTIVE?

In addition to the horrendous human costs, war inflicts extraordinary economic costs on societies. And no wars inflict such damage as civil wars. The destruction of homes and facilities, the disruption of commerce, and the killing and maiming of citizens have impoverished all the states we have analyzed in this volume. Paul Collier and Anke Hoeffler have attempted to quantify some of the economic costs of civil war. They find that on average civil wars reduce prospective economic output by 2.2 percent per year for the duration of the conflict.[1] However, once peace is restored, economic activity resumes and in a number of cases, the economies grow.

Collier and Hoeffler examine various policy options to reduce the incidence and duration of civil wars. They find post-conflict military intervention to be highly cost-effective, in fact, the most cost-effective policy that they analyze.[2] The historical record demonstrates that unless peacekeeping forces are deployed as part of the international community's overall response, most societies emerging from conflict return to it within a few years, no matter how much money, advice, or other forms of assistance they may receive. By contrast, the majority of post-conflict societies where peacekeepers have been deployed remain at peace after the international troops are finally withdrawn.

---

[1] Paul Collier and Anke Hoeffler, "The Challenge of Reducing the Global Incidence of Civil War," Centre for the Study of African Economies, Department of Economics, Oxford University, Copenhagen Challenge Paper, April 23, 2004, p. 3.

[2] Collier and Hoeffler (2004), p. 22.

Our analysis supports this conclusion. The UN success rate among missions studied—seven out of eight societies left peaceful, six out of eight left democratic—substantiates the view that nation-building can be an effective means of terminating conflicts, insuring against their reoccurrence, and promoting democracy.

The effects of such successful interventions may also be measured in a sharp overall decline in deaths from armed conflict around the world over the past decade. During the 1990s, deaths from armed conflict were averaging over 200,000 per year. In 2003, this number had come down to 27,000, a fivefold decrease in deaths from civil and international conflict.[3] This figure presumably rose in 2004 as a result of the conflicts in Iraq and Sudan, but probably not to these earlier levels.

The cost of UN nation-building tends to look quite modest when compared to the cost of larger and more demanding U.S.-led operations. At present, the United States is spending some $4.5 billion per month to support its military operations in Iraq. This is more than the United Nations will spend to run all 17 of its current peacekeeping missions for a year. The cost for one year of U.S. operations in Iraq thus could approach the cost for all UN peacekeeping from 1945 to the present day. The United States pays only one-quarter of the UN peacekeeping budget. Thus the annual U.S. contribution for all UN peacekeeping is less than the cost of one week's operations in Iraq.

This is not to suggest that the United Nations could perform the U.S. mission in Iraq more cheaply, or perform it at all, but simply to underline that there are 17 other places where the United States will probably not have to intervene because UN troops are doing so a tiny fraction of the cost.

CONTINUING DEFICIENCIES

Even when successful, UN nation-building only goes so far to fix the underlying problems of the societies it is seeking to rebuild. Francis Fukuyama has suggested that such missions can be divided into three distinct phases: (1) the initial stabilization of a war-torn society, (2) the recreation of local institutions for governance, and (3) the strengthening of those institutions

---

[3] Jean-Marie Guèhenno, "Giving Peace a Chance," in *The World in 2005* (2004), p. 3; Human Security Centre, ed., *Human Security Report 2004*, London: Oxford University Press, forthcoming.

to the point where rapid economic growth and sustained social development can take place.[4] Experience over the past 15 years suggests that the United Nations has achieved a fair mastery of the techniques needed to successfully complete the first two of those tasks. Success with the third has largely eluded the UN, as it has the international development community as whole.

Despite the United Nations' significant achievements in the field of nation-building, the organization continues to exhibit weaknesses that decades of experience have yet to overcome. Most UN missions are undermanned and underfunded. UN-led military forces are often sized and deployed on the basis of unrealistic best-case assumptions. Troop quality is uneven and has even gotten worse as many rich Western nations have followed U.S. practice and become less willing to commit their armed forces to UN operations. Police and civil personnel are always of mixed competence. All components of the mission arrive late; police and civil administrators arrive even more slowly than soldiers.

These same weaknesses have been exhibited most recently in the U.S.-led operation in Iraq. There it was a U.S.-led stabilization force that was deployed on the basis of unrealistic, best-case assumptions and U.S. troops that arrived in inadequate numbers had to be progressively reinforced as new, unanticipated challenges emerged. There it was the quality of the U.S.-led coalition's military contingents that proved distinctly variable, as has their willingness to take orders, risks, and casualties. There it was U.S. civil administrators who were late to arrive, of mixed competence, and never available in adequate numbers. These weaknesses thus appear endemic to nation-building, rather than unique to the United Nations.

CONCLUSIONS

Difficulties encountered by the United States in Afghanistan and Iraq put earlier UN failings in some perspective. UN-led nation-building operations have been smaller, cheaper, and, at least by this sampling, more successful than American. On the other hand, U.S.-led operations have taken place in more-demanding circumstances. Indeed, several—in Somalia, Haiti, and Bosnia—came in the wake of failed UN ef-

---

[4] Francis Fukuyama, *State-Building: Governance and World Order in the 21st Century,* Ithaca, New York: Cornell University Press, 2004, pp. 99–104.

forts. Experience demonstrates that neither the United States nor the United Nations is yet fully equipped for these tasks, and both have much to learn. Overall budget aside, the most serious limitation on the UN's capacity for nation-building is the increasing reluctance of First World governments to commit their forces to UN operations. Nevertheless, it is important to recognize that despite these shortcomings UN- and U.S-led nation-building efforts have saved millions of lives and freed many societies from war and oppression.

Although the U.S. and UN styles of nation-building are distinguishable, they are also highly interdependent. It is a rare nation-building operation in which both are not involved. In Somalia, for instance, a U.S.-led coalition rescued a faltering UN-led operation, then UN-led troops came to the rescue of beleaguered American Rangers. Blue-helmeted UN troops covered the American withdrawal and remained in Somalia for another year until finally the U.S. Navy and Marines returned to extract the remaining UN forces. In Haiti, UN-led missions have twice relieved U.S.-led intervention forces over the past decade. In Bosnia, the United Nations supplied the police components of a NATO-led peacekeeping mission. In Kosovo, the United Nations and NATO divided responsibility for securing and governing that territory between them. In both Afghanistan and Iraq, the United States turned to the United Nations to oversee the process of government formation and the organization of elections.

Assuming adequate consensus among Security Council members on the purpose for any intervention, the United Nations provides the most suitable institutional framework for most nation-building missions, one with a comparatively low cost structure, a comparatively high success rate, and the greatest degree of international legitimacy. Other possible options are likely to be either more expensive (e.g., coalitions led by the United States, EU, or NATO) or less capable (e.g., coalitions led by the African Union, the Organization of American States, or the Association of Southeast Asian Nations). The more-expensive options are best suited to missions that require forced entry or a total troop strength of over 20,000 men. The less-capable options are suited to missions where there is a regional but not a global consensus for action or where the United States simply does not care enough to foot 25 percent of the cost of a UN-run operation.

At mid-decade, both UN and U.S. nation-building efforts stand at near historic highs. Demand for UN-led peacekeeping operations far exceeds the available supply, particularly in sub-Saharan Africa. U.S. armed forces, by far the world's most powerful, also find themselves badly overstretched by the demands of such missions. A decade ago, in the wake of UN and U.S. setbacks in Somalia and Bosnia, nation-building became a term of opprobrium, leading a significant segment of American opinion to reject the whole concept. Ten years later, nation-building appears ever more clearly as a responsibility that neither the United Nations nor the United States can escape.

Abdullah, Ibrahim, "Bush Path to Destruction: The Origin and Character of the Revolutionary United Front/Sierra Leone," *The Journal of Modern African Studies,* Vol. 36, No. 2, June 1998.

Agreement on a Comprehensive Political Settlment of the Cambodia Conflict, 1991, http://www.usip.org/library/pa/cambodia/agree_comppol_10231991_toc.html (accessed November 20, 2004).

Alden, Chris, *Mozambique and the Construction of the New African State: From Negotiations to Nation Building,* New York: Palgrave, 2001.

America's Watch, *El Salvador's Decade of Terror: Human Rights Since the Assassination of Archbishop Romero,* New Haven, Conn.: Yale University Press, 1991.

Amnesty International, *Indonesia and Timor-Leste: International Responsibility for Justice,* New York, 2003.

———, *1999 Annual Report on Sierra Leone,* http://www.amnesty.org/ailib/aireport/ar99/afr51.htm (accessed November 20, 2004).

Anderson, Benedict, *Imagined Communities: Reflections on the Origin and Spread of Nationalism,* New York: Verso, 1991.

Asian Development Bank, *Sixth Progress Report on Timor-Leste,* Dili, 2003.

———, *Asian Development Bank Outlook 2003,* Mandaluyong City: Asian Development Bank, 2003.

———, *Trust Fund for East Timor,* Lisbon, Portugal, 2000.

Ball, Desmond, "Silent Witness: Australian Intelligence and East Timor," *Pacific Review,* Vol. 14, No. 1, 2001.

Beauvais, Joel C., "Benevolent Despotism: A Critique of UN State-Building in East Timor," *New York University Journal of International Law and Politics,* Vol. 33, 2001.

Berman, Eric, *Managing Arms in Peace Processes: Mozambique, Disarmament and Conflict Resolution Project,* United Nations Institute for Disarmament Research, Geneva: United Nations Publications, 1996.

Bernath, Clifford, and Ayre Nyce, "UNAMSIL—A Peacekeeping Success Lessons Learned: Report on the United Nations Mission in Sierra Leone," Washington, D.C.: Refugees International, 2002.

Binford, Leigh, *The El Mozote Massacre: Anthropology and Human Rights,* Tucson, Ariz.: University of Arizona Press, 1996.

"Birth of a Nation: East Timor Gains Independence, Faces Challenges of Economic Management, Poverty Alleviation," *IMF Survey,* Vol. 31, No. 11, June 10, 2002.

Blaxland, Joan, *Information-Era Maneuver: The Australian-Led Mission to East Timor,* Duntroon, Australia: Land Warfare Studies Centre, June 2002.

Bostock, Ian, "East Timor: An Operational Evaluation," *Jane's Defence Weekly,* Vol. 33, No. 18, May 3, 2000.

Boyce, James K., ed., *Economic Policy for Building Peace: The Lessons of El Salvador,* Boulder, Colo.: Lynne Rienner Publishers, 1996.

"Bremer: US in Tough Fight in Iraq," BBC News Online, November 16, 2003, www.news.bbc.co.uk, accessed November 16, 2003.

Brown, Macalister, and Joseph Jermiah Zasloff, *Cambodia Confounds the Peacemakers, 1979–1998,* Ithaca, N.Y.: Cornell University Press, 1999.

Brown, Susan, "Diplomacy by Other Means," in Leys and Saul (1995).

Brownmiller, Susan, *Against Our Will: Men, Women, and Rape,* New York: Simon and Schuster, 1975.

Call, Charles T., "Democratization, War, and State-Building: Constructing the Rule of Law in El Salvador," *Journal of Latin American Studies,* Vol. 35, No. 4, 2003.

Campbell, Greg, *Blood Diamonds: Tracing the Deadly Path of the World's Most Precious Stones,* Boulder, Colo.: Westview Press, 2002.

Caplan, Richard, *A New Trusteeship? The International Administration of War-Torn Territories,* Adelphi Paper 41, London: International Institute for Strategic Studies, 2002.

Center for International Development and Conflict Management (CIDCM), *State Failure: Internal Wars and Failures of Governance, 1955–2002,* data set, University of Maryland, www.cidcm.umd, accessed November 22, 2004.

Central Bureau of Statistics of the Republic of Croatia, *Statistical Information,* Zagreb, 2003.

Centre for Defence Studies, *Independent Study on Security Force Options and Security Sector Reform for East Timor,* London: King's College, London, August 8, 2000.

Chandler, David P., *The Tragedy of Cambodian History: Politics, War and Revolution Since 1945,* New Haven, Conn.: Yale University Press, 1991.

———, "Three Visions of Politics in Cambodia," in Doyle (1997).

Charter of the United Nations, June 26, 1945, http://www.un.org/aboutun/charter/ (accessed November 8, 2004).

Chester, Cara, Eben Forbes, Tasha Gill, Heather Kelly, Heather Kulp, Jeff Merritt, and Sharon Otterman, *Bridging the Gap: An Assessment of IOM's Community Assistance Programs in East Timor,* New York: Columbia University School of International and Public Affairs, 2000.

Chesterman, Simon, *You, The People: The United Nations Transitional Administration, and State-Building,* New York: Oxford University Press, 2004.

Childress, Michael, *The Effectiveness of U.S. Training Efforts in Internal Defense and Development: The Cases of El Salvador and Honduras,* Santa Monica, Calif.: RAND Corporation, MR-250-USDP, 1995.

Chopra, Jarat, "The UN's Kingdom of East Timor," *Survival,* Vol. 42, No. 3, Autumn 2000.

Claiborne, William, "Namibian Agreement Threatened," *Washington Post,* April 2, 1989.

Clark, Dick, *The Challenge of Indochina: An Examination of the US Role,* Congressional Staff Conference, April 30–May 2, 1993, Aspen Institute for Humananistic Studies, 1994.

Cliffe, Lionel, *The Transition to Independence in Namibia,* Boulder, Colo.: Lynne Rienner Publishers, 1994.

Coalition Provisional Authority (CPA), Interim Iraqi Government Press Packet, June 24, 2004.

———, Working Papers: Iraq Status, Unclassified Briefing, June 29, 2004.

Coleiro, Christine, *Bringing Peace to the Land of Scorpions and Jumping Snakes: Legacy of the United Nations in Eastern Slavonia and Transitional Missions,* Clementsport, Nova Scotia: Canadian Peacekeeping Press Publications, 2002.

Collier, Paul, and Anke Hoeffler, "The Challenge of Reducing the Global Incidence of Civil War," Centre for the Study of African Economies, Department of Economics, Oxford University, Copenhagen Challenge Paper, April 23, 2004.

Collins, Joseph J., Deputy Assistant Secretary of Defense for Stability Operations, DoD News Briefing, February 25, 2003, available at http://www.CENTCOM.mil/CENTCOMNews/transcripts/20030225.htm, accessed June 2004.

Constitution of the Democratic Republic of East Timor, Section 67.

Conteh-Morgan, Earl, and Mac Dixon-Fyle, *Sierra Leone at the End of the Twentieth Century: History, Politics and Society*, New York: Peter Lang Publishing, 1999.

CPA—*See* Coalition Provisional Authority.

Croatia: History, http://www.encyclopedia.com/html/section/Croatia_History.asp (accessed November 16, 2004).

Dayal, Rajeshwar, *Mission for Hammarskjöld: The Congo Crisis,* Delhi: Oxford University Press, 1976.

de Mello, Sergio Vieira, Address at the First CNRT Congress, Dili, August 21, 2000.

de Witte, Ludo, *The Assassination of Lumumba,* London, New York: Verso, 2001.

del Castillo, Graciana, "The Arms-for-Land Deal in El Salvador," in Doyle (1997).

———, "Post-Conflict Reconstruction and the Challenge to International Organizations: The Case of El Salvador," *World Development,* Vol. 29, No. 12, 2001.

Dobbins, James, John G. McGinn, Keith Crane, Seth G. Jones, Rollie Lal, Andrew Rathmell, Rachel M. Swanger, and Anga Timilsina, *America's Role in Nation-Building: From Germany to Iraq,* Santa Monica, Calif.: RAND Corporation, MR-1753-RC, 2003.

Donnan, Shawn, "Evidence Grows Over Jakarta Hand in Violence," *Financial Times,* November 25, 1999.

Dowell, William, and Douglas Waller, "When the Peace Cannot be Kept," *Time,* Vol. 155 No. 21, May 22, 2000.

Doyle, Michael W., *UN Peacekeeping in Cambodia: UNTAC's Civil Mandate,* Boulder, Colo.: Lynne Rienner Publishers, 1995.

———, "Authority and Elections in Cambodia," in Doyle et al. (1997).

———, "War and Peace in Cambodia," in Doyle et al. (1997).

Doyle, Michael W., Ian Johnstone, Robert C. Orr, eds., *Keeping the Peace: Multidimensional UN Operations in Cambodia and El Salvador,* New York: Cambridge University Press, 1997.

Durch, William J., ed., *The Evolution of UN Peacekeeping: Case Studies and Comparative Analysis.* New York: St. Martin's Press, 1993.

———, *UN Peacekeeping, American Politics, and the Uncivil Wars of the 1990s,* New York: St. Martin's Press, 1996.

"East Timor: UN Indicts General Wiranto for Crimes Against Humanity," ABC Radio, February 25, 2003.

Eriksson, John, Alcira Kreimer, and Margaret Arnold, *El Salvador: Post-Conflict Reconstruction,* Washington, D.C.: World Bank, 2000.

Fearon, James D., and David D. Laitin, "Neotrusteeship and the Problem of Weak States," *International Security,* Vol. 28, No. 4, Spring 2004.

Findlay, Trevor, *Cambodia: The Legacy and Lessons of UNTAC,* New York: Oxford University Press, 1999.

Fleitz, Frederick H., Jr., *Peacekeeping Fiascos of the 1990s: Causes, Solutions, and U.S. Interests,* Westport: Praeger, 2002.

Freedom House, *Freedom in the World Country Ratings, 1972 Through 2003,* New York: Freedom House, 2003.

"From Madness to Hope: The 12-Year War in El Salvador," Report of the Commission on the Truth for El Salvador, S/25500, April 1, 1993.

Fukuyama, Francis, *State-building: Governance and World Order in the 21st Century,* Ithaca, NY: Cornell University Press, 2004.

Further Report of the Secretary-General Pursuant to Paragraph 7 of Resolution 840, S/26260, August 26, 1993.

Garvin, Glenn, "Civil War Over, But Violence Goes On," *Miami Herald,* August 4, 1997.

Gellner, Ernest, *Nations and Nationalism,* New York: Columbia University Press, 1983.

George, Alexander L., "Case Studies and Theory Development: The Method of Structured, Focused Comparison," in Paul Gordon Lauren, ed., *Diplomacy: New Approaches in History, Theory, and Policy,* New York: Free Press, 1979.

Global Witness, *Forests, Famine, and War: The Key to Cambodia's Future,* London, 1995.

Godwin, Peter, and David Hughes, "Thatcher Helps Keep Namibia's Peace," *The Times (London),* April 2, 1989.

González, Armando Duque, Francesco Mezzalama, and Khalil Issa Othman, *Evaluation of United Nations System Response in East Timor: Coordination and Effectiveness,* JIU/REP/2002/10, Geneva: United Nations Joint Inspection Unit, 2002.

Goodspeed, Peter, "UN Flirting With Disaster," *Toronto Star,* February 28, 1993.

Gordon, Stuart, and James Higgs, "Peace: At What Price?" *Jane's Defense Weekly,* September 27, 2000.

Guèhenno, Jean-Marie, "Giving Peace a Chance," in *The World in 2005* (2004).

Hainsworth, Paul, and Stephen McCloskey, *The East Timor Question: The Struggle for Independence from Indonesia,* New York: I. B. Tauris, 2000.

Halchin, L. Elaine, "The Coalition Provisional Authority: Origin, Characteristics, and Institutional Authorities," CRS Report for Congress, RL32370, Washington, D.C.: Congressional Research Service, April 29, 2004.

Hansen, Annika S., *From Congo to Kosovo: Civilian Police in Peace Operations,* Adelphi Paper 343, New York: Oxford University Press, 2002.

Harris, Robin, "Blair's 'Ethical' Policy," *The National Interest,* No. 1, Spring 2001.

Hearn, Roger, *UN Peacekeeping in Action: The Namibian Experience,* New York: Nova Science Publishers, 1999.

Helman, Gerald B. and Steven R. Ratner, "Saving Failed States," *Foreign Policy,* No. 89, Winter 1992–93.

Hersh, Seymour M., "Offense and Defense: The Battle Between Donald Rumsfeld and the Pentagon," *The New Yorker,* April 7, 2003.

Hirsch, John, *Sierra Leone, Diamonds and the Struggle for Democracy,* Boulder: Lynne Rienner Publishers, 2001.

Hochschild, Adam, *King Leopold's Ghost: A Story of Greed, Terror, and Heroism in Colonial Africa,* Boston: Houghton Mifflin, 1998.

Holiday, David, and William Stanley, "Building the Peace: Preliminary Lessons from El Salvador," *Journal of International Affairs,* Vol. 46, No. 2, Winter 1993.

Horta, José Ramos, and Emilia Pires, "How Will the Macroeconomy Be Managed in an Independent East Timor? An East Timorese View," *Finance & Development,* Vol. 38, No. 1, March 2001.

Human Rights Watch, *An Exchange on Human Rights and Peace-Keeping in Cambodia,* New York, September 1993.

——, *Land Mines in Mozambique,* New York, 1994.

——, *Justice Denied for East Timor,* New York, 2002.

Human Security Centre, ed., *Human Security Report 2004,* London: Oxford University Press, forthcoming.

Huxley, Tim, *Disintegrating Indonesia? Implications for Regional Security,* Adelphi Paper 349, London: International Institute for Strategic Studies, 2002.

ICG—*See* International Crisis Group.

IMF—*See* International Monetary Fund.

Inspector General, Coalition Provisional Authority, Initial Report to Congress, March 30, 2004.

Inspector General, Coalition Provisional Authority, "Audit Report: Management of Personnel Assigned to the Coalition Provisional Authority in Baghdad," Report Number 04-002, June 25, 2004.

Institute for Security Studies (ISS), *Sierra Leone: Building the Road to Recovery,* ISS Monograph No. 80, Pretoria, South Africa, March 2003.

Instituto Universitario de Opinión Pública in San Salvador, Evaluación del pais a finales de 1998, San Salvador: El Instituto Universitario de Opinión Pública, Universidad Centroamericana, 1999.

International Crisis Group (ICG), *Indonesia: Implications of the Timor Trials,* Jakarta and Brussels: ICG Asia Briefing, 2002.

——, *Sierra Leone: Time for a New Military and Political Strategy,* Freetown/London/Brussels: ICG Africa Report No. 28, 11 April 2001.

International Institute for Strategic Studies (IISS), *The Military Balance, 1991–1992,* London: Oxford University Press, 1992.

——, *The Military Balance, 1992–1993,* London: Oxford University Press, 1993.

International Monetary Fund (IMF), *Namiba: Recent Economic Developments,* Washington, D.C., December 1997.

——, *International Financial Statistics 2002,* Washington, DC., 2002.

———, *Cambodia: Selected Issues and Statistical Appendix,* IMF Country Report No. 03/59, Washington, D.C., March 2003.

———, Public Information Notice, No. 03/90, Washington, D.C., July 28, 2003.

———, *Democratic Republic of Timor Leste: Selected Issues and Statistical Appendix,* No. 03/228, Washington, D.C., July 2003.

———, *Republic of Mozambique: Ex Post Assessment of Mozambique's Performance Under Fund-Supported Programs,* Country Report No. 04/53, Washington, D.C.: International Monetary Fund, March 2004.

International Republican Institute, *IRI in Cambodia,* Washington, D.C., 2004.

Isaacman, Allen, and Barbara Isaacman, *Mozambique: From Colonialism to Revolution, 1900–1982,* Boulder, Colo.: Westview Press, 1983.

ISS—*See* Institute for Security Studies.

Jabri, Vivienne, *Mediating Conflict: Decision-making and Western Intervention in Namibia,* Manchester, UK: Manchester University Press, 1990.

Jacobson, Harold Karan, "ONUC's Civil Operations: State-Preserving and State-Building," *World Politics,* Vol. 17, No. 1, October 1964.

Jane's Information Group, Jane's Online, www.janes.com, accessed December 23, 2004.

Jaster, Robert S., *The 1988 Peace Accords and the Future of South-Western Africa,* Adelphi Paper 353, London: Brassey's, 1990.

Jetley, Vijay Kumar, "Report on the Crisis in Sierra Leone," http://www.sierra-leone.org/jetley0500.html, accessed November 20, 2004.

Johnstone, Ian, "Rights and Reconciliation in El Salvador," in Doyle et al. (1997).

Kaela, Laurent C. W., *The Question of Namibia,* New York: St. Martin's Press, 1996.

Kato, Elisabeth Uphoff, "Quick Impacts, Slow Rehabilitation in Cambodia," in Doyle et al. (1997).

Kelly, Sean, *America's Tyrant: The CIA and Mobutu of Zaire*, Washington, D.C.: American University Press, 1993.

Kiernan, Ben, "The Failures of the Paris Agreements on Cambodia, 1991–1993," in Clark (1994).

Killick, John, *The United States and European Reconstruction 1945-1960*, Edinburgh: Keele University Press, 1997.

Kim, Cheryl M. Lee, and Mark Metrikas, "Holding a Fragile Peace: The Military and Civilian Components of UNTAC," in Doyle et al. (1997).

King, Gordon, *The United Nations in the Congo: A Quest for Peace.* Washington, D.C.: Carnegie Endowment for International Peace, 1962, p. 67.

Kitchen, Helen, ed., *Footnotes to the Congo Story: An Africa Report Anthology*, New York: Walker and Company, 1967.

Kpundeh, Sahr John, "Limiting Administrative Corruption in Sierra Leone," *The Journal of Modern African Studies,* Vol. 32, No. 1, March 1994.

Kreilkamp, Jacob S., "UN Post-conflict Reconstruction," *International Law and Politics,* Vol. 35, No. 3, 2003.

Human Rights Watch, *Landmines in Cambodia: The Coward's War,* New York, September 1991.

Lawyers' Committee for Human Rights, *El Salvador's Negotiated Revolution: Prospects for Legal Reform,* New York, 1993.

Lefever, Ernest W., *Crisis in the Congo: A United Nations Force in Action,* Washington, D.C.: Brookings Institution, 1965.

Letter Dated 8 October 1991 from El Salvador Transmitting the Text of the Geneva Agreement signed on 4 April 1990 by the Government of El Salvador and the FMLN, A/46/551-S/21328, 9 October 1991.

Letter dated 8 October 1991 from El Salvador Transmitting the Text of the Mexico Agreement and Annexes Signed on 27 April 1991 by the Government of El Salvador and the FMLN, A/46/553-S/23130, October 9, 1991, in United Nations Department of Public Information (1995b).

Letter dated 7 January 1993 from the Secretary-General to the President of the Security Council Concerning Implementation of the

Provisions of the Peace Agreements Relating to the Purification of the Armed Forces, S/25078, January 9, 1993, in United Nations Department of Public Information (1995b).

Letter dated 4 October 1999 from the Secretary-General Addressed to the President of the Security Council, S/1999/1025, October 4, 1999.

Letter dated 15 October 1999 from the Secretary-General Addressed to the President of the Security Council, S/1999/1072, October 18, 1999.

Letter dated 29 October 1999 from the Secretary-General Addressed to the President of the Security Council, S/1999/1106, October 29, 1999.

Levine, Mark, "Peacemaking in El Salvador," in Doyle et al. (1997).

Leys, Colin, and John S. Saul, *Namibia's Liberation Struggle: The Two-Edged Sword,* Athens, Ohio: Ohio University Press, 1995.

Luke, David Fashole, and Stephen P. Riley, "The Politics of Economic Decline in Sierra Leone," *The Journal of Modern African Studies,* Vol. 27, No. 1, March 1989.

Mabusa, Basile, *The Crisis in Education: A Congolese View,* in Kitchen (1967).

Malan, Mark, "The Challenge of Justice and Reconciliation," in ISS (2003).

———, "UNMASIL After the Elections," in ISS (2003).

Malan, Mark, and Sarah Meek, "Extension of Government Authority and National Recovery," in ISS (2003).

Malan, Mark, Phenyo Rakate, and Angela McIntyre, *Peacekeeping in Sierra Leone: UNAMSIL Hits the Home Straight,* ISS Monograph 68, Pretoria, South Africa, ISS, January 2002.

Marshall, Monty G., and Keith Jaggers, *Polity IV Project: Political Regime Characteristics and Transitions, 1800–2002, Dataset Users' Manual,* College Park, MD: Center for International Development and Conflict Management, September 2002.

Martelli, George, *Experiment in World Government: An Account of the United Nations Operation in the Congo,* 1960–1964, London: Johnson Publications, 1966.

Martin, Ian, *Self-Determination in East Timor: The United Nations, the Ballot, and International Intervention,* Boulder, Colo.: Lynne Rienner Publishers, 2001.

Mason, Linda, and Roger Brown, *Race, Rivalry, and Politics: Managing Cambodian Relief,* South Bend, Ind.: University of Notre Dame Press, 1983.

McCarthy, Terry, "Rising From the Ashes," *Time,* March 20, 2000.

McCormick, David H., "From Peacekeeping to Peacebuilding," in Doyle et al. (1997).

McGinn, John G., "After the Explosion: International Action in the Aftermath of Nationalist War," *National Securities Quarterly,* Vol. 4, No. 1, Winter 1998.

Megalli, Mona, and Heba Kandil, "Iraq Donors Commit About $1 Billion to Iraq Funds," Reuters, February 29, 2004.

Memorandum to President Ford from Henry A. Kissinger, "Your Visit to Indonesia," CA. November 21, 1975. National Archives, Record Group 59, Department of State Records, Executive Secretariat Briefing Books, 1958–1976, Box 227.

Mitchell, B. M., *International Historical Statistics: Europe 1750-1988,* 3rd Edition, New York: Stockton Press, 1992.

———, *International Historical Statistics: Africa, Asia & Oceania 1750-1993,* 3rd Edition, New York: Grove's Dictionaries, Inc., 1998.

Montague, Dena, "The Business of War and the Prospects for Peace in Sierra Leone," *The Brown Journal of World Affairs,* Vol. IX, No. 1, Spring 2002.

Montgomery, Tommie Sue, "Getting to Peace in El Salvador: The Roles of the United Nations Secretariat and ONUSAL," *Journal of Interamerican Studies and World Affairs,* Vol. 37, No. 4, Winter 1995.

Morrow, Jonathan, and Rachel White, "The United Nations in Transitional East Timor: International Standards and the Reality of Governance," *The Australian Year Book of International Law,* Vol. 22, Canberra, Australia: Centre for International and Public Law, Australian National University, 2002.

Mozambique, Internal Affairs, *Jane's Sentinel Security Assessment—Southern Africa*, posted January 14, 2004, at http://www4.janes.com, accessed April 15, 2004.

Mozambique Ministry of Foreign Affairs and Cooperation, *Annual Report: Mine Action Programme, 2003*, Maputo, February 2004.

Munck, Gerardo L., and Dexter Boniface, "Political Processes and Identity Formation in El Salvador: From Armed Left to Democratic Left," in Munck and de Silva, eds. (2000).

Munck, Ronaldo, and Purnaka L. de Silva, eds., *Postmodern Insurgencies: Political Violence, Identity Formation and Peacemaking in Comparative Perspective*, New York: St. Martin's Press, 2000.

Murray, Williamson, and Major General Robert H. Scales, Jr., *The Iraq War: A Military History*, Cambridge, Mass.: The Belknap Press of Harvard University Press, 2003.

Namikas, Lise A., "Battleground Africa: The Cold War and the Congo Crisis, 1960–1965," Dissertation, University of Southern California, 2002.

National Democratic Institute for International Affairs, *Nation Building: The U.N. and Namibia*, Washington D.C., 1990.

———, *Cambodia*, Washington, D.C., 2004.

Ninth Report on the United Nations mission in Sierra Leone, 14 March 2001.

Oakley, Robert B., Michael J. Dziedzic, and Eliot M. Goldberg, eds., *Policing the New World Disorder: Peace Operations and Public Security*, Washington, D.C.: National Defense University, 1998.

Operation Order No. 2 for the Joint Military Component of UNTAC, issued December 9, 1992.

Organization for Security and Cooperation in Europe (OSCE), "Report of the OSCE Mission to Croatia on Croatia's Progress in Meeting International Commitments Since September 1998," Vienna, Austria, January 26, 1999.

———, Mission to Croatia, "Background Report: Implementation of the Constitutional Law on the Rights of National Minorities and Related Legislation," Zagreb, Croatia, May 12, 2003, available through osce-croatia@oscecro.org.

Pastor, Manuel, and Michael E. Conroy, "Distributional Implication," in Boyce (1996).

Pearce, Jenny, "From Civil War to 'Civil Society': Has the End of the Cold War Brought Peace to Central America?" *International Affairs,* Vol. 74, No. 3, 1998.

Perito, Robert M., *The American Experience with Police in Peace Operations,* Clementsport, Canada: Canadian Peace Keeping Press, 2002.

Pisik, Betsy, "UN Sides with US on Voting in Iraq," *Washington Times,* January 16, 2004.

———, "UN Iraq Advisor Issues Vote Warning," *Washington Times,* January 28, 2004.

Power, Samantha, *A Problem From Hell: America and the Age of Genocide,* New York: Basic Books, 2002.

Pratt, David, "Sierra Leone: The Forgotten Crisis," Report to the Minister of Foreign Affairs, the Honorable Lloyd Axworthy, P.C., M.P. from David Pratt, M.P., Nepean Carleton, Special envoy to Sierra Leone," April 23, 1999, http://www.sierra-leone.org/pratt042399.html, accessed November 16, 2004.

Ramsbotham, Oliver, and Tom Woodhouse, *Encyclopedia of International Peacekeeping Operations,* Santa Barbara, Calif.: ABC-CLIO, 1999.

Razzall, Katie, "Looting Rife," Channel Four News-United Kingdom, April 11, 2003, http://www.channel4.com/news/2003/04/week_2/11_war.html, accessed November 20, 2004.

Recknagel, Charles "Iraq: Al-Basrah Riot Underlines Frustration With Energy Shortages," Radio Free Europe, Washington, D.C., August 11, 2003.

A Review of Peace Operations: A Case for Change, London: King's College, 2003.

Rohland, Klaas, and Sarah Cliffe, *The East Timor Reconstruction Program: Successes, Problems and Tradeoffs,* CPR Working Paper No. 2, Washington, D.C.: World Bank, 2002.

Roos, Klaas, *UNTAC Evaluation Report, UN CIVPOL,* Phnom Penh, Cambodia: UNTAC, August 1993.

Ryan, Alan, *Primary Responsibilities and Primary Risks: Australian Defence Force Participation in the International Force East Timor,* Duntroon, Australia: Land Warfare Studies Centre, 2000.

———, "The Strong Lead-Nation Model in an Ad Hoc Coalition of the Willing: Operation Stabilise in East Timor," *International Peacekeeping,* Vol. 9, No. 1, Spring 2002.

Sankoh, Osman Benk, "In Diamonds We Trust," *Concord Times,* Freetown, March 23, 2004.

Schiavo-Campo, Salvatore, *Financing and Aid Management Arrangements in Post-Conflict Situations,* Washington, D.C.: World Bank, 2003.

Schwarz, Benjamin C., *American Counterinsurgency Doctrine and El Salvador: The Frustrations of Reform and the Illusions of Nation Building,* Santa Monica, Calif.: RAND Corporation, 1991.

Second Progress Report of the Secretary-General on the United Nations Transitional Authority in Cambodia, S/24578, September 21, 1992.

Segovia, Alexander, "The War Economy of the 1980s," in Boyce (1996).

Seventeenth report of the Secretary-General on the United Nations Mission in Sierra Leone. S/2003/321, March 17, 2003.

Seventh Report of the Secretary-General on the United Nations Mission in Sierra Leone, S/2000/1055, October 31, 2000.

Seventh Report of the Secretary-General on the United Nations Observer Mission in Sierra Leone, S/1999/836, July 30, 1999

"Sierra Leone: Getting Away with Murder, Mutilation and Rape, New Testimony from Sierra Leone," Human Rights Watch Report, Vol. 11, No. 3(A), July 1999.

Skehan, Craig, Hamish McDonald, Lindsay Murdoch, and Mark Dodd, "Jakarta's Bloody Hands: Military Backs Violence," *Sydney Morning Herald,* September 6, 1999.

Smith, A. V., *Equipment for Post-Conflict Demining: A Study of Requirements in Mozambique,* Working Paper No. 48, Coventry, United Kingdom: Development Technology Unit, University of Warwick, January 1996.

Smith, Christopher, "The International Trade in Small Arms," *Jane's Intelligence Review,* Vol. 7, No. 9, 1995, http://www4.janes.com, accessed April 15, 2004.

Smith, Michael G., *Peacekeeping in East Timor: The Path to Independence,* Boulder, Colo.: Lynne Riener Publishers, 2003.

Sparks, Donald L., and December Green, *Namibia: The Nation After Independence,* Boulder, Colo.: Westview Press, 1992.

Special Report of the Secretary-General on the United Nations Mission of Support in East Timor, S/2003/243, March 3, 2003.

Special Report of the Secretary-General on the United Nations Mission of Support in East Timor, S/2003/243, March 2, 2003.

Spence, Jack, et al. *Chapúltepec: Five Years Later: El Salvador's Political Reality and Uncertain Future,* Cambridge, Mass.: Hemispheric Initiatives, 1997.

Stanley, William, and Robert Loosle, "El Salvador: The Civilian Police Component of Peace Operations," in Oakley et al. (1998).

Statistical Yearbook of Yugoslavia 1997, Belgrade: Federal Statistical Office, 1997.

Steele, Jonathan, "Nation Building in East Timor," *World Policy Journal,* Vol. 19, No. 2, Summer 2002.

Strohmeyer, Hansjorg, "Collapse and Reconstruction of a Judicial System: The United Nations Missions in Kosovo and East Timor," *The American Journal of International Law,* Vol. 95, No. 46, 2001.

Suntharalingam, Nishkala, "The Cambodian Settlement Agreements," in Doyle et al. (1997).

Suny, Ronald Grigor, *The Revenge of the Past: Nationalism, Revolution, and the Collapse of the Soviet Union,* Stanford, Calif.: Stanford University Press, 1993.

Sutter, Valerie O., *The Indochinese Refugee Dilemma,* Baton Rouge, La.: Louisiana State University Press, 1990.

Synge, Richard, *Mozambique—UN Peacekeeping in Action 1992–94,* Washington, D.C.: United States Institute of Peace Press, 1997.

Taylor, John G., *East Timor: The Price of Freedom,* New York: Zed Books, 1999.

Thatcher, Margaret, *The Downing Street Years,* New York: HarperCollins, 1993.

Torres-Rivas, Edelberto, "Insurrection and Civil War in El Salvador," in Doyle et al. (1997).

"Transfer Does Not Affect Troops," BBC News Online, November 16, 2003, www.news.bbc.co.uk, accessed November 16, 2003.

Traub, James, "Inventing East Timor," *Foreign Affairs,* July/August 2000, Vol. 79, No. 4.

UN—*See* United Nations.

UNAMSIL Press Briefing, 21 February 2003.

UNDP—*See* United Nations Development Programme.

UNIDR—*See* United Nations Institute for Disarmament Research.

UNSCR—*See* United Nations Security Council Resolution.

UNTAC—*See* United Nations Transitional Authority in Cambodia.

USCR—*See* U.S. Committee for Refugees.

United Nations, *An Agenda for Peace: Preventive Diplomacy, Peacemaking, and Peacekeeping,* New York, 1992.

——, *El Salvador—ONUSAL: Facts and Figures,* 1995.

——, *The United Nations Transitional Administration in Eastern Slavonia, Baranja and Western Sirmium (UNTAES) January 1996–January 1998: Lessons Learned.*

——, *East Timor: Building Blocks for a Nation,* New York, November 2000.

——, *Report of the Independent Panel on the Safety and Security of UN Personnel in Iraq,* October 20, 2003.

——, *A Strategy for Assistance to Iraq,* draft for stakeholder consultation, February 7, 2004.

——, *Evaluation of UNHCR's Repatriation and Reintegration Programme in East Timor,* 1999–2003, EPAU/2004/0, New York, February 2004.

——, The Political Transition in Iraq: Report of the Fact-Finding Mission, S/2004/140, February 23, 2004.

————, "Iraq Situation Report," July 18–24, 2004, www.who.int/disasters/repo/14032.pdf (accessed November 22, 2004).

United Nations Department of Peacekeeping Operations, http://www.un.org/Depts/dpko, accessed December 23, 2004.

United Nations Department of Public Information, *The United Nations and Cambodia, 1991–1995,* New York: United Nations, 1995a.

————, *The United Nations and El Salvador, 1990–1995,* New York: United Nations, 1995b.

————, *The United Nations and Mozambique,* New York: United Nations, 1995c.

————, *The Blue Helmets: A Review of United Nations Peace-Keeping,* 3rd Edition, New York: United Nations, 1996.

————, *UN Peace Operations Year in Review 2002,* "Sierra Leone," New York: United Nations, December 2002.

United Nations Development Programme (UNDP), *The Way Ahead: East Timor Development Report, 2002,* Dili, East Timor, 2002.

United Nations Development Program and World Bank, *Joint Iraq Needs Assessment,* Washington, D.C.: UNDP and World Bank, October 2003.

United Nations Electoral Law for the Conduct of a Free and Fair Election of a Constituent Assembly for Cambodia, March 31, 1992.

United Nations High Commissioner for Refugees, *Statistical Yearbook,* Geneva, Switzerland: UNHCR, various years.

United Nations Institute for Disarmament Research (UNIDR), *Managing Arms in Peace Processes: Nicaragua and El Salvador,* Geneva, 1997.

United Nations Office for Coordination of Humanitarian Affairs (UNOCHA), *Multi-Country Mine Action Study: Mozambique,* Maputo, Mozambique, 1997.

United Nations Transitional Authority in Cambodia (UNTAC), UNTAC Daily Press Briefing, April 30, 1993.

————, *UNTAC Facts and Figures,* New York: United Nations, 1993.

Urquhart, Brian, "The Tragedy of Lumumba," *The New York Review of Books,* Vol. XLVIII, Number 15, October 4, 2001.

U.S. Committee for Refugees (USCR), *World Refugee Survey: Country Report: El Salvador,* Washington, D.C., 1997.

———,*World Refugee Survey: Country Report: East Timor,* 2003, 2002, 2001, http://www.refugees.org/ (accessed November 16, 2004).

———, *World Refugee Survey: Country Report: Croatia,* 1996, 1997, 1998, 1999, 2000, http://www.refugees.org/ (accessed November 16, 2004).

U.S. Department of Defense, Iraq Status Report, June 29, 2004.

———, Directorate for Information Operations and Reports, http://www.dior.whs.mil/, accessed December 23, 2004.

U.S. Department of Justice, *East Timor Project Overview,* Washington, D.C.: International Criminal Investigative Training Assistance Program, U.S. Department of Justice, 2002.

U.S. Department of State, *Occupation of Germany: Policy and Progress 1945–1946,* Washington, D.C.: United States Government Printing Office, 1947.

———, Briefing Paper, "Indonesia and East Timor," November 21, 1975. National Archives, Record Group 59, Department of State Records, Executive Secretariat Briefing Books, 1958–1976, Box 227.

———, *Communist Interference in El Salvador: Documents Demonstrating Communist Support of the Salvadoran Insurgency,* Washington, D.C., February 1981.

———, *2003 Human Rights Reports,* Washington, D.C., 2004.

U.S. Government Accountability Office (GAO), *Rebuilding Iraq: Resource, Security, Governance, Essential Services, and Oversight Issues,* GAO-04-902R, Washington, D.C., June 2004a.

———, *Rebuilding Iraq: Fiscal Year 2003 Contract Award Procedures and Management Challenges,* GAO-04-605Washington, D.C., June 2004b.

U.S. War Department, Strength of the Army, Washington, D.C., December 1, 1945.

U.S. War Department, Strength of the Army, Washington, D.C., December 1, 1946.

Valdivieso, Luis M., *East Timor: Building Blocks for a Nation,* New York: United Nations, November 2000.

Valdivieso, Luis M., and Alejandro López-Mejía, "East Timor: Macroeconomic Management on the Road to Independence," *Finance and Development,* Vol. 38, No. 1, March 2001.

Valdivieso, Luis M., Toshihide Endo, Luis V. Mendonca, Shamsuddin Tareq, and Alejandro López-Mejía, *East Timor: Establishing the Foundations of Sound Macroeconomic Management,* Washington, D.C.: International Monetary Fund, 2000.

Vilas, C., *Between Earthquakes and Volcanoes: Market, State, and the Revolutions in Central America,* New York: Monthly Review Press, 1995.

Wainwright, Elsina, *New Neighbour, New Challenge: Australia and the Security of East Timor,* Barton, Australia, Australian Strategic Policy Institute, 2002.

West, Robert L., "The United Nations and the Congo Financial Crisis," *International Organization,* Vol. 15, No. 4, Autumn 1961.

Wheeler, Nicholas J., and Tim Dunne, "East Timor and the New Humanitarian Interventionism," *International Affairs,* Vol. 77, No. 4, 2001.

Wilkins, Timothy A., "The El Salvador Peace Accords: Using International and Domestic Law Norms to Build Peace," in Doyle et al. (1997).

Williams, Brian, "Returning Home: The Repatriation of Cambodian Refugees," in Doyle et al. (1997).

Woods, James L., "Mozambique: The CIVPOL Operation," in Oakley et al. (1998).

Woodward, Robert, *Plan of Attack,* New York: Simon and Schuster, 2004.

World Bank, *Cambodia: Agenda for Rehabilitation and Reconstruction,* Washington, D.C., June 1992

———, *Cambodia Rehabilitation Program: Implementation and Outlook,* Report No. 13965-KH, Washington, D.C., February 1995.

———, *El Salvador: Meeting the Challenge of Globalization,* Washington, D.C., 1996a.

———, *World Bank Yearbook 1996,* Washington, D.C.: World Bank, 1996b.

———, *Cambodia: Progress in Recovery and Reform,* Report No. 16591-KH, Washington, D.C., June 1997.

———, *Bosnia and Herzegovina: 1996–1998 Lessons and Accomplishments,* Washington, D.C., 1999a.

———, *Report of the Joint Assessment Mission to East Timor,* Annex 1, Washington, D.C.: World Bank, 1999b.

———, *Trust Fund for East Timor,* Update No. 2, Dili: World Bank, September 6, 2000.

———, *Kosovo, Federal Republic of Yugoslavia Transitional Support Strategy,* Washington, D.C.: 2002a.

———, *Participatory Potential Assessment (PPA): East Timor,* Dili, East Timor: UNDP, ADB, ETTA/ETPA, 2002b.

———, *Namibia: Country Brief,* Washington, D.C., 2004a

World Bank Development Indicators database, Washington, D.C.: World Bank, 2004b. .

World Bank-Administered Trust Fund for East Timor, *Fact Sheet,* Washington, D.C.: World Bank, April 11, 2000.

World Food Program, "World Hunger—Iraq," May 2004, http://www.wfp.org/country_brief/index.asp?region=6 (accessed November 20, 2004).

The World in 2005, London: The Economist, 2004.

Young, M. Crawford, "Post-Independence Politics in the Congo," *Transition,* Vol. 26, 1966.

Ziemke, Earl F., *The U.S. Army in the Occupation of Germany, 1944-1946,* Washington, D.C.: Center of Military History, 1975.